He Said, She Said

He Said, She Said

✦

A Father-Daughter Perspective

Ken Klarfeld
Jasmyn Klarfeld

iUniverse, Inc.
New York Lincoln Shanghai

He Said, She Said
A Father-Daughter Perspective

iUniverse books may be ordered through booksellers or by contacting:

iUniverse
2021 Pine Lake Road, Suite 100
Lincoln, NE 68512
www.iuniverse.com
1-800-Authors (1-800-288-4677)

ISBN-13: 978-0-595-36991-1 (pbk)
ISBN-13: 978-0-595-81397-1 (ebk)
ISBN-10: 0-595-36991-X (pbk)
ISBN-10: 0-595-81397-6 (ebk)

Printed in the United States of America

Contents

Preface

Relationships between parents and their teen-agers are notoriously difficult and often painful. My relationship with my daughter defined the stereotype in many ways; we shouted, we cried, we punished each other, and we loved each other. We survived the misunderstanding and the pain.

As we looked back over the past 20 years and tried to figure out what went wrong, what went right, and what we could have done differently, it became apparent that the stories remembered were different depending on who was telling them. We decided to tell the stories from both points of view. First, the following stories are told as remembered by me, the father, and then by Jasmyn, my daughter.

We hope this book will enlighten teens and parents about the perceptions of both groups, so that they will gain valuable insights leading to the understanding of each other's point of view.

Prologue

I met Eden, my daughter's mother, in the Navy in 1978. We were both stationed in Hawaii and fell in love with being in love. But life with Eden was no paradise. I remember thinking about the attributes my next wife would have even before marrying this woman.

Eden and I fought continually. Being young, we thought having a child would fix our marriage. Our daughter Jasmyn was born, but of course, things did not get better. I decided to separate from Eden, but I didn't know how to do it and still keep my daughter. While I was trying to figure this out, Eden became pregnant with our second child.

When I was discharged from the U.S. Navy, we moved to my wife's hometown of Sunnyvale, in California's Silicon Valley. We had our second child, a boy, and I resigned myself to staying with her for our children's sake. Because I was in electronics in the service, I had no problem finding a job. I had aspirations of becoming an attorney, so I also started school.

What I didn't know was that before joining the Navy, Eden was a PCP addict. PCP is an animal tranquilizer. When humans take it, they achieve a utopian high by killing massive amounts of brain cells. When we returned to Sunnyvale, she fell back in with her old friends and resumed her drug use. We tried a drug rehabilitation program, but somehow she managed to have drugs smuggled into her and was thrown out of the facility. I decided it would be best for the kids and me if I filed for divorce. My daughter was three and my son eight months. Thankfully, I was employed as an engineer and made enough money to hire full time live-in help. I dropped out of school. I resolved never to speak ill to the children about their mom and made sure they visited her often.

I met Lynn on a blind date in 1983 and fell head over heels in love. We dated, were engaged after three weeks, and married in August of 1984. We started our lives together with the kids. As the kids grew up, we had as normal a life as possible. My ex-wife was difficult to deal with at best, but we continued to encourage visitations on a scheduled basis. There were times when

Eden would show up stoned to pick up the kids for a visit, and we would not let them go with her. I'm sure this had an effect on my daughter.

Eventually my ex-wife was involved in an incident, a result of her drug use, that killed her best friend. They were high and arguing. Eden told her friend to get out of the car. She did. Unfortunately the car was traveling at 60 miles per hour. After a 6-month term in jail, she went back to rehab. This time it stuck; she met a great guy in rehab, married, and, thank God, has been clean and sober ever since.

She was still very difficult to deal with and contradicted my wife and me whenever possible. She undermined my wife's authority with our daughter. My daughter and wife had become very close, and Jasmyn started calling Lynn "Mom" at the age of four. This made things worse as Eden developed a deep-seated hatred for my wife. Despite all this, we had a typical life for the next few years. Jasmyn was a brilliant child and very outgoing. My son, Joshua, was a well-adjusted boy; they both played sports and did well in school.

When Jasmyn turned 12 or 13, things started to change. She got into minor trouble at school. We did her homework together, but for some reason she would not turn it in. She wanted to date and wear make-up, but I felt she was too young. Lynn thought she smelled cigarette smoke on Jasmyn's hair, but Jasmyn denied smoking. She started sneaking out at night through her window. She wanted to go live with Eden, but that was not an option. She started running away at age 14. The problem was she did not care about consequences. Her attitude was, "It's my life; why do you care?"

We tried counseling, putting her in private school, and turning the household upside down, but despite all our efforts, she was still uncontrollable. So we began our long battle to save our child and our family. The next six years were traumatic for all of us. Only now, with the benefit of hindsight, can we begin to understand what happened.

1

A New Family

Father's story

The decision to end my first marriage was not difficult, although I avoided it for a long time. After being discharged from the Navy and moving to my wife's hometown, I had no trouble finding a job. The electronics industry, particularly defense, was booming. I had six job interviews and five job offers. I took a job on the swing shift of a local telecommunications firm, which left my days free to pursue a degree; I hoped to attend law school and have a career as an attorney. I took advantage of the GI Bill benefits for school.

My wife Eden was a full-time mom, at home with our two children. We were saving for a house and had well over $15,000 in the bank, enough for a substantial down payment. Eden was not easy to live with; she was confrontational most of the time, but I had grown used to her ways. Most likely, her behavior explained why I was content to work eight hours a day and then attend school full time. She managed our finances; my job was to deposit the checks.

Then I started to notice strange things at home. She was gone quite often when I called from work in the evenings, and I found drug paraphernalia around the house on a few occasions. When I confronted her, we fought. I threatened to divorce her and have her declared unfit. During one incident, she held a large butcher knife to her wrist and screamed, "I'll kill myself if you leave me!" All the while our three-year-old daughter played in her room within earshot. I never considered that she might be affected by our arguments. I was more concerned about her and her brother's safety when I was at work or school.

On the way to work one day, I stopped at our bank's ATM to withdraw some money, but the screen reflected an overdrawn balance. Thinking I was very aware of our financial position, I went to the bank the next day to see why they mistakenly listed the account as overdrawn. To my surprise, I learned that withdrawals for the maximum allowed amount had been made nearly every night between 5:00 and 10:00 p.m. They were all charged to Eden's ATM card, and the balance in our savings account was now less than a thousand dollars. The teller suggested I speak to my wife.

I rushed home and confronted her. At first, she claimed her ATM card had been stolen and she forgot about it. "That's ridiculous," I shouted. "I can't believe you think I would accept such an absurd explanation. The bank has pictures of you making the withdrawals from the ATM."

She cried and sobbed. Finally she said, "I owed money to a dealer. I had to pay him; I don't know what might happen if I didn't pay him."

Eventually, she acknowledged she had a serious problem, and for the sake of the kids, she would go into rehab. I told my wife I would stick by her, but if she continued with the drug use and the lies, I would divorce her and have her declared an unfit mother. This was her last chance. We found a live-in facility with a three-month program, and she went into rehab the next day. We agreed that I would now handle all financial activity. My mother came to stay and help with the children, and I quit school so I could be at home as much as possible.

While Eden was in rehab, I took our two babies to see her often, but it was an ordeal for us all. The visits were supervised in a group room, and the children were not comfortable with the environment. My wife spent most of the time pleading with me to get her out. According to her, she was not an addict like the other people in there. She always asked for money for cigarettes and other incidentals.

After a few weeks, she called and said I needed to pick her up. The rehab center had thrown her out because one of the other residents had framed her by putting drugs in her belongings. It wasn't her fault, and besides, she didn't belong there in the first place. I had no choice. I went to get her. My daughter Jasmyn, who was then three, was thrilled to have her mom back home. I told Eden that I wouldn't tolerate any further drug use or deception. She convinced me that she was committed to cleaning up her act. No more drug use or lies. I wanted desperately to believe her and I did.

Having been burned by my trust in her before, I kept a close eye on her behavior and our finances. It only took a week until she made a $200 withdrawal from our bank. I had destroyed her ATM card, so I knew she was the only person who could have made the withdrawal. When I confronted her, she told a long sob story about an old debt to a dealer. I wasn't buying it. I believed Eden was incapable of shaking her drug habit and felt it was best for the children if we divorced.

I was relieved when Eden created a situation that allowed me to divorce myself from this nightmare while retaining full custody of Jasmyn and Joshua. I put an ad in the paper and hired a full-time live-in nanny. My mom went home and life returned to something resembling normal. My soon-to-be ex-wife was living with friends, and we set up a visitation schedule for the children. All went well for the next few months. My mother-in-law, who visited the kids often, once talked to me about dating and getting out of the house. I told her I was fine. Even after the divorce was final, I still wasn't interested in dating. Between the children and my job, I had my hands full.

About three months later, a colleague at work suggested I meet a girl who was "perfect for me." I decided it was time to get out a little.

I met Lynn on a blind date and fell head over heels in love. She was, and still is, the girl of my dreams. Shortly after we met, I explained to her that the kids and I were a package deal. Although she had not spent much time around small children, it wasn't long before she was part of the family. Jasmyn and Joshua both took to her almost as quickly as I had. She assumed the roll of "mom" for a one-year-old boy and a four-year-old girl, although her friends told her she was nuts and should run for her life.

After dating for a few weeks, we were engaged and living together. The kids loved having Lynn around; at one point, I remember being amazed at how unaffected they were by the last year's activities. Lynn and I were married seven months later with Jasmyn as our flower girl. Our new family was doing great.

We decided to re-locate and raise the children in a country environment. We found a wonderful home on three acres in a community that was only a two-hour drive from my ex-wife's house. We had a horse stable so we bought a pony for Jasmyn. Jasmyn and Lynn grew closer and closer. To our amazement, one day Jasmyn called her "Mom." Lynn was thrilled. After a few weeks, we asked Jasmyn why she had decided to call Lynn "Mom". Jasmyn replied, in her cute little four-year-old voice, that she wanted to because it made everybody feel happy. We told her she was right and left it at that.

Three weeks later, Jasmyn and Joshua went to visit Eden for the weekend. When Jasmyn returned, she reverted to calling her new mom, "Lynn." We asked why, and she said Eden had told her that she wanted to be her only mom; she didn't want her calling Dad's new wife "Mom."

We called Eden and asked what was going on. "Oh, Jasmyn misunderstood me," she replied. "It's fine for her to call your new wife 'Mom.' I just don't want her to forget about me, you know?"

We put her on the phone with Jasmyn and listened on the extension. "But you said you're my only mom," Jasmyn insisted. Eden tried to explain herself to Jasmyn, but it was obvious to us she was dancing around the truth. After that, Jasmyn called Lynn "Mom."

Daughter's story (Age 4)

When I was four years old, my Dad met a woman named Lynn. My parents were divorced, and as I got to know Lynn, I started to love her as much as the other adults in my life.

I remember she and my dad giving me a choice. I could call this new woman Lynn, or I could call her Mom. As a four-year-old who wanted to make her daddy happy, I thought I would call her Mom. But when I told my mom, (who at the time I thought of as my Real-Mommy), she got really sad. She said that *she* was already my mom and that she was the only one I should call "Mom." I remember feeling very guilty. I *really* didn't want Mommy to be sad! I felt that *I* was making her sad. I agreed with her that she was my mommy, and I would call Lynn "Lynn." Now I just had to tell my dad.

When I told my dad that I had made the choice, and I wasn't going to call Lynn "Mom," he wasn't happy.

"No," he said. "You will call her 'Mom.' That is the final decision."

"Okay," I said. But I was mad. I remember thinking that my mom would find out and then she would be *very* sad and it would be my fault! I hoped she wouldn't think I loved my dad and Lynn more than I loved her. I loved both my parents, but I remember thinking Daddy's decision was going to make my Real-Mommy pretty mad at me.

2

Dealing with the Ex

Father's story

The next few years were uneventful for the most part. We lived on a nice piece of property in the country, and the kids had many friends living close by. My wife and I tried to teach the children responsibility and instill the morals that would carry them through life.

It was hard to carve out quality time with the children. We both worked full time and commuted an hour each way to and from work. We spent our evenings supervising homework with the kids and completing all the chores involved in maintaining chickens, a pony, a few dogs, and a cat. Jasmyn took care of her pony. Joshua helped feed the chickens and clean up after the other animals.

Visitation with their mother was sporadic. We had agreed that we would meet halfway between our homes to transfer the kids, but this never seemed to work out. Eden always had an excuse and couldn't make it. My wife and I started planning trips to visit relatives near my ex-wife's home so she could see the children without driving to pick them up.

One day when we were on our way to meet Eden, I said, "You know, I'm really beginning to resent the fact that we make all the arrangements, do all the driving, and incur all the costs of these visits."

"But it's important for the children to see their mom," Lynn reminded me. "If she won't take the responsibility, then we have to make it happen."

It was always difficult letting them go for the weekend. We suspected Eden was still using drugs, and we didn't want to put the children in harm's way. The children loved visiting their mom and we could not keep them from her, but sometimes we did cancel the visit to keep them safe.

Eden was a PCP addict. Because she had been doing this drug for quite a while, she had learned how to function while on it. On one planned visitation, Eden came to my mother-in-law's home to pick up the kids. When she came inside, she seemed confused and disoriented, asking the same questions over and over. It took a while to gather up the kids and get them out the door.

After they left, Lynn and her sister were very concerned. They thought Eden was under the influence of drugs. "Are you sure?" I asked. My cautious nature led me to require proof. "I know she was acting strange, but was she high?"

After a brief discussion, we decided we couldn't take the chance. My wife ran out to the car; although it had been a full five minutes since the kids went outside, Eden was still trying to navigate the buckles on the car seat. She looked at Lynn and asked, "How do I get out of here?"

My wife looked at her and said, "The same way you came in."

"Which way was that?" That confirmed Lynn's suspicions. She grabbed the kids out of the car and told Eden they couldn't go with her. We rushed the children into the house and closed the door.

Eden followed, knocking on the door and asking calmly, "What's wrong? Where are the kids?"

"That does it," I told Lynn. "If she were sober, she'd be screaming at the top of her lungs." After we told her we thought she was high and she could not have the kids, she left.

Why hadn't I acted right away, as soon as I noticed Eden's odd behavior? One of the challenges I had was the continuous battle over who to believe and what actions to take. I felt pulled between my wife's beliefs and desires and those of my daughter and her mother. This indecision would become a much larger problem as Jasmyn got older. She quickly picked up on my inner conflict and learned how to use it to her advantage.

Daughter's story (Age 5)

It was almost Christmas and my Mommy-Eden was going to come pick up my brother Joshua and me so we could spend some time at her house. I was very excited. Being with Mom was fun! She was beautiful. She had really long hair and a powdery face, and I thought she looked almost exactly like a princess.

She got to Grandma's house and put us in the back seat of her car. I was sitting in the middle and Joshua was sitting by the window. Normally, I probably would have complained about these seating arrangements, but that night, I was too excited. We were going to our mom's! My Mom-Eden started the car and…

"Eden, wait!" yelled Mom-Lynn, running full speed out of Grandma's house.

"What's wrong?" Mom asked. Mom-Lynn opened the door next to my brother. "Lynn, what are you doing?"

"Hold on," Mom-Lynn told Mom–Eden as she pulled my brother out of the car and started to unbuckle my seat belt. "I just need to see something with Jasmyn."

Jasmyn? Uh-oh. Had I done something bad? Was there something wrong or weird about me? Why did she need to look at me?

But she didn't look at me. She just pulled us right into that house and locked the door and said we weren't going to our mom's after all. But I *wanted* to see my mom! And I could tell that my mom really wanted to see me. I could tell because she was knocking on the door and calling my name.

"Jasmyn, open the door! Let me in!" she cried. I wanted to open the door but my dad said I couldn't. I remember thinking that I wanted to do what Mommy wanted and I wanted to see her 'cause I really loved her, but I *had* to do what Daddy said. Mom knocked some more and called to me, but then I guess she decided to go home.

At nighttime, Dad and Mom-Lynn put me to bed at my grandma's house. We were spending the night there instead of my mom's. I remember feeling sad. It wasn't fair. Mom-Lynn had said she had to see something with *me* so I knew that it was my fault that Mommy and I didn't get to see each other, but I didn't know what I had done. I wished I could find out so I could not do it anymore.

3

The Early Years

Father's story

I look back on my daughter's grammar school years as the calm before the storm. Jasmyn was bubbling with excitement over the prospect of starting school and being a "big girl." I knew she was very intelligent and would do well, and she didn't disappoint me. Her teachers sent notes home singing her praises. We looked forward to parent-teacher conferences like a well-advertised and anxiously awaited movie. Her teachers often describe Jasmyn in glowing terms such as "a pleasure and always does her best."

She was tested for scholastic aptitude and scored in the top two percent nationally in her age group. My wife and I were not surprised. It was as obvious to us as it was to everyone who knew Jasmyn that she was gifted. Her teachers suggested she be tested for the GATE, a program for "gifted and talented, exceptional children." It's funny what news about his child's successes does to a father's ego. My chest expanded two or three inches, and I found myself working the news about my daughter's brilliance into conversations with anyone who would listen. Okay, maybe the information operators didn't care, but they heard about it nonetheless.

My wife and I discussed the advanced program at school and decided we would let Jasmyn progress and excel without the added pressures and increased workload the GATE program would involve. We wanted her to enjoy her childhood.

Jasmyn's home life was also what I considered typical for a kindergarten student. Lynn and I tried to balance her social activities with responsibilities around the house. This was somewhat difficult because of another gift Jasmyn possessed. Even at this early age, Jasmyn could argue a point to exhaustion. We had decided chores were an excellent tool to build character and self-esteem. Jasmyn had her fair share. She was responsible for kitchen cleanup or family room clean up on a week-by-week rotating basis. She also had to keep her room picked up and feed her animals.

Like most kids, she would blow through her chores to get to play time. Like most parents, we found her habits frustrating. We tried to instill in her the attitude to accomplish her assigned tasks correctly the first time around. Although this took slightly longer than her chosen path, in the long run it was much quicker because she didn't have to do everything twice.

I'm sure this struggle was played out in virtually every household on the planet, but in our home, the problem always increased after a visitation with Eden. It seemed at mom's house, there were no rules. She could do whatever she wanted without consequences. There were no chores and no responsibilities. Her mother's attitude was consistent with many parents with the two-day-a-month visitation agreement. She felt the children spent so little time with her that while they were there, it should be 48 hours in heaven. No chores or responsibilities. When the children returned from this utopia they resented having to once again assume their slave routine.

We fought this battle constantly. With enough arguing, Jasmyn could always wear me down. She was less successful with my wife, which often led to conflict between Lynn and me. Usually, the conflict ended with one of us saying, "Fine! You decide what to do!" If the argument grew heated enough, Jasmyn was sure to get her way—a neat trick for a child of five or six to learn. As the years passed, she honed this skill and used it often.

Daughter's story (Age 5–8)

I remember going to sign up for kindergarten. I was so proud. I was to be just like a big girl! I was going to carry my own lunch box and sit at those little tables made just for one person! My dad said they were called "desks."

Mom-Lynn took me to sign up. We met the teacher, and she showed us around the classroom and playground. I was a little bit disappointed because the tables were actual tables and not desks, but the playground was great. I couldn't wait to be a big girl!

When we got home my dad asked how it went, and we told him "good." I was so excited that I could hardly even stand still.

"Will she be going a half day or full day?" Dad asked Mom-Lynn.

"FULL DAY! FULL DAY!" I exclaimed, hopping up and down.

"She'll be going for half the day," Mom-Lynn told him, laughing. "She starts full days next year."

Oh well, I thought happily, I'm *still* a big girl!

Kindergarten was really fun but first grade was even better! The best part was that during that year, we were going to learn to read! It didn't seem too hard and I was really proud when I was able to sound out words all by myself.

That year I was thrilled to get a desk and even homework!

Our teacher divided us into different reading groups according to skill, and I was in the highest one. I decided that I must be really smart.

I really liked my third-grade teacher. I thought she was pretty and nice and she liked my work. I did a good job and got good grades on my report card. I thought it was important to be smart, but in third grade that wasn't the most important part of school for me.

My favorite time was recess! We played this really great game called handball, and I thought I was one of the very best players. I loved being better at it than other kids. When I played, I imagined that everyone was admiring my speed and skill. PREPARE yourselves, ladies and gentleman, I would think; it's Jasmyn, the greatest handball player in the WORLD!

After school, I went home with my best friend Johnny. He was my age. His mom, Linda, used to pick us up from school, and we would usually go right to his house, but sometimes I had to go with him to his Boy Scout meetings. I didn't like doing that. The boys got to do lots of stuff, and I just had to sit and wait. I liked being at Johnny's house, though.

Johnny's parents had lots of acres. We lived right below Johnny and had three acres. Below us were the Rivera's. They had six kids and five acres. Their daughter, Vanadale, was a friend of Johnny's and mine. So between Vanadale's, Johnny's, and my house, it seemed to us kids that we had a hundred million miles of forest to run around in. We had lots of adventures, and Johnny's mom always had ice cream or Popsicles for us. My parents didn't buy a lot of sweets.

One of my favorite things about Johnny's was that he got to do almost whatever he wanted! I was amazed that he didn't even get into trouble for talking back to his parents. I wasn't allowed to talk back to my parents.

Johnny and I loved spending the night at each other's houses. At night we pretended that everything was really scary. We'd say things like, "Hey look at that shadow; that wasn't there before." Then we'd look at each other seriously and say together; "Some*thing's fishy!*" We usually played that game until we *really* got scared and then we'd stop.

I loved when we spent the night together, but I liked spending the night at my house more than his. When his dad got mad, he yelled. I didn't like that. When my dad got mad, he just talked to me and sent me to my room or something. Also, if Johnny kept the refrigerator open too long, his mom would tell him he was throwing away money. She'd look up into the air like things were flying away and say things like, "There goes a nickel! There goes a quarter!" That seemed pretty sarcastic to me. Mom-Lynn would've just told me to close the fridge.

Chores at our house started off as small tasks that my little brother and I could be proud of doing (clearing the table after dinner, for instance). But they soon escalated into an overwhelming amount of responsibility, taking up to two hours each day. Clearing the table after dinner soon turned into washing all of the dishes, scrubbing the pots and pans, sweeping, mopping, and scrubbing the kitchen counter tops as well.

Before my seventh birthday, I was responsible for kitchen duty every other week for the whole week. When I wasn't on kitchen duty, I was responsible for living room duty. Cleaning the living room included cleaning up after Dad and Mom-Lynn, vacuuming the living room and hallway, sweeping the entryway, wiping down the living room tables, cleaning the entire bathroom, and sometimes doing household laundry. I was always responsible for feeding the animals and doing my own laundry while also keeping up with the more typical childhood responsibilities like homework and packing my lunch for school. When trying to do laundry, I was too small to reach down and take clothes out of the washing machine, so I had to pull a chair over to finish the job.

My many chores caused me much anxiety; I was constantly in trouble for not being able to keep up with my laundry or for doing my chores incorrectly or too slowly. When that happened, Mom-Lynn would get really mad and insist that it was taking too long. She would show me how to do it and expect me to do it with the same speed and efficiency she had demonstrated. I never seemed to be able to get it right, no matter how hard I tried. This seemed a constant source of frustration to Mom-Lynn, and I started to feel anxious when she was home. If my brother and I were relaxing when she came home from work, we would both jump up and try to look productive.

Since Mom-Lynn wanted the chores done perfectly and was so quickly frustrated, I soon started to resent her. Frustration for her usually equaled punishment for me, and when it didn't it was only because my dad stepped in. Seeing this as highly unfair, (after all I *was* my dad's kid, not *hers),* I started to imagine that life would be smooth sailing for my brother and me if not for her. Although I would always love my dad, I felt that he was more concerned with being *her* husband than *my* dad.

Sometimes on weekends my brother and I would get to go to our Mom-Eden's house. The drive seemed long, but we usually got to stop for fast food, (a very special treat), and I always looked forward to seeing her.

Once at her house, she tried to make our visits special. I remember her packing picnic lunches for us with sandwiches, juice, and Twinkies, and taking us to the park. When she met my step-dad, Raul, he would get up early in the morning while we were still watching cartoons and ask us what we wanted for breakfast. We could pick out any kind of breakfast cereal we wanted, no matter how sweet, and Raul would run right out to the store and get it for us. My brother and I didn't even have to agree on what kind we wanted, because Raul would get us each our own.

When we would complain to our mom about our household chores, she would get mad that we had to take on so many adult responsibilities. Her anger helped to confirm my belief that I had a good reason to be angry with the adults who were raising me. While at her house we didn't have any responsibilities beyond picking up after ourselves and obeying the rules, and I loved just being able to be a kid without worrying about evoking grown-up anger.

At first our visits with our mom were pretty sporadic. She and my dad would plan an outing, but after each visit I didn't know when the next one was going to be. At some point, though I'm not sure exactly when, I remember my dad telling us that we would start going to see Mom-Eden during the third weekend of every month. By this time, my mom and Raul were married with two new babies, and I was thrilled that I was going to be able to see them so often.

There were definite advantages to having more than one set of parents. At Christmas time and birthdays I got *tons* of presents. I'd get a bunch of presents from each set of parents, and then they would each get me additional presents from "Santa Claus." I loved stuffed animals and had so many that if

I tried to set them all up on my queen-sized bed, there wouldn't have been any room left for me!

There were, however, disadvantages as well. Dad and Mom-Eden didn't seem to agree on who should pay for the extra things I wanted to do, like karate or acting lessons, for example. Although Mom-Lynn and Dad did pay for a lot of extras throughout my childhood, there were numerous times when they would tell me I should ask my mom for the money. Most of the time, I would not. Mom had told me that she was paying something called "child support" and that she sent Dad money every month for things like that. Dad said that he paid to support me, too, and that if I asked my mom, the worst that could happen was she would say no. He and Mom-Lynn didn't understand why my brother and I were so hesitant to ask our mom for things.

How could we explain it to them when we didn't understand it ourselves? One time when I asked Dad and Mom-Lynn to pay for something and they said I should ask my Mom-Eden, I asked them to intervene.

"Will *you* ask her?" I begged.

"Honey, why don't you want to ask her?" Mom-Lynn asked.

I thought about it and said, "I don't know. I just don't."

"Well," said my dad, "If you ask her and she says no, we'll pay for it, but you have to ask her."

I didn't end up doing whatever it was I wanted to do.

In retrospect, I think that not asking my mom for things was a form of self-protection. I was with my dad every day, so I knew that I was absolutely his daughter. I was an important part of his family. That was not the situation with my mom. She had a whole separate family and two other kids that she took care of completely. She was with them every day and paid for all of their extracurricular activities, whereas I only got to visit. If I would have asked her to pay for something and she had refused, I would have felt even less a part of her new life then I already did. I would have felt that my little brother and sister were more her children than I was. Although I couldn't articulate it at the time, I was more willing to miss out on activities than I was to deal with that anticipated rejection.

4

The First Move

Father's story

As time went on, life in the country became less appealing. The winters were particularly hard. The water for our home was pumped from a well. On very cold mornings, the mechanism that turned on the pump would freeze. I would get up and go outside with a propane torch to heat it up enough to supply water to the house.

In addition, our home was located at the top of a large hill—some might consider it a mountain—up a very steep, winding dirt road. A loosely formed homeowners association maintained the road. Our hill was like a little community complete with lower, middle, and upper income families. In the worst of winter, the road became impassable to all but four-wheel drive vehicles, but this did not stop the residents who did not own these vehicles from trying to get their cars to the top. Consequently, they often abandoned cars, usually at the steepest areas.

One evening, I returned from work in the midst of a particularly bad storm. I stopped at the base of our hill and put chains on my four-wheel drive truck. I then drove up to our home, hoping the road would not be littered with abandoned cars in the morning. An hour or so later, a neighbor knocked on my door. His car was stuck half way up the road and he needed a tow. I agreed to help.

The temperature had dropped considerably. We started down the road and found the steepest part had turned to a solid sheet of ice. We started to slide out of control. On the right side was the wall of the hill that had been cut out long ago to construct the road. On the left side was a nearly vertical drop to the street far below. All I could do was steer toward the wall and hope to regain control. Then we hit a stump buried deep in snow and ricocheted over the steep side of the road. The truck rolled over three full times, picking up speed as it descended the hill. Amid the crashing glass and imploding roof, all at once the truck stopped. We were inverted and suspended above the last 30-foot drop to the road below. A rickety old barbed-wire fence had stopped our descent. I crawled out through the opening where seconds before the window had been intact.

I decided it was time to move from the country.

We sold our rural home and moved back to suburbia. We purchased a home with a large backyard and a built-in pool. These attributes were nice but for me the piece de resistance was curbside garbage pick-up. No more hauling mounds of trash to the county dump! Things were good.

We were concerned about how successful the children would be making new friends in the community. For the past four years, they had lived on top of a mountain with the same close-knit group of peers. Now, they would have to make new friends. Jasmyn found a little girl a few houses down who was close to her age. It wasn't long until she became her new best friend. The two girls were inseparable.

Although we no longer lived in the sticks, we were still in a small community. We were not concerned with child abductions or other crimes associated with larger communities. Still, we wanted to teach the children to be safe. We required them to let us know where they were at all times. We didn't allow them to walk by themselves to the strip mall almost a mile away. One day, a friend mentioned to my wife that she thought she saw our children alone at the strip mall earlier in the week. Wondering if Jasmyn had been sneaking off, we confronted her.

Jasmyn denied ever being there. Being Mr. Logic, I felt inclined to believe her because we didn't have absolute proof, but Lynn was sure she was lying. She had better radar than I did in this area. So we pushed a little harder. We told Jasmyn she had been spotted at the mall. She denied being there. We told her we had proof. She denied being there. We told her it was easy for us to go and check with the people who worked at the mall. She denied being there. We told her if she ever were caught going to the mall by herself or with friends without permission, she would be in big trouble. She denied being there. We left it at that. Subsequently, we found out that she had been at the mall. Once again, Jasmyn learned a lesson in avoiding the truth with ease.

Daughter's story (Age 8–11)

Growing up, I was a tomboy. I loved playing with the boys, and although I loved stuffed animals, I thought playing with dolls was weak and stupid. I would have chosen GI Joe over Barbie any day. However just playing *with* the boys wasn't enough; I loved trying to prove that I could play *better* than the boys. Instead of merely trying to keep up in boy games, I felt compelled to jump higher, run faster, and hit harder than any of my friends. Not only did I pride myself on finding ways to be tougher than my peers; I felt I should be smarter and more clever as well.

I found numerous ways to confirm my intelligence. At first, I felt satisfied earning good grades on my report card, and through third grade my grades were almost perfect. On the comparative SAT tests required every couple of years, I was in the top 95–98 percentile in most subjects. I was smart and tough and *no one* could take that away. Soon however, earning good grades didn't satisfy me. After all, school wasn't hard; other people earned good grades, too. I started looking for other ways to prove myself superior in the cleverness category.

The first couple of times I shoplifted, I didn't even leave the store. I would get permission from whatever adult I was with to go look at toys while they shopped and then I would grab a candy bar off the rack (Babe Ruth's were my favorite.) I would take the candy bar, find a place in the store with low visibility, and eat it right on the spot. That was too easy, however, and I soon wondered if I could get the candy out of the store. I decided to scope things out.

I noticed that most stores had big plastic-looking alarms by the doors and figured that they would beep if I tried to smuggle the candy past them. But there was nothing inside chocolate or peanuts that would set off an alarm, so I decided to solve the problem by taking the wrapper off the candy and then sneaking just the bar out of the store. It worked! But after doing it numerous times, it became too easy to be very exciting. *Could I sneak bigger things out of the store?* I wondered. Would the alarm go off? Maybe the alarm was just for show. Since the last thing I wanted to do was get caught stealing with my parents standing there, I had a problem. I wanted to test the alarms, but I wasn't allowed to go to the store by myself.

It didn't even occur to me that if I got caught without my parents, the store would call them. I was confident in my ability to talk myself out of trouble. My friends and little brother had seen me do it many times. My friends came to me when they needed excuses to tell their teachers or parents and, in private, my little brother called me the "Queen of Excuses." "Don't worry," he'd proudly tell other kids we were causing mischief with, "if we get caught, my sister will talk us out of it."

I found a solution to my supervision dilemma when I met a little girl named Fiona. Fiona and I were the same age, and her family lived just down the street from mine. I would get permission from my parents to go play at Fiona's house, and once there, Fiona's parents, (who were a lot less strict than mine) would give us permission to take a walk. Free from the stifling supervision of adults, we would walk to the store. We decided to test the alarm by walking out at the same time as some teenagers who were in the store. We figured if it beeped, the teenagers would get stopped and we—being sweet-looking little girls—would just keep walking. The alarm didn't beep.

Fiona and I started going to the stores as often as we could. But sometimes, when I went to play, my parents made me take my little brother with me. Soon, he started shoplifting too.

One day my parents asked me straight-out if I'd been walking to the stores. I knew I wasn't allowed to go to the stores by myself and would get into *big* trouble if my parents found out I had.

"The stores?" I echoed, arranging my face into my best-confused look.

"Yes," Mom-Lynn said, without taking her eyes off me. "The stores down the street that you're not allowed to walk to."

"No, when would I have time to do that? You guys always know where I am."

"One of our friends saw you," my dad informed me.

Was he bluffing, I wondered? "Musta' been a different kid," I said aloud, trying to look unconcerned.

Both parents looked at me. Hard. "She must think we're idiots," Mom-Lynn said to my dad. "Jasmyn, lying will only make things harder on you," she warned in her firmest tone.

"I'm not lying," I stubbornly insisted.

"Well," my dad said, looking at Mom-Lynn. "We can easily find out. We'll just go down to the stores and ask all the cashiers if she was there. They won't lie." They both looked at me. "Jasmyn," my dad asked, "Would you like one last chance to tell the truth?"

Damn, I thought. *This guy is good.* There was no way I was talking myself out of this one. They had won, which meant I wasn't quite as clever as I'd thought.

Ready to spill the beans, I opened my mouth. "Well, I—"

"No," Mom-Lynn interrupted. "Before you say anything else, I want you to think about what we've said. Dad and I will go into the other room for a few minutes, and when we come back, I hope you're ready to tell the truth."

"But I don't *need* time to think!" I protested. I knew when I was beat.

"Take it anyway," Dad told me, as they walked out of the room.

How unnecessary, I thought. If they had *listened* they would already have known the truth and could even have been discussing my punishment by now. But then I *did* start to think about it.

The cashiers at the store saw hundreds of people shopping every day. They probably wouldn't remember whether they had seen a couple little kids. Even if they did, they didn't all work there all the time. My parents had no idea what days or times I had gone, so they really had no way of figuring out which employees might have been there at that time.

Furthermore, I reasoned, my parents were pretty adamant about getting me to tell the truth. Why hadn't they just told me that they knew I had lied and punished me? Then it dawned on me.

They didn't know for sure. I still had a chance! Not only did they not know I was lying, I realized, they also had no way of finding out. And I had almost told on myself! I had almost made a Stupid Move. But they had underestimated me. They forgot how smart I was and gave me time to think. I forgave myself for almost acting dumb, since I had learned a lesson. I promised myself I would never tell the truth and get myself in trouble without thinking about it first.

When my parents came back and asked for the truth, I maintained that I'd been telling it all along. I had a method for lying. Once I decided to lie, instead of trying to lie well, I pretended my lie was the truth and then acted accordingly. It was usually pretty convincing. Although this time my parents weren't sure whether to believe me, they didn't punish me. They did, however, reiterate the rule about not walking to the stores. I did not do it again.

Although my brother and I did not walk to the stores alone anymore, we did not stop shoplifting. When we went to visit my grandma, she would let us look around the store while she shopped. My brother and I competed in our shoplifting skill and started gaining more confidence. We stole all kinds of things. We stole things for our friends and ourselves. We stole magazines we didn't read and cigarettes we didn't smoke. There was nothing quite as satisfying as looking small and innocent while walking out of a store with our pockets stuffed with things we weren't supposed to have.

We did have morals, however. We would not steal from people or homes, just stores. One day when we were with my grandma, my brother got caught stealing a Ninja Turtle action figure. I had wandered off to look at books, he had gone off to look at toys, and we were all supposed to meet in the front of the store. When I got there, my brother was crying, and my grandma was furious.

"Joshua got caught stealing," she told me.

"That was dumb," I said, looking at my brother.

"I know," he said, looking down. Although my grandma thought I was telling him stealing was dumb, my little brother understood that I was telling him that getting caught had been dumb. A Stupid Move.

What was most baffling to the adults around us was that Joshua had had enough money in his pocket to pay for the Ninja Turtle. Why hadn't he? Joshua couldn't explain that it was not the *things* we stole that we enjoyed; it was the actual *activity* of stealing. We didn't ask permission to steal and knew that it was forbidden. Yet, it was our choice. When we were stealing, we were the ones in control. The fact that adults wouldn't have liked what we were doing was irrelevant in that part of our lives because they couldn't stop us.

5

The Trouble Begins

Father's story

During this same time, the company I worked for was going through major changes. I was in management and found out I was going to be let go. Lynn and I discussed the situation, and together we decided on a plan for the future. We took a second mortgage on our home and I started my own business. We struggled financially for two years, finally losing our home. The business was doing better, but it was too little, too late.

We had to move again, and once again the children said good-bye to their old friends and started over. We were lucky and found a nice home to rent in a community closer to the major city in our area. There was a community health club within walking distance with activities for kids. Jasmyn made new friends at the center and started socializing more. By the time we moved, she was thirteen and had decided she was old enough to start wearing make-up and dating. As her father, I thought she was much too young for either activity. I thought sixteen was a more appropriate age. The storm was about to hit, and I never saw it coming.

In the middle of the ongoing battle over make-up and dating, Jasmyn's grades started to decline. When we asked Jasmyn what was going on, she said it was not her fault that her teachers didn't like her. The strange thing was it was not all of her grades. Her report card would show two A's, two C's, and a D. We set up a conference with her teachers to get to the bottom of the problem. Apparently, Jasmyn was not turning in her homework, so the classes that relied heavily on homework to derive the grade were affected most.

Although this was disturbing, we thought we could solve the problem easily. We told Jasmyn that if her grades continued to fall, she would be grounded. I checked her homework daily and helped her with anything she found difficult. I also asked if she turned in the homework. Jasmyn always had a satisfactory answer.

But the next report card was even worse. For the first time, she made an "F." I was furious. How could this be? Had I not asked her every day about homework? Had I not sat for hours working with her? I knew the work was done. How could she receive an "F"?

As promised, we grounded her until her grades improved, which was at least a full semester. "What happened?" I asked. "I know you did the homework."

"Yes, I did the homework. I just didn't turn it in," Jasmyn replied.

"But why?" I couldn't imagine a logical reason for not turning in completed work.

"I don't know."

"That's all you can say? You don't have a reason?"

Jasmyn shrugged. "I don't know."

It seemed that "I don't know" became her standard answer to most questions. How I came to despise those three words over the next few years!

"Fine," I said. "We'll have to think of a way to make you turn in the homework." I met with her teachers and asked them to sign a homework-verification note every day. Looking back, I realize this must have embarrassed Jasmyn, but I wasn't concerned with her feelings. I was going to nip this problem before it got out of hand.

My strategies didn't work. Things were spiraling out of control, and Jasmyn was depressed all of the time. I decided it was time for a change. We would wipe the slate clean and start a new.

Daughter's story (Age 12–13)

As my boredom with school grew, my grades started to fall. I thought learning was important, but once I'd learned something, I wasn't willing to practice it until everyone else in the class had learned it as well. As I grew older, my group of friends shifted from kids who cared about school to other kids who, like me, had better things to do than homework. I loved my friends, and at first our mischief was minor.

By age thirteen, I had a best friend named Cherry whom I respected as my intellectual equal. She and I cooked up many minor schemes to amuse ourselves. We loved to steal makeup from the supermarkets and then meet older boys, telling them we were 17-year-old twins.

One Saturday afternoon while we were sitting around my room trying to think of something fun to do, one of us came up with a Brilliant Idea. We didn't have any money and thought we would have more options if we did. We decided that we would go door to door in our P.E. clothes, asking people for donations for our school volleyball team. (Neither of us played volleyball or were even sure our school had a volleyball team). I found a flat, white cardboard box and even attached a homemade deductible sheet so people could write down their names, addresses, and how much they'd donated. We explained to homeowners that our school didn't have enough money for uniforms and that it was really embarrassing to play in our P.E. clothes when everybody else had nice uniforms to play in. We collected about thirty dollars, a small fortune to thirteen-year-olds at the time.

Eventually, Cherry and I started hanging out with some girls at school who were into smoking and drinking. Although I didn't smoke because I thought it was gross, drinking was fun, and I started taking alcohol from my parents' cupboard. I brought it to school in anything from washed out shampoo bottles to Tupperware containers. I loved how it tasted going down and the way it warmed my throat and stomach. My friends thought it was hilarious when I swigged out of shampoo bottles.

At about the same time, I started to feel school was a huge waste of time. I hated spending more than a day on any new concept or lesson, and once I had learned the material I was no longer willing to practice it. When my dad asked me if I had homework, I would only tell him about the things I didn't yet know how to do. He would show me, and once I was confident I had grasped the concept, I wouldn't bother with similar assignments. I saw no point in learning things I already knew. I lied to my dad about the assignments I wasn't willing to do, and soon I found myself grounded for a whole semester.

A semester was a long time, and even if I'd been willing to improve my grades, I wouldn't have seen any immediate rewards. Being grounded meant I couldn't see my friends, talk on the phone or watch television. I felt that life was bleak without anything immediate to look forward to. The only time I was allowed out of the house was to go to school, and I wasn't about to waste all of that freedom by going to classes. I loved reading and during homework time would tell my parents I had book reports due so I could read. I started cutting school with my friends to gain back some semblance of a social life.

Although I felt the semester would never end, it eventually did, but my grades were predictably horrible. My grounding was extended another semester, and I couldn't believe my parents were taking away a whole year of my life with their constant grounding. Why would they possibly think this would motivate me? I hated my life and couldn't stand my parents' house.

To make sure I was getting my homework done, my dad decided that I had to get my teachers to sign a homework note each day, as if I were in first grade. I hated doing this, and soon just started forging my teachers' signatures. I didn't feel motivated to do anything. I didn't care what punishments my parents came up with. I wasn't quite fourteen, and I didn't care about life.

6

A New Start

Father's story

Around Jasmyn's fourteenth birthday, I decided we all needed a fresh start. No more grounding. I purchased a phone just for her. We would experience a new openness overnight, and Jasmyn would start doing well in school again. All would be right with the world.

Unfortunately, the new openness shut down almost immediately. I don't remember what triggered it, but I believe it was the first time Jasmyn was suspected of smoking. She came home from being out with her friends, and Lynn smelled the aroma of cigarette smoke on her clothes. She told me Jasmyn had been smoking and we needed to do something about it.

I remember thinking, "Here we go again." When we confronted Jasmyn with our suspicions, she was furious. According to her, she didn't smoke; the smell was from someone else smoking near her. Given her recent history, we didn't believe her. We grounded her again, but she didn't seem to care. She just went to her room, which was on the ground level of our home. It had a large sliding-glass window with a screen. A few days later, I noticed that the screen had been removed. The sneaking out stage had begun.

Daughter's story (Age 14)

On my fourteenth birthday, I was able to get out of the house. My dad was taking me out to dinner, just him and me. He took me to have sushi, which I loved. During dinner, Dad handed me an envelope. I opened it, but wasn't sure why he'd given it to me. It looked like a phone bill. I didn't recognize the number at the top.

"What's this?" I asked.

"That's you're new phone number; we got you your own phone line," he said, smiling.

Phone line? Wasn't I grounded for the next six months?

Dad must have seen my puzzlement because he went on. "Jasmyn, we've decided to give you another chance. We're going to wipe the slate clean. You're not grounded anymore, and we're going to give you back our trust even though you lied about your grades."

Awesome! I felt like a black cloud had been lifted from around my head. I could breath again. I decided that I would work my butt off in school to get good grades, and I would stop cutting classes. I wouldn't lie to my parents. I had a feeling that this newly awarded confidence I was being given was primarily my dad's doing. I wouldn't let him down.

Although we were making a lot of new friends, Cherry and I were still best friends and constantly did things together. My parents knew her and often gave us rides to places like the mall or skating rink.

On one such trip to the mall, shortly after my grounding had been lifted, my Mom-Lynn told me to pick out some school clothes. She was going to drop us off, and we were to call her when we were done so that she could pay for my things. I was very excited, for this was the first time I had been allowed to do my school shopping myself. Cherry and I spent hours going from store to store, picking out just the right things, right down to accessories such as belts.

Finally, I called Mom-Lynn and she came to get us. I was feeling particularly happy, and my animosity had mostly diminished since my parents had given me a new chance. When Mom-Lynn started walking us into the mall however, her face froze.

"You've been smoking," she informed me. It was a statement, not a question.

What?!? I thought. I hadn't been smoking. In fact, I had never even wanted to try smoking.

"No, I haven't," I protested, even though a small ball of fear had coiled itself into my stomach. I knew she wouldn't believe me. She *never* believed me. "Smell my breath!" I suggested, knowing that it didn't smell like smoke.

She did, but said that it smelled like smoke and took me home without purchasing the clothes I had picked out. Although my dad said he wasn't willing to punish me without proof, Mom-Lynn made it clear that she didn't believe me, and I was furious. Not only did I resent that defending myself against her false accusations bruised my pride, I felt that her adamancy had also erased my dad's confidence in me. I was right.

A few days later, my parents said that they needed to talk to me. They had reconsidered their decision not to punish me. Mom-Lynn was 100 percent positive that I had been smoking, and that was enough for my dad. Despite how hard I'd been trying to meet all my parents' expectations, I was grounded again.

This time however, I wasn't so compliant. I was grounded for an indefinite amount of time and was back to not caring about anything. I had met a boy at the skating rink during my brief period of freedom, and he soon became my boyfriend.

Tommy was living in a group home for delinquents, but he could get phone calls at certain hours. I'd sneak onto the phone to call him and, since I was grounded, we'd arrange to see each other after my parents were asleep so that I could sneak out my bedroom window.

Although I hadn't smoked before, I soon started. One night, when I was out with Tommy, he asked someone for a cigarette. The guy gave him two, thinking I smoked, too.

"Want one?' Tommy asked, not knowing I'd never smoked before.

It was a cold night, and the lit tip of his cigarette looked warm and toasty. Besides, what did I have to lose? Since I was grounded for smoking anyway, I might as well try it. "Sure," I said.

"It's a menthol," he said, making a face.

"No problem," I said, not knowing what "menthol" meant but not wanting to appear naive.

As Tommy lit the second cigarette and passed it to me, I tried to remember how to smoke. I'd seen my friends teach other kids, and I remembered that in order not to cough, I'd have to mix the smoke with air as I slowly inhaled. I tried it.

I didn't cough, and a surprised grin spread across my face. "This tastes like mint!" I exclaimed to Tommy in wonder.

"Well, yeah," he said, "That's why it's called a menthol."

"Great!" I told him. "I *love* mint!" We both laughed.

7

The Suicide Attempt

Father's story

A few weeks later, my wife and I were working at our business location and received a call from Jasmyn's school. She had been caught smoking pot and was suspended. She was a freshman in high school. The principal said, "Jasmyn is so stoned, she doesn't know what day it is." We were skeptical because Jasmyn seldom knew what day it was, stoned or sober. We rushed to the school to pick her up. We decided we needed to come down hard on her. When we returned home we took the door of her room off the hinges and stored it in the garage. We then removed all of her posters, her phone and the grunge clothes she had grown attached to.

We decided that being suspended from school should not be a holiday. Lynn came up with a list of chores for Jasmyn to accomplish while home from school, such as scrubbing the toilet with a toothbrush. The next morning, Lynn was getting ready for work and told Jasmyn to take the trash bag full of her grunge clothes and put them by the car. She was going to take them to the Goodwill store. Jasmyn became very upset. She argued but Lynn insisted we were going to stick to her punishment. The clothes were part of the whole thing. Her grunge, her music, her smoking pot—all of it was leading to these problems.

On her way to work my wife called from the car. "Jasmyn," she said crying, "I really am not doing this to hurt you but rather to help you."

"Are you still going to get rid of my clothes?" Jasmyn asked.

"Sorry, yes," Lynn answered.

Jasmyn went to the medicine pantry and found a bottle of penicillin. She took 20 or so. Then she accompanied her grandmother to her physical therapy appointment. We got a call from my mother—something was wrong with Jasmyn. She had taken some pills. We agreed to meet her at home.

"What the hell do you think you're doing?" Lynn asked Jasmyn. "Do you think this is going to work?"

I took Jasmyn to the hospital, and the doctor gave her some medicine to induce vomiting. When we returned home, Jasmyn was throwing up in the bathroom. My wife patted her head and tried to comfort her. I was very distraught and decided if she was that upset; we should give her back her clothes. I was close to tears. "I just don't want to lose her," I told my wife.

Lynn was distraught with the whole situation and once again said, "Do what you think is right." I gave the bag of clothes back to Jasmyn.

After the suicide attempt, I was concerned about disciplining her at all. If she didn't get her way, would she go off somewhere and try again? What if she were successful? We decided we needed professional help, so we made an appointment with a therapist.

Jasmyn was falling deeper and deeper into an abyss. She did not want to go to the therapist, but we persuaded her to give it a try. The deal was that if she didn't want to continue after a few sessions, we wouldn't make her go. Jasmyn had a talent for completely shutting down at will. The therapist saw this and, to our amazement, told Jasmyn if she didn't cooperate, she could and would have her thrown in jail. Needless to say Jasmyn lost all trust in this woman and saw her as another adult out to get her. She did not want to continue with the therapy. My wife and I were desperate to reach Jasmyn.

Daughter's story (Age 14)

After being grounded for a while, I was bored and needed something new to do. Smoking was getting less exciting, and my parents' alcohol wasn't much fun anymore. I had sneaked it so often that the bottles had gotten noticeably emptier until I finally had to add water to the alcohol in order to restore liquid levels and avoid getting caught. I started smoking weed.

I smoked my first bowl in the backyard by myself. I had bought some in history class from a kid at school with a reputation for being a troublemaker. He charged me twenty dollars for an eighth and threw in a cool-looking pipe as well. "Brown or green?" he'd asked me when I'd first approached him.

I'd never even seen weed before and imagined that it looked like white powder. I had no idea that I'd have to choose a color.

"Uh, green," I answered, since green was a much prettier color than brown.

Being a reader, I had read about smoking weed and knew that in order to get stoned, one had to hold the smoke inside the lungs until it felt like they were about to burst. I did that a few times, but it didn't seem like anything had happened. *Oh well,* I thought, going inside the house and sitting down in my room. I looked around the room, but when I stopped, my head kept moving by itself, in the same pattern as I'd moved it in to search the room. I laughed, and my laughter sounded musical and far away. Laughing some more, I tried moving my head in a figure-eight pattern. Again, when my effort stopped, my head kept going! Suddenly, I realized how funny I must look, sitting in the middle of my room, moving my head around and laughing. That made me laugh even harder.

I was hooked. By smoking weed, I didn't have to sneak out in order to have fun. Being high made everyday things fun and silly. Even walking around my house because I was grounded was fun when I was high. I started carrying my pipe everywhere and began ducking out of classes in order to smoke a quick bowl in the bathroom at school. After about six months, I got caught.

The school monitor who had discovered me in the bathroom brought me to the office, where school authorities contacted my parents. While I was waiting for them to arrive, the school nurse questioned me. She was talking really slowly so, in order to save her some time, I informed her that she could talk normally since I wasn't too high to understand her. Not believing me, she asked me what day it was.

"I don't know," I truthfully answered. She smirked.

"I never know what day it is," I told her in a flat voice.

When my parents arrived, they found out I was suspended. They were furious, and my dad let Mom-Lynn decide on what my punishment would be during my suspension. She gave me an exhaustive list of chores to do each day, including scrubbing several bathroom areas with an old toothbrush. She kept me busy every waking moment of my day and never allowed me any time to relax. The idea was that I would be so miserable with these consequences that I would strive to do better. The result was that I felt even more alienated from the family fold, even more out of control over my life, and even more desperate to regain that control.

Next, my parents decided to take away all of my clothes and my make-up, with the exception of some old things I had worn in elementary school that still fit me. These were mostly T-shirts with kissing koalas or smiley faces on the front. Being fourteen, I was beyond these baby-themes. The theory was that if I didn't look so much like the kids I hung out with, I wouldn't be as welcome or willing to be around them. I was angry that my parents were taking away my clothes, and decided that if I changed one thing about myself, including my behavior, I would lose and they would win. They had taken my clothes, but I vowed not to let them take my self.

At first the clothes sat in my parents' room, and I assumed I would get them back when my parents decided the punishment was over. One morning, however, I found out this was not true. I saw Mom-Lynn dragging the bags out to the car.

"What are you doing?" I demanded.

"I'm taking these to the Goodwill," she icily informed me.

"You can't do that!" I screamed. "Those aren't yours!" It was true. Though she and Dad had bought a lot of those clothes, some of them were gifts from my mom, and some were even borrowed from friends.

"Everything in this house belongs to your father and me," she insisted before getting into her car and driving away. Crying, I went back into the house.

My parents had taken the door to my room off its hinges and had torn down all of my posters. They had thrown away my makeup and CDs and now they were getting rid of all of my clothes. Nothing in my life belonged to me- except my attitude.

The phone rang. It was Mom-Lynn. She had called to tell me that she was still getting rid of my clothes but that she was doing it to help me. I hung up.

She couldn't help me. She didn't know me. They could control my belongings but not my actions. I'd show them that. I opened the pantry and looked at the medicine bottles. I took one down and looked at it. Something-acyclyn, an antibiotic. It couldn't kill me, but it could make me sick. If I were sick, I wouldn't have to clean their damn house. I took a bunch of them and then went back to work.

Although I don't remember being brought to the hospital, I do remember that once there a hospital social worker kept asking me why I tried to kill myself. That wasn't what I was trying to do, I told her. She spoke to my father and finally we went home. At home my dad said the social worker in the hospital said we had to go to counseling.

The first counselor was a drug counselor. I sat and stared at him. Didn't talk. He told me that just by looking at me he could tell I was smoking a lot of weed. Within my group of peers, that was something to be proud of. I smiled. He told me he could tell because weed caused one's eyelids to collect little telltale rolls of fat. I didn't like the idea of having fat eyelids. I glared at him. Didn't talk. My parents didn't bring me back.

The second counselor was a woman who asked me a lot of questions about my feelings and my mom. I liked her. I went to see her about three times. I liked her because before I went in to see her I would decide what I wanted her diagnosis to be and then see if I could act in a way that would make her say what I had already decided she would. It worked, and it was a lot of fun. I think she might have figured it out and told my parents, though, because after the third session we didn't go back.

The third and final counselor was a middle-aged, dumpy lady with a sterile office and a hard couch. I didn't like her, so I stared at her without talking. She acted like she had the most magical touch and thought that her brilliance would get me to open up. I didn't. I just stared at her face while she asked me question after question. I watched her grow uncomfortable and finally irate. I could tell that she was taking this personally. What an idiot. I kept on staring. Finally she told me that if I didn't answer her questions she could declare me mentally ill and have my parents put me in a lock-up facility.

I started crying, big, silent, angry tears. I wasn't scared; I was angry. This lady thought that she could scare me just because I was a kid. She thought that I would believe her lies and open up to her. Yeah, right. I wasn't stupid. I didn't talk to her, and I never went back. That was the end of counseling for me.

After my suspension was over, my parents started bottling me, (testing urine for drugs) once a month. Weed stays in the system for thirty days, and I couldn't get high without getting caught. I was still grounded and couldn't stand it.

I talked to some of my friends and found out that alcohol is only detectable in urine for about three days, so I could still drink while I was supposed to be at school. But alcohol was less accessible than weed, and besides, that wouldn't help me at home. Drunkenness was more noticeable than being stoned. I needed something that would whisk my cares away but not show up on drug tests.

I soon found out that LSD, or acid, didn't show up on drug tests, and was incredibly cheap. I cut school, and some of my friends hooked me up for free since I'd already gone a couple of months without drugs and they felt bad for me. I put three doses on my tongue and waited. And waited.

Just when I'd decided it was bunk, I noticed that the ground around me, which had been level before, was now sloped downward. I moved my hand over the ground to try and see if the ground had really moved or if I was hallucinating. When I ran my hand over the ground, it left a colorful trail behind that didn't fade for a few moments. I looked at the walls and saw with amazement that they were breathing. I looked at my friends, who were just beginning to trip, too. They looked ugly. Like aliens, all sharp angles and long limbs. I hated how their skin was breathing.

We got up and went over to sit on the grass, and I felt one with the grass and the trees. I wasn't only sitting on a grassy hill; I was part of the grassy hill. The individual blades seemed as much a part of me as my own fingertips. After a while we started to peak.

I was so high that I couldn't talk. I just walked around with my friends, pointing and laughing at all the beautiful things. Even the air was beautiful, full of colors that swirled around and moved aside when I made color trails with my hands. I couldn't believe that I had been alive for fourteen years but had never seen the air before.

I started tripping as often as I could.

8

Foreign Exchange Student

Father's story

Lynn and I thought if we could expose Jasmyn to kids her own age who were doing well, she might turn around. We found out about a foreign exchange program in our area. There was a French girl a few years older than Jasmyn who wanted to complete her senior year of high school in the United States. She was a straight "A" student and spoke four languages fluently. This was the kind of girl we needed to mentor Jasmyn.

We applied to the program. Jasmyn was actually excited with the prospect of having a big sister in the house. We purchased twin beds for her room in preparation for Monique's arrival. All was ready as we went to the airport to pick up Monique. She was somewhat shy, but we moved her into Jasmyn's room and they became friends. What we didn't anticipate was Jasmyn's affect on Monique. Monique thought Jasmyn was the coolest and wanted to be more like her. Although she kept her grades up, she started getting into the same type of mischief as Jasmyn. I remember having to go to the mall to pick Monique up from security because she had been caught shoplifting with four pairs of pants on. When I arrived, she was embarrassed and shut down. Not wanting to be responsible for two troubled teenage girls, I explained to Monique that if her behavior didn't improve drastically, she would have to go back home to France. That was the last time she emulated Jasmyn.

My business was doing quite well. We had expanded our coverage area to include a radius of around 500 miles. I was spending a few days a week on the road with my employees. It was a stressful time, and my wife wanted to do something for me to get my mind off work and the constant challenges Jasmyn presented us. I had earned my private pilot's license 15 years earlier while in the Navy and stilled talked about how nice it would be to start flying again. Lynn purchased a certificate for a weekend flight seminar flying WW2 war birds. I was thrilled. I knew getting back in the cockpit of an aircraft would rekindle my desire to fly. I thanked my wife and convinced her to return the certificate and allow me to take lessons toward my instrument rating.

I started lessons a week later. I found learning to fly an aircraft on instruments to be an all-encompassing experience. It was like walking through a door into a room the rest of the world couldn't and wouldn't follow me into. For a few hours a week I would totally immerse myself in flying on instruments without room for even the minutest thought other than the task at hand. This mental vacation became my salvation from the overwhelming problems at home.

Daughter's story (Age 14)

I was excited when my parents told me they'd decided to accept a foreign exchange student into our home. I wanted a boy, they said absolutely not, so I was happy to have a girl. I had always wanted a big sister and was looking forward to having one for a year.

Even though Monique was pretty hard to understand at first because of her accent, she was awesome. She was eighteen years old. We shared a room and quickly became close. I was going into ninth grade, and was happy that Monique gave me a reason to hang with the seniors. Even though she got all good grades and seemed preppy at first, she was boy crazy and we had a lot in common.

Although she loved my parents, she couldn't believe how strict American parents were. I agreed that they were incredibly strict and loved hanging out with Monique. She showed me how to roll a French joint, a big, fat blunt rolled with tobacco as well as weed. My parents had stopped bottling me because it was too expensive and I had done so well the first couple times. Things in my life were okay again, except for the fact that Mom-Lynn and I were constantly at each other's throats.

9

Runaway

Father's Story

While I was on the road for a job, my wife called me at my hotel. Someone had broken into our house and taken our most precious belongings. Lynn was at work when the burglary occurred, and the thieves must have spent quite some time ransacking every corner of the house. Understandably, Lynn was distraught and did not want to spend any time in the house alone, so I returned immediately and started the cleanup. We were fully insured, but the insurance company could do nothing to alleviate the loss of security we felt in our own home. We decided to move once again.

Not wanting to relocate the children to yet another school, we looked only in the local area. We found a huge home across town. The house was large enough for everyone, including Monique, to have his or her own room, But Monique and Jasmyn pleaded to stay together. Not seeing any harm in the arrangement, we agreed. We moved into our new residence, which was only a block from Jasmyn's school.

Jasmyn's grades continued to worsen. Before long she was failing all her subjects and cutting most of her classes. The high school had a self-paced program for troubled teens, and the guidance counselor suggested Jasmyn give it a try. Actually, it was more than a suggestion; it was the only way they would allow Jasmyn to stay in school.

Jasmyn did quite well. The self-paced nature of the program suited her intellect; she was able to go as fast as she liked and was proud of her accomplishments. It seemed things were starting to turn around. She was still smoking and hanging out with the wrong crowd, but we adopted a "one thing at a time" attitude with her. We hoped the worst was behind us.

Jasmyn and Lynn continued to get into arguments. It seemed they couldn't be together for more than 15 minutes without a screaming match that ended with Jasmyn being sent to her room. After one such episode, we woke the next morning to find Jasmyn gone.

I called the police and reported her missing. They asked if she had any disciplinary problems, and of course, we had to say yes. They said she was probably a runaway, but they would put her description out to the patrol cars. We were pretty sure she had run away, but there was a lingering doubt. We changed her access code for the alarm system. If she did return when we were out, we would know. Later that day, she tried to get into the house to get some of her clothes. Now we knew for sure.

We talked to her friend Greg in Sacramento. He was a really nice kid and cared about Jasmyn a lot. He did well in school and was pretty responsible. He agreed to meet us with his mom and take us to Jasmyn's boyfriend's house to show us where she was staying. I went to the door and asked the guy who opened the door if she was there. "No way," he said. "I haven't seen her for a long time."

We were pretty sure she was there but not positive. As we were leaving, the boyfriend's mother came home and angrily told us, "Jasmyn isn't here; I would have known."

What a joke. The house was a mess; she was obviously never there. The children had the run of the house. But we didn't press the issue with her. We talked to a counselor who advised us that since we knew where she was and she was safe, we should take this time as a respite, try to enjoy the harmony in our home, and wait for Jasmyn to come back. The counselor felt sure she would return on her own; after all, she couldn't stay there forever. She would have to come back for clothes, putting us in the driver's seat. We would have more negotiating power if she asked to come back, and we could then set some rules for her to agree. It was the old tough-love scenario, but it sounded good.

We tried to take her advice. A full week went by, and finally we had had enough. "Lets' go get her; this is crazy." We assembled a "posse." We stationed a good friend at one corner with her two Great Dane dogs, another friend down at the other end of the street and Lynn in the middle. We all had our cell phones. I then went to the house were she was staying. I knocked on the door and a teenage boy opened the inner door to talk to me through the ragged screen. I told him who I was and asked if my daughter was there. He said he didn't know my daughter. I told him I was coming in to see for myself. He didn't have much choice; I was six feet tall and a very lean 210 pounds. All that was standing between me and confirming my daughter was alive and well was the resemblance of an old screen door and a teenage kid half my size.

I pushed my way in; the house made a pigpen look homey. There was trash everywhere. The sheetrock had large holes from a runaway fist. I could smell urine everywhere. I looked through the house and didn't see Jasmyn. The older kid said, "See asshole, I told ya she ain't here!"

I got close up to his face. Without resorting to any additional dramatics, I said, "I know that you know where my daughter is, and I'll stop at nothing to find her. When I leave here, I'm going to the police and tell them you are hiding her. I'm going to watch you like a hawk." As I talked, his expression changed from cocky to bored to terrified; I convinced him that I wasn't an enemy he wanted to have.

He told me to wait a minute. He went into the back of the house and a minute later came back with Jasmyn in tow. She had been hiding under one of the endless stacks of laundry. When he saw me he started pleading, "She made me promise not to tell you she was here." He repeatedly apologized. I took my daughter and left.

Daughter's story (Age 14)

Mom-Lynn and I were constantly fighting. I hated being around her and she obviously hated me. I was anxious whenever she was home and tried to stay in my room as much as possible. No matter how hard I tried, she always found something wrong with my chores, my actions, or even my tone of voice. I always felt like I was walking on thin ice and could fall through, without warning or notice, at any moment.

I had a new boyfriend now, a boy named Alan whom I'd met while ditching school. He was sixteen, and his house was really cool. He had two little brothers, ages 14 and 13, and since their mom was gone for days at a time, the boys could do whatever they wanted. I talked to Alan about my problems at home, and after a particularly huge fight with my step-mom, I called to tell him I was running away. I asked if I could stay at his house. He agreed.

His house was about fifteen minutes away from mine by car, which neither of us had, and not wanting me to walk the whole way by myself, he agreed to meet me halfway. I waited until my parents were asleep, got dressed, grabbed my steel toed combat boots and a knife, and left. The first half of the walk took about 45 minutes, and when I saw Alan, he looked like he was going to cry.

"I was so worried about you," he said.

Uh-Oh, I thought. *I hope he's not gonna get all weak on me now.* "Chill," I told him. "I can take care of myself."

We walked to his house and went inside. There were holes all over the walls, and the house was a mess. But there were no adults. I could go a whole day without being screamed at or confronted; I never wanted to go home.

One day there was a knock on the door. Adults never came over, and the kids didn't bother to knock. Alan looked at me, scared, and I told him to answer the door while I went to hide in his room. "I'm not here," I reminded him.

From his room, I heard my dad's voice and the sound of arguing. I felt bad for my dad, but knew that things would be even worse between Mom-Lynn and me if I went home now. Then I heard a women's voice that I didn't recognize, and the arguing stopped. I heard the sound of the TV and waited for Alan. After about an hour, he came in. I was still hiding. "What happened?" I asked.

"My mom told your dad that you weren't here. I had to spend some time with her before I came in here so she wouldn't think you were here."

"Your mom's here? Should I leave?"

"Naw," he assured me, "she's leaving tomorrow. Just stay in here and be really quiet."

Alan's mom left the next day, and everything was cool for a while. Alan was getting pretty attached to me. "I love you," he told me one day.

"Uh, love you, too," I said, not wanting to hurt his feelings and knowing he expected that response. A couple of days later, my dad was back. I went to go hide, and this time my dad demanded Alan let him come in and look for me himself. I had hidden in the laundry hamper beside Alan's dresser and pulled a bunch of clothes on top of me so that it looked like the basket was overflowing. I heard my dad come in and heard him opening and closing the dresser drawers as he searched for me. *Why was he looking in the dresser?* I wondered. *I wasn't that skinny.* I held my breath. Finally he left the room, I let my breath out but stayed hidden. I heard muffled voices outside the room and a couple of minutes later someone coming back into the room.

"Jasmyn," Alan called, not knowing where I was hiding. I shook the clothes off and looked at him. My dad was right behind him. I glared at Alan and walked out of the room. "I'm sorry," he lipped to me, right before he started apologizing to my dad.

We got into my dad's car, and I expected him to lecture me and tell me how mad he was. He didn't. He just sighed and told me I was going to live with my mom. Although I'd wanted to live with her for years, I had friends here now, and I would miss Monique. I was happy to go live with my mom, but sad to leave my friends.

10

Changing Families

Father's story

We called Eden; Jasmyn was out of control and needed a change. We agreed that she would stay with her mom for a while. Jasmyn had been asking for this for quite some time, so we were surprised at her response when we told her she could go. She wanted to go but not until after the summer because she had plans here with her friends. Considering her last week with "her friends," we knew it was best for her to go now. She wasn't happy about it, but she went.

I was unhappy over my daughter leaving. Ever since I divorced Eden, my primary goal had been to keep my family together. I had failed. But perhaps she was better off at her mom's. It didn't take a Ph.D. to realize the constant fighting within our home was not healthy for anyone. Life at our house returned to a peaceful calm. We missed Jasmyn but did not miss the fights and the constant struggle. I spoke to her on the phone and that was pleasant.

Jasmyn had been living at her mom's house for about a month when Eden and her husband left for a trip to Hawaii. They left Jasmyn and their young twins at home with a babysitter. Then one day, Eden called from Hawaii to tell us that someone had stolen her husband's truck. Jasmyn swore she was at the park and had nothing to do with it, but Eden said her husband would not come home if Jasmyn were still there. They were convinced Jasmyn was responsible. I told my wife what had happened and drove the two and a half hours to pick her up.

Daughter's story (Age 15)

At my mom's in San Jose, I was bored. It was summer and without being enrolled in school, I didn't have a chance to meet any friends. Besides that, however, life was great. My mom never yelled at me; she told me I could tell her the truth about anything without her getting mad. I tested it out by telling her I smoked. She wasn't mad, but told me it was bad for me and asked me not to smoke around my little brother and sister.

I loved how cool my mom was with me and how I could talk to her about anything. I didn't have to lie or hide things. Also, she understood the importance of makeup and clothes. While she always gave me her opinion about how my makeup and clothes looked, she never demanded I change. I wasn't grounded and no one yelled at me. Raul, my step-dad, jokingly called me Casper because I was so white. I loved having a nickname and felt like a real part of the family, instead of the evil bad-child who's every step had to be closely monitored.

Because my mom regarded me in a respectful way and talked to me without suspicion, I felt an enormous amount of respect toward her. I volunteered to do dishes after dinner because I was so grateful that it wasn't a requirement. Although I missed having friends, the contrast between this new home and my previous one was a huge one. Being at home here was a relaxing and safe experience, instead of one where I felt I had to be anxious, alert, and constantly on edge.

One day while my mom was at work, I walked over to a local park to look for someone who had a cigarette. As I was walking, a couple of boys called out to me. I walked over to them and bummed a cigarette.

"Do you get high?" one of the boys asked me after I'd thanked them for the cigarette.

"Hell, yeah!" I said, grinning. I hadn't smoked any bud in months.

The boys and I introduced ourselves. Mark was Black, tall, and very athletic looking. He obviously had the weed, and therefore on this day seemed to be the leader of the two. Ross, the other boy, didn't seem to be in any condition to lead anyway. He was drunk and high and kept looking at me with a tilted head and comical bird-like movements. Despite his obvious inebriation, this boy was *fine*. He had milky brown skin and unique features that made it hard to guess his ethnicity. I found out later that he was Black, Mexican, and white.

As I got to know Ross I discovered that he was highly intelligent. He was probably one of the most persuasive people I've ever met and could talk anybody into almost anything. Although I have always prided myself on my logical thinking skills, I discovered Ross could spin the facts around so much that he always seemed to be right in the end. I was convinced that Ross would grow up to be a high-powered attorney.

Mark, Ross, and I walked to a more secluded park to smoke some bowls. Later, we went to the store and the boys had someone buy us a couple of forties (beers). I had made new friends.

That night when I got home I had the munchies. I had just started making myself a snack when my mom came into the kitchen. We had only been talking for about thirty seconds when she looked at me funny.

"What?" I asked.

"Are you stoned?"

I couldn't have lied even if I'd wanted to. She trusted me too much. I definitely didn't want to tell the truth though. I settled for just looking at her.

"That's answer enough," she said.

"Sorry," I mumbled.

She explained that she didn't want my little brother and sister to see me stoned and asked me not to come home high anymore. I told her I wouldn't and she sent me to my room. A few minutes later she brought me something to eat. I was surprised that she was still being nice to me right after I'd done something she didn't like. This seemed too good to be true.

For years as I'd gotten up early to make myself breakfast and lunch, and while feeling anxious over my never-ending chores, I'd envied my little brother and sister whose mom made them breakfast every morning and, once they started school, packed their lunches for them every night. "Wow," I would think, watching her with them. "I wish I had a mom like *that*." Now I did. And she shared everything she had with me. She had drawers full of cute clothes that she let me borrow whenever I wanted and tons of makeup. I finally felt like a wanted daughter.

I started going to the park every day while my mom was at work and soon met about a dozen of Mark and Ross's friends. We'd chill at the park all day getting stoned and only leave to chase the ice cream truck or ride our bikes to the store and get something to eat. I would stop smoking about an hour or two before I was going to go home so that I wouldn't be high when I got there.

One day one of the guys brought some girls by. I didn't really like to kick it with girls because I thought they were stupid and whiney, but one of them, Sara, was pretty cool. We got high, and she and I started talking about having kids.

"I'm never having kids!" I said, sure as could be at fourteen. "And if I do, I'm naming him fartface!"

"Fartface?" she asked, cracking up.

"Yeah," I explained, "can you imagine? On his first day of kindergarten his teacher will ask him his name, and he'll look at her and say 'Fartface!' She'll be like 'Don't call me names young man or I'll call your mom! Now tell me your name!' And he'll say '*Fartface.*"

Sara was laughing her butt off by now, so I grinned and kept going. "Then that night I'll be home making dinner and the phone will ring. I'll answer it and it'll be Fartface's teacher calling to tell me that all she did was ask my son his name and he started using vulgar language. 'I'm so sorry.' I will say, 'I just don't know *where* he gets it. Let me call him to the phone.' Then I'll put the phone down on the counter and yell, 'Hey, Fartface! Get out here *now!*'"

I had to stop then because she and I were *rolling* with laughter. We became good friends and had many similar intellectual discussions while stoned.

Eventually, one of the park's neighbors started calling the police and soon they started rolling up onto the grass and searching us for drugs. At first the boys just gave their stuff to us girls and we shoved it into out bras and down our pants. The cops were almost always men, and we knew it was illegal for them to search female minors thoroughly without parental consent. When the searches became almost daily occurrences, however, we found an easier and less scary solution. Since we always sat in the same spot at "our" park, we dug a hole in the grass big enough to hide things in. When the cops started rolling up, we would throw all our stuff in there and cover it with a grass cap and then toss additional grass on top to camouflage the hole. The police never found our spot.

The park was a cool spot because we could go there almost any time of the day and find our friends without arranging to meet beforehand. There were a bunch of regulars, but our group changed sometimes. Whenever anybody walked through whom we didn't know, we'd call him or her over and see if he or she were cool to kick it with. Also, the people who came regularly brought other people sometimes. It was summer vacation, and there were a lot of bored kids around.

One Saturday, Mark and one of the newer kids, Jared, came to the door looking for me. I wasn't home but my mom asked me about them when I got there. She'd met Mark, and knew we were just friends, but she'd never seen Jared before.

"Who's Jared?" she asked.

"A friend."

"Do you like him?"

"Naw. I already have a boyfriend." I was still with Alan.

"Good," she said, "he's ugly!"

I smiled. My mom was a trip.

Jared and I started hanging out more often, and he chilled with older guys at night. I wanted to go and meet them, but I had to be in my room with lights out by one a.m. and I didn't want to disobey my mom's rules. I decided that if I went out the front door after she and my step-dad were asleep, but was back before one, I wouldn't *technically* be breaking the rules. Jared and I arranged to meet at midnight, and I told him to bring me some pickles.

"Pickles?" he asked, puzzled. "Why?"

"Because I'm hungry and I want some," I told him. "Don't come without pickles." I ordered, thinking that a seventeen-year-old boy who let a fourteen-year-old girl boss him around wasn't worth much.

At midnight I went outside, and there was Jared, sitting on the curb with a damn jar of pickles. "I'm not hungry anymore, but thanks anyway." I said, smiling sweetly.

He shoved the pickles into his pocket, and we walked over to his friend's house. The people there were all guys in there early to middle twenties. They had CD cases out, straws, and razor blades. They were sniffing lines of some powdery white stuff through hundred dollar bills. "Want some?" one of them offered.

"What is it?" I asked.

"CR," he informed me. "CR" meant crank, and I would later hear it called C, dope, powder, and shit, the last being the most accurate description.

"Sure," I said. I was ready for a new drug. Jared told him it was my first time and not to make the line too big. The guy cut a small line and showed me how to hold one nostril closed and sniff with the other one. I thought it would burn big time and hoped I wouldn't cry or embarrass myself. I braced myself and sniffed. No pain! I expected that I would feel like I did when I was stoned but after a few minutes I realized I felt invincible. I didn't feel the foggy vagueness of being stoned but felt more clearheaded and ready for life then ever before. I felt fresh and alive. Ready for anything.

Jared pulled me onto his lap. "Yeah, right," I said, laughing and getting up.

"Just kiss me once?" he begged. I wouldn't, and it was pathetic. He kept begging. I'd never had a guy beg me to kiss him before, and it was disgusting. Jared was disgusting. Still, I was in a garage with all his friends. I decided not to be too bitchy.

"Jared," I said sweetly, pushing some hair back from his forehead, "you're *such* a good friend, I really don't want to ruin it."

"Come on," he said gruffly. "Friends want to make each other happy."

What an idiot, I thought. *Didn't he realize that he was making a fool of himself, with all his friends watching?*

I looked around, wondering if he even remembered that there were people around. One of the older guys must've thought I was looking for help 'cause he stepped in.

"Jared, be a man; she said no. Jasmyn, you need another line?"

"Sure." I said, grinning. This stuff was better than weed.

After I'd done my line, I realized that it was pretty late and told Jared I needed to leave. He said he'd walk me back to my mom's house. Once we got outside, the cold air hit us, feeling great on my face. I felt great. I smiled up at Jared, feeling benevolent. "Let's *run!*" I exclaimed, as if it were a brilliant idea.

"Naw, chill," he told me, laughing.

Once I got home I went into the bathroom. I took a shower and then spent about fifteen minutes brushing my teeth before it was time to go to bed. This drug made me feel like doing everything thoroughly.

I went into my bedroom to lie down. I couldn't sleep. I was full of energy and my mind was racing. I got up and wrote a poem.

I started spending more and more time at the park, and I was tired of being stoned. I wanted to do CR again, but I definitely didn't want to hang out with Jared by ourselves anymore. One day someone brought a new girl, Jessi, to the park. Jessi was moving around a lot and was full of energy.

"What's up with you?" I asked.

"I'm wired," she told me. "Wired" meant under the influence of crank. When I asked her if she had anymore, she shook her head.

Just then Ross, who was walking back from buying ice cream from the ice cream man yelled "five-oh!" (That's what we called the police.) Everyone passed their stuff to Mark who threw it in our stash spot and put the cap on, just as the police cars rolled onto the grass.

As they were searching one of the boys, Jessi, who had sat by me when the officers had ordered us to sit down, whispered into my ear.

"I've got a bag of CR in my pocket."

Since Jessi was new, she hadn't known about the stash spot. But hadn't this girl just told me she didn't have anything? I decided to help her anyway. She could pay me back later.

"All right," I whispered, "slowly reach into your pocket." She did. "Now grab the bag and leave your hand there till I tell you to take it out. When I tell you, take your hand out of your pocket and lean back in the grass like this." I leaned back on my arms, hands behind me.

"Now." I whispered, while both officers were looking through a pack of cigarettes they'd found in the boy's pocket. She leaned back so that our hands were almost touching. "Let go." She dropped the bag behind her and we both started slowly tossing grass on top. She was the next to be searched.

"Thank you so much!" She told me after the cops left. "Dude, my mom would've killed me if she'd found out I was doing this."

"No problem," I told her. "So, you gonna kick down?" (Kick down means share.)

"Sure," she said. I grinned. How could she refuse?

Jessi and I became good friends. She always had CR.

Another time, a boy named Gary came by the park. Gary wasn't cute, but he wasn't ugly either. On a scale of one to ten, I would've rated him a six. I liked how he kicked back and watched what was going on. He didn't brag like all the other boys, and he had a nice smile.

The first time I saw him, I didn't even remember his name. Soon, however, he started coming to the park more often, and all my friends already knew him. He and I started to become friends.

Shortly after I met Gary, school started. I was enrolled and went to about a week of classes before I got bored. I had tons of new friends and better things to do than sit in the classroom. One day on the way to science class, Gary, who went to the same school, walked up behind me and put his arm around me, acting all confident.

"What's up?" he asked.

"Not much," I said, deciding not to shrug his arm off since he was being so cute about it.

"Well, see ya later!" he said, walking off. I watched him go, thinking he looked a lot cuter than when I'd first met him.

One of his friends, Ron, liked me, too. No one really liked Ron, and I talked to him because I felt sorry for him. Later on in the day I saw him and stopped to talk to him. We talked about how boring school was, and he asked me if I wanted to skip school that day. "Naw," I said. Talking to Ron was one thing, but hanging out with him would've been a little too much.

"That's cool," he said. "I guess it'll just be me and Gary."

Gary? "Well, actually, I guess I could," I said. "I wouldn't want you guys to have to go by yourselves."

After that a lot of my friends and I started cutting school almost every day and hanging out at the park.

Alan and I still talked on the phone every night, but I was starting to like Gary. I decided to break up with Alan and got a chance the next time he called.

"I miss you," he told me.

"I miss you, too." I said.

"I love you," he said.

"Well," I replied, "about that…"

"What?"

"I don't think we should be together anymore." I held my breath. I'd never been broken up with and hated always having to be the one to do it.

"Fine!" he said. "If that's the way you want it—"*click.* He'd hung up on me. I looked at the phone and smiled. That was easier then I thought. Nice and quick.

The next day Gary, Sara, and I were ditching school. I looked at Gary and wondered when he was going to ask me out. *Now would be a good time,* I thought. I looked at Sara, whose boyfriend had just broken up with her. "Hey, Sara, I broke up with my boyfriend last night."

"Yeah?" she asked.

"Yup. I was thinking since neither of us have boyfriends now, we should go and find some. C'mon." I got up with Sara and acted like I was about to walk away. "Later, Gary!" I said nonchalantly over my shoulder.

"Wait!" he said.

"What?" I asked, stopping and rolling my eyes like I was in a hurry.

"I'll be your boyfriend," he said in his quiet voice.

"Cool," I said, grinning and plopping back down beside him. Boys were *so* easy.

For the next couple of months, Gary, my friends, and I had lots of fun together. We all cut school, and would chill at the park or someone's house if the parents happened to be out of town. I had lots of access to drugs and very rarely had to pay for them myself. San Jose had lots of gangs and crews, and wanting to be like the older kids we deemed ourselves a crew and called ourselves "TDS," which stood for "True Dank Smokers."

Eventually, my mom and step-dad decided to go out of town. They were going on a vacation to Hawaii. Not wanting to leave me responsible for my little brother and sister, my mom got a friend of hers from work to come and look after the house and us. While they were gone, my friends and I kicked it at my house for a couple of days during school. Being there made me nervous, however, because I was worried something might get broken, and I wouldn't have a way to explain it since I was supposed to have been at school. I decided we wouldn't kick it at my house during school anymore.

The day after I'd decided that, I went to some of my classes. After school I went to the park looking for my friends, but no one was there. When I walked into my house, I jumped. About fifteen of my friends were sitting in my mom's living room. I looked around, furious.

"Damn, Jasmyn, you scared us!" said Ross. "We thought you were that lady!" 'That Lady' meant the woman my mom had gotten to watch the house while she was gone.

"Well, I am *so* sorry for walking into my own house and scaring you!" I yelled at Ross. "What do you think you're doing? *Get out!!*" I screamed at my friends, who didn't see why I was so mad.

They left, and after changing my clothes I went to the park. Some of my friends were there and they apologized and smoked me out. We were all chillin' and just when it started to get dark the babysitter drove up with my little brother and sister in the car.

"Jasmyn!" she screamed, getting out of the car. "You need to come home right now!"

Not knowing what was going on, I went and got in the car. Sara came with me. The lady explained that my step-dad's new truck had been stolen. "I went to pick you up at the mall, but you weren't there," she said, glaring at me.

"Why would I be at the mall?" I asked, confused.

"You called and asked me to come and get you at the mall, and when I left to get you the truck was stolen."

"I wasn't at the mall," I told her. "I didn't call you. I've been at the park all night. Ask Sara."

Sara nodded. We figured someone who knew my parents were out of town got a girl to call in order to get everyone out of the house and then stole the truck.

Sara and I cooperated with the police, and they found the truck.

My mom was furious. She called from Hawaii and told me she was in the hospital. She and my step-dad had gotten into a car accident. They didn't need this. I told my mom that I was sorry and that it wasn't my fault. I'd never steal from them. She said we'd talk about it when they got home.

These last few months were the first time I'd felt I'd had a secure home, and now I was worried it would all be ruined. I talked to Gary about my fears the next day.

"I'm gonna get kicked out," I said.

"No, you're not," he said. "Your mom loves you."

He didn't understand. My mom did love me, but she had a new family now. A long time ago she and my dad had made a mistake and married. Then they had corrected their mistakes, fixed their lives, and done it right. I was what was leftover. I wasn't someone my parents and their lifelong spouses had planned for and wanted. I was just accepted. Unless I became unacceptable.

When my mom and Raul got back my mom explained to me that I would have to leave. She said I was tearing apart the family and she had to think of my seven-year-old brother and sister. I understood. They were little kids. They needed their parents. I was fifteen—a grownup. I didn't need anybody.

11

Halloween

Father's story

Jasmyn was home again. Halloween was just around the corner. Knowing she had a better chance of getting a yes from me, Jasmyn came to me and asked, in only a way a daughter can melt her father's heart, "Daddy, since I'm doing so good in school, can I please go out trick-or-treating with my friends on Halloween?" How could I say no? Things were looking up and I desperately wanted my little girl to be happy. I convinced my wife we should let her go and then gave the good news to Jasmyn. She was thrilled.

Halloween came and she dressed up and was ready to go. Lynn dropped her off at her girlfriend's house and reminded her to be home by eleven. She had assured me she wouldn't be late, but eleven o'clock came and went, then midnight, then 1:00 a.m. She didn't come home. I was sure something terrible had happened to her. There was no way she would run away after assuring me she would be home by eleven.

The next day we called all her friends, but they all claimed they hadn't heard from Jasmyn. I made a missing poster with a recent picture and took it to the print shop. Armed with a hundred copies, I visited all her old haunts and hung up posters. I asked any and all kids I ran into if they had seen her. All replied no. I didn't go to work. The search for my daughter was all consuming. I started thinking if I hadn't let her go trick-or-treating, this wouldn't have happened.

Daughter's story (Age 15)

After my dad picked me up from my mom's and brought me home, I re-enrolled in the self-paced alternative program at school. I was doing pretty well grades-wise, but I was still doing drugs and hanging out with my old friends.

One day while I was chillin' in the hallway at school smoking a cigarette, a girl walked up to me. I'd never met her before, and I tensed up. I didn't like her walking up to me like we were old friends or something.

"What are you *doing?*" she asked me, wide eyed, looking at the cigarette.

"What, you don't smoke?" I asked her.

"Sure," she said. "In the bathrooms, or out back in the field. Never right in the hallway where it's easy to get caught."

"Ever been caught in the bathroom?" I asked her.

"Yes."

"Me, too," I explained. "The school has people check the bathrooms and the fields to see if we're smoking. They don't check in the halls because they figure nobody's stupid enough to smoke right out in the open."

She laughed as I took another drag and stubbed out my cigarette. "You're Jasmyn Klarfeld, right?"

"Yeah," I confirmed, wondering how kids always seemed to know my name even though I'd never seen them before.

"Well," she told me, "my boyfriend likes you."

Too bad for her. I was prettier. "Who's your boyfriend?"

"Barry."

"Oh," I assured her, "I think he's ugly."

The girl looked kind of confused, like she didn't know whether to be appeased or insulted. Her name was Elle, and she soon decided we were best friends. I didn't mind. Her mom spoiled her and she had a ton of cute little clothes that she let me borrow often, since we were *best* friends and all.

On Halloween I asked my dad if I could go trick-or-treating with her. He let me go, since I was doing okay in school, but made me promise to be home by eleven. I promised with every intention of doing so.

I got dressed up and Mom-Lynn drove me over to Elle's house. We had a fight in the car, however, and I was in a bad mood when I got there.

We started trick-or-treating and soon ran into a group of boys who were busy drinking. We all introduced ourselves, and the guys were willing to share their alcohol. They even had some weed. By the time eleven o'clock rolled around, we were all pretty sloshed. "Don't we have to go home?" asked Elle.

"I'm not going home," I announced, deciding as I said the words. Mom-Lynn was already mad at me and going home drunk and stoned wouldn't make matters any better. Last time she'd seen me stoned I'd gotten all my belongings torn up or taken away, plus I'd had to scrub the house for two weeks. And besides, I missed Gary. If I stayed here, I'd never get to see him. "Can I stay at your house?" I asked Ron, one of the older boys.

"Sure," he said, while Elle glared at me. She'd already decided that she liked Ron. I smiled at her. That's what happened when you got all emotionally attached to people five minutes after meeting them.

"Me, too?" she asked, and I laughed.

"Sure," I answered before Ron could say anything. She'd be fun to have around.

We stayed at Ron's house for a couple of days, leaving only to go to the grocery store to steal some hair dye. The same day I dyed my hair black, Ron invited a bunch of friends over to his house. They were all pretty drunk when his roommate came home and said everybody had to leave.

Elle and I didn't have a place to go, but one of the girls said we could stay with her. She was nineteen and living with her boyfriend, who was twenty-one. She had a little sister our age and felt bad for us. We spent the night at her house. The next day, she and her boyfriend, Roger, had a huge fight. She kicked him out and we went with him.

Father's story

Looking back, it is easy now to realize what was happening within our family. If this were a script in a play the major players would include Jasmyn, my wife, my ex-wife, and me. In my daughter's eyes, my wife was the evil step mom, and she was very observant about Jasmyn's behavior and mannerisms. She was quick to point out to me whenever Jasmyn was going astray. She didn't need absolute proof; instead, she relied on her intuition and Jasmyn's behavior. In retrospect, she was correct 95 percent of the time. Jasmyn's mom was as quick to point out to Jasmyn that Lynn and I were much too strict. Jasmyn did not need to listen to what we said because her real mom would support her. Because of this attitude, our daughter was rebellious and extremely argumentative. I was caught in the middle, constantly cast in the role of referee and decision maker.

My wife was so frustrated with Jasmyn's behavior that she took every opportunity to point out when she thought Jasmyn needed to be disciplined. She criticized Jasmyn so often that I started automatically defending unless we had absolute proof of her guilt. I was literally blind to Jasmyn's actual behavior because I believed Lynn was too critical, and Lynn couldn't back off and let me see for myself what Jasmyn was doing. My wife was convinced she could get through to Jasmyn with just one more lecture; Jasmyn responded by rolling her eyes and displaying attitude. This sparked a frenzy of yelling and screaming, which always ended with Lynn's announcement, "You're grounded!"

Years later, we realized that if Lynn had stopped continuously pointing Jasmyn's faults and let me see for myself, we could have approached the problem more as a team. Jasmyn resented my wife for her perception. Jasmyn said often in private and sometimes in the heat of an argument, "I'm Dad's daughter, not yours! Why can't you leave me alone?" Of course, this was far from the truth. My wife had raised Jasmyn from the age of three. She had earned the title "Mom."

12

Another New Home

Daughter's story (Age 15)

Roger took us to one of his friend's houses and we all stayed there over the weekend. He and I kicked it a lot and messed around a little bit. On Monday, he had to go to work. He worked in Fairfield, which was halfway to San Jose. I convinced him to take us with him and we would hitchhike from there to San Jose.

Once in Fairfield, however, Elle didn't want to go. "You have a boyfriend there and I don't," she whined.

I wasn't going back and I felt responsible for her. She was so stupid that she'd get herself killed if I let her take off by herself. "Okay," I said. "You want a boyfriend; I know lots of guys in San Jose." I tried to think of the two who were least useful to me. Useful guys weren't worth much once they had a girlfriend, so I wasn't going to give Elle anybody I might need sometime. After a moment, I'd decided on two who weren't TDS. "You can have Ryan or Jed," I told her. "Jed would be more convenient since he's Gary's brother, but Ryan would be cool, too." She agreed and we hitchhiked to San Jose, passing up rides that I thought looked sketchy. Roger had given me a knife, but we still had to look out for ourselves. I was trying to see my boyfriend and have some fun, not *die*.

Once I got to San Jose, I saw all my friends again. Elle loved Jed. Literally. After about three days, they told Gary and me that they were going to get married someday. I was getting tired of her. She was whiny, clingy, and emotional. Her personality reminded me of all the reasons I had for not hanging out with girls. Besides Sara and another girl from the park, Ruby, all of my friends whom I liked and respected were guys.

We spent the night at Gary and Jed's house when they could sneak us in, but we usually had to stay out pretty late in order to make sure their parents were asleep. One night the police picked us up for being out past San Jose's eleven o' clock underage curfew. They took us to a shelter for homeless kids. The shelter had a lot of rules, and I didn't like it there. I called my mom. She came and picked me up. I told her I was fine and asked her to drop me off at a friend's house. She did, but told me to call her if I needed anything.

The shelter wouldn't let my mom take Elle, and she ended up going home. I asked her to tell my dad I was okay and was glad she was going. I hated having somebody else to take care of.

Father's story

After a few days, we knew that Jasmyn had run away again. The mom of girl with whom she had gone out on Halloween called to tell us her daughter said Jasmyn had gone back to the Bay Area. I couldn't understand it. She was doing well in school. Things at home seemed to be looking up. Why would she run away again? I asked my wife if anything happened when she dropped her off at her friend's house. She replied they had an argument, but it wasn't major. It occurred to me that Jasmyn's response to any negative situation at home or in school was the same: run away.

I truly had no idea what to do next. I was powerless. I reported her as a runaway to the local police department and hoped for the best. A few days later the phone rang again. When you have a child who is a chronic runaway, the phone ringing becomes a scary sound. I found myself saying little prayers on the way to pick it up: "Please let her be OK" or "Please let her not be dead" but most often "Please let it be her calling to say she wants to come home." This time, it was Jasmyn's mom in the Bay Area. The police had picked her up for breaking curfew. Her mom had picked her up but dropped her off at a friend's house. Since the truck incident, her mom's home was not an option, and Eden didn't want to risk disturbing her family's tranquility.

What could we do? Jasmyn wasn't allowed anywhere near her mom's house, and she didn't want to come back and live with us. She wanted to stay in the Bay Area. My wife's sister Anne lived there with her husband in a nice three-bedroom home and had no children. They were loving people and wanted to help Jasmyn, so they offered her a home with them. They lived very close to Jasmyn's mom so she could visit often.

It seemed like a solution; however, I had a problem with it. I knew my daughter. She would eat these people up. But seeing no other alternative, I agreed Jasmyn should give it a try. Jasmyn moved in with her aunt and uncle. Lynn and Anne were extremely close and spoke many times a day; they came up with a plan for Jasmyn to do chores and earn her keep. If she needed extra curricular items, she could earn them by doing additional chores.

Of course, Jasmyn hated this arrangement. She wanted no responsibilities or restraints whatsoever. To her, going to school was a waste of good partying time. It wasn't long before her uncle noticed the screen had been removed from Jasmyn's window. It was obvious that she was sneaking out at night, but to no one's surprise, she denied it when confronted. Apparently the screen that had been in place for the past twenty years started mysteriously falling out of the window. Anne tried to punish Jasmyn for sneaking out and lying. Within a few months, Jasmyn ran away again. I can't say I was surprised. I am ashamed to remember feeling a sense of redemption. Because I couldn't understand why Jasmyn kept running away from our home, I had hoped secretly that she would do the same wherever she went, proving it was not my fault. This was Jasmyn's third home spanning a short period of time.

All adults have rules they truly believe to be reasonable and just. It's called society. Jasmyn was determined not to live within the constraints of anyone's rules. She knew she was a minor and believed she could suffer no real consequences for her actions. Sadly, she was correct. Everyone tried to explain to her she was ruining her life and her future, but she was unconcerned. She was living for today. She believed it was her life to do with as she pleased. How dare any adult tell her differently? It was a few weeks before we heard from Jasmyn again.

Daughter's story (Age 15)

I called each of my parents a couple of times a month in order to let them know I was okay. My dad always asked me if I wanted to come home. I didn't. I liked being with my friends and doing whatever I wanted. I liked not having someone yell at me or suspect me constantly. One day my dad asked me to lunch and I accepted.

While we were at lunch, he told me he was worried about me. He said he understood that I didn't want to go home, but he didn't like me living on the streets. I was only fifteen and it was dangerous. He had talked to my aunt and uncle and they had said I could live with them. I could tell my dad was pretty worried, so I agreed.

Once at my aunt's, things seemed to be okay. Aunt Anne was a genuinely warm person and I thought we'd get along, but after awhile, that didn't seem to be the case. She and Mom-Lynn talked on the phone regularly and decided that I needed to learn the value of money. I thought that this was ridiculous. After all, I'd been living on the streets where money meant food. I'd gone whole days without eating if I hadn't had any money and often times 99 cents seemed like a fortune. Ninety-nine cents could buy a Whopper at Burger King.

The plan was that I'd work out in the yard in order to earn money. I would be paid $4.25 an hour, which was minimum wage. I worked the first couple of hours willingly, so I could earn bus money to see Gary and my friends. I liked being able to earn money whenever I wanted it, but it took less than a week for the novelty to wear off. I had enrolled in school by then and was expected to earn the bus money to get to school. If I didn't have any money, I could walk. I chose to walk rather then waste money.

I had planned on going to school every day and had every intention of avoiding cutting class. I did pretty well for the first couple of weeks. But P.E. was my first period class and I needed a uniform to participate. The uniform cost $25; when I asked for the money, Aunt Anne said I'd have to earn it. I couldn't believe it—over five hours of raking leaves to earn an ugly uniform. I didn't want to participate in P.E. anyway. I still showed up at my first period class every day, and every day the teacher made me sit out. Finally, at the end of the second week, she came up to me as the class was beginning.

"You know," she said, "if your parents can't afford to buy a uniform you can have them call the school to see if we can lend you one."

"Thanks," I said, embarrassed. I did not go back to the class. I still planned on attending school. I'd just find something else to do until second period. I did find other things to do, and by the time second period rolled around every day I was already busy. I still raked from time to time in order to earn money for the bus. I didn't even feel guilty about spending my bus money to see friends instead of using it to ride to school. After all, it was *my* money; I'd worked for it.

During this time, Gary and I broke up. He'd heard I was sleeping with an older boy named Neil. I wasn't.

When Neil heard that we'd broken up he asked me why. I told him.

"That's not true," he said, kissing me. We'd never kissed or even flirted before, and I wrinkled my nose at him. Then I laughed. Everybody already thought I was sleeping with him anyway, and he *was* cute. "What're you doing later?" he asked.

"Same thing as you," I answered, raising my eyebrows.

We ended up going over to his house but I was surprised to find that it wasn't even really *his* house. He was nineteen, and I'd expected him to live alone. He lived with his mom, who ran a daycare center. She was home with about ten little kids. Yuck. Besides family, I didn't really have any fondness for little kids. They always seemed to be dripping fluids. I'd take a puppy any day.

Neil led me through his house and to his room. He kissed me, a big, wet, slobbery kiss. Yuck! Neil was leakier than all the little darlings who were currently banging on the door and screaming for Neal to come out and play with them. I had to get out of here. I told Neal we'd chill again later.

It was a promise I didn't intend to keep and I stopped kicking it with my old friends. I didn't want to see Gary, anyway. I'd never been broken up with before, and I didn't like it at all. Instead, I decided to spend my school days at the mall, where I soon met a guy named David. He was nineteen, too, and lived with his dad, who didn't care that David didn't work or pay rent. He also didn't mind if I chilled at his house with his son all day, drinking beer and smoking weed instead of going to school. Perfect. David became my new boyfriend.

One day when I got home my aunt told me that the school had called and said I'd been skipping school. Although I tried to act surprised, I was still grounded. I promised I'd go to school.

Before I left for school the next day, though, Sara paged me. She said that Gary had been asking about me and asked if I could come kick it. I still liked Gary and readily agreed. When I got to the spot, everybody was there. Gary asked what I'd been doing, and I told him I had a boyfriend. I didn't want him to think I was hurt or anything. He was selling doses (acid) and Sara and I bought some and left. We went back to her house and fried. I had been planning on getting back to my aunt's house at the same time I would've gotten home from school had I gone, but time lost all meaning during the majority of my trip. By the time I remembered to look at the clock, it was nine-thirty at night.

"Is that clock right?" I asked the people at Sara's house. It was. "Damn!" I said, "I'm grounded." We all laughed.

When I felt able to talk on the phone without laughing, I called my aunt who said she'd come and pick me up. I was having a good trip and wasn't at all concerned with getting in trouble. Besides, I knew the worst anyone could do was ground me and I didn't have to stay grounded unless I chose to. When my aunt arrived, she was mad. I got in the car and looked ahead. There was rain on the windshield and it was dripping down in beautiful gobs of color. I sat back in the car, content.

"Did you go to school today?" Aunt Anne asked.

"Huh," I said, distracted and needing to reconstruct the question in my head. "Oh...naw," I finally answered, too distracted by my hallucinations to lie.

Aunt Anne blew up. "You don't even care! I used to wonder how Lynn could lose her temper with you so easily and now I know! You just don't CARE!" Aunt Anne screamed at the top of her lungs, pounding on the steering wheel. I watched her outburst, mildly amused and only slightly interested in all her movement, before turning my attention back to the pretty windshield water.

The next day I saw David for the last time, although not by any prior planning on my part. We were lying in his bed when he turned to me and said something stupid. "You know Jasmyn, you're really special to me."

"Uh yeah, you're special to me too," I muttered, not knowing what else to say and hoping that'd be the end of it. It wasn't.

"I hope that one day we'll get married and have kids," he said smiling. "I'll cook breakfast for you every morning..."

What? I thought, as he continued to daydream. *I've known this guy for less then a month. Plus, I'm only fifteen. And he's in love? This guy needs to get a life.*

"Mmmm, that'd be nice," I said aloud, stretching and sitting up. I looked at the clock. "I've gotta go; I'm still grounded," I said, kissing him.

"See you tomorrow?" he asked.

"Of course."

Luckily, I'd only given him my pager number. He paged me for months, but I never talked to him again. Instead, I started hanging out with my old friends again, and found better ways to scam up money than raking. Soon Gary and I were back together; he was acting cooler than ever. All it took was my ignoring him for a couple of weeks. We'd had a long talk and he'd begged me to get back with him. I'd pretended to think about it for a few days and then finally agreed, telling him that if he was ever even slightly less than a sweetheart, I would never talk to him again.

I still didn't have a P.E. uniform and wasn't going to school. None of my friends did, and I felt like I'd miss out on life if I spent my days in the classroom. The only time I went to school was to sell cigarettes or CR, and then I'd leave before having a chance to go to class. As a result, it just wasn't working out at my aunt's house. My aunt and uncle were driving themselves crazy trying to control me. I left.

13

Group Home or Jail

Father's story

Jasmyn was on the streets again. We didn't know exactly where she was, but we did know she had been spotted around town. I worried about her constantly. I couldn't chain her to the house or escort her around school. All I could really do was hope she would come to her senses before she lost them to a rapist or a murderer.

Life in our home was also moving on. Lynn and I had been married for over ten years and wanted children of our own. Lynn longed to be a mom without the baggage that was associated with dealing with Eden. We had put off having children of our own because of the turmoil with Jasmyn. We decided together we had delayed long enough.

But there were problems. After Joshua was born, I'd decided to get a vasectomy. I had a beautiful daughter and son and was convinced I wouldn't want more children. When Lynn and I married, I knew Lynn wanted us to have children of our own someday, so I went to the doctor and had the vasectomy reversed. Although the operation was successful, we were unable to conceive. We consulted a fertility expert. We tried artificial insemination. The emotional roller coaster was exhausting. Lynn wanted to be pregnant more than anything else. She purchased home pregnancy tests every month and repeatedly tested three or four times, hoping to get a positive result. With every negative result, her spirits plummeted. The doctor asked if we were under any stress at home. He said the problems we were experiences could result from stress. We continued to try to conceive and continued to add to the stress.

I started looking for ways to relieve some of the anxiety that was overwhelming Lynn. She had always been very close to her family. Before we married, she had always lived within 15 minutes of five siblings. She needed this support now more than ever, so I decided to move back to the Bay Area. My business was thriving there, and I could easily open another location; my business partner agreed it would be a positive move for the company.

I also reasoned that Jasmyn kept running away because of her desire to live in the Bay Area close to friends and her biological mom. If we moved, she could live at home and be happy. My family would be back together again. I proposed the move to Lynn and she was thrilled. Before long, we had rented a nice home and moved.

Shortly after the move, we received a call from the juvenile division of the local police department. Jasmyn had been arrested the night before for breaking into a train station. I thought, "What next?" I went to juvenile hall and picked her up. Lynn was not thrilled with the prospect of having Jasmyn back in the house. She didn't need any more stress in her life.

"Don't you think I've been through enough?" she asked. "Why can't Eden take her in?"

"Eden doesn't want to jeopardize her marriage and current family by catering to Jasmyn," I explained.

"Oh, I see. And why don't we have that option? Why do we have to jeopardize our marriage and family?"

"Look, Lynn. I'm the only person Jasmyn can count on in her life. No matter how hard she falls, I want her to know I'll always be there to pick her up and love her. I'll always give her a home in my house; I won't—I can't—take that away from her."

Lynn could have demanded I make a choice—my daughter or her. I can't imagine how many marriages break up as a result of situations like ours. But Lynn made no demands. Although we both wanted the chaos to stop, she never gave me an ultimatum. Once again my wife told me to do what I felt needed to be done. I went to pick Jasmyn up.

Jasmyn was not happy to be home. She wanted to be free to do as she pleased. I had hoped her time in juvenile hall would have scared some sense into her, but that was not the case. In fact, she thought it was a breeze, just another part of being a bad-ass kid. She had no intention of staying home, but I explained that she had been released to me and had an appointment with a probation officer the next day. If she bolted, they would throw me in jail. This was not true, but it worked. That night, we fought and she stomped off to her room. The next day, I took Jasmyn to the probation officer. They gave her two options: Go back to juvenile hall, or go to a live-in group home for troubled teens. She chose the group home.

Daughter's story

My friends and I did pretty much whatever we wanted, and one of them always sneaked me and whoever else needed a place into a house at night. Although some of them always went home after a couple of days or weeks, there was seldom a time during my homelessness that a few of my friends weren't homeless as well. Eventually I grew tired of couch hopping, and Ruby emptied out her closet and made me a nice little bed inside. It was like my own little room and I kept all of my stuff there. Gary was into CR by now, as were most of my friends, and we usually had one or two moneymaking schemes going on, ranging from stealing to selling drugs.

Ross was one of the only ones who wouldn't touch crank. He said it was nasty and always lectured the rest of us on it. He used his money to buy weed.

We never got caught for anything major. When we did get caught, it was for something pretty stupid.

One night, when Gary and I were on the streets, we were kicking it with some of his older friends. We were selling crank at the time and had just bought an eight ball and gotten it all chopped up and ready to sell. We had plenty leftover for personal use, and each of us had done a couple of rails. A rail is a really big line.

I bought a pack of Magic Markers with the intention of taking out the felt insides and stashing our stuff inside the markers before putting them back inside the box. One of the guys we were with, Daryl, didn't like the idea. "No," he insisted, "you're too young. If we get caught, your life will be messed up. I'll hold it."

"No," I argued, "Since I'm a minor, I can't get into much trouble. They'll think I didn't know better. Besides, if they open the box, they'll just see markers."

He wouldn't 't budge. Thinking we wouldn't get busted anyway, as we never had before, I shook my head and handed over the stuff. We went on with our day.

That night I started getting a weird feeling in the pit of my stomach. I felt anxious. It was almost midnight and the four of us were sitting at a park downtown, talking. I looked around, alert. Everything looked normal. I looked at Gary, and suddenly knew the feeling had something to do with him. He was going to go away or get sick or something. A bolt of fear shot through me. I was with Gary because I loved him. All of my other boyfriends had either gotten annoying after a couple of weeks or had been easily disposable when their usefulness ran out. He wasn't, and suddenly I was worried about losing him.

I looked at him closely. He seemed suddenly kind of quiet. "You okay?" I asked him.

"Yeah," he said. "Just a little thirsty."

"All right," I said, worried. "Let's go get something to drink." The four of us walked to the nearest fast food restaurant. It was closed. We walked to the next one, only to find it closed as well. After walking all through downtown and not finding anything open, the others wanted to give up.

"I'm okay," Gary told me. "*Really.*"

That wasn't good enough for me. That weird feeling hadn't gone away, and I was determined to get Gary something to drink. "Okay," I said, "let's just find a water fountain." The others agreed and we began our search again. We still hadn't found one as we neared the Amtrak station. It was now about two-thirty in the morning.

"There!" I said triumphantly. "They've *got* to have a water fountain." We walked up to the station, past a homeless man sleeping on a bench. They did have a water fountain, but it was inside. The station was closed. *Damn.* I looked around. Whoever had last closed up had forgotten to close the window to one of the bathrooms. I crawled through the window and then went around and opened the station's front door for my friends. We all went in, got a drink, and left. When we came out the bum was gone. The weird feeling in the pit of my stomach was not.

We had not walked far when we heard sirens. Three police cars rolled up to us, cops pouring out. "What's going on, officer?" one of us asked.

"Four people of your description just robbed the Amtrak station," one of the officers replied as his co-workers began searching our belongings and us. We all had to sit on the curb with our hands behind our back. I watched as one of the cops grabbed my backpack and started to look through it. He pulled out the box of markers and tossed it to one of the other cops. The guy opened it and glanced inside. "Markers," he declared as he closed the box and gave it back to his partner. "You like to color?" he asked me as I watched the box disappear back into my backpack.

"Uh, yeah," I said absentmindedly, wishing Daryl had trusted me. I watched him get up to be searched. I watched the officer pull a pack of cigarettes out of Daryl's pocket. I watched him flip open the top and look inside.

"Bingo," said the searching officer, showing the bagged-up drugs to a partner. "Possession with the intent to sell."

"It's mine," I said, panicked. "He was just holding it for me." I would get a lot less time then he would.

"No, it's not," argued Daryl.

The officers ignored him. "How old are you?" one of them asked me, frowning.

"Fifteen," I answered, truthfully. "I needed the money," I said, feeling like I should add something.

"She's lying," said Daryl.

"Both of you shut up," said one of the cops. "It's in his possession. I'll take him."

All of us ended up getting arrested that night, Daryl for possession with intent to sell, and the rest of us for breaking and entering. I was taken to the juvenile hall in San Jose and booked.

Juvie had rules like everywhere else, just stricter. "All you bitches wake up!" the female guards would yell, walking up and down the halls at five-thirty in the morning. The showers were all grouped together with towels too little to cover anything. Each girl got to have a turn in the shower every other day. Since showering in front of fifty other people was not my idea of a good time, I felt lucky to be able to leave before my turn came up. My charges had been dropped.

Daryl spent about three years in jail.

14

Jail Break

Daughter's story

After my dad picked me up from juvie, things at home had not changed. Needless to say, Dad and Mom-Lynn were not happy with me or my current circumstances. Almost as soon as we got home, we all had a huge fight, which resulted in my stomping upstairs to the guestroom. My parents thought I should have learned from getting arrested and felt that I should be ready to admit they were right, settle down, and atone for my past behavior. They seemed to think that my remorse would put them in a better position to maintain control.

The problem with the theory was that I did not possess the expected remorse. Once when I was about twelve, I had tried to apologize voluntarily to Mom-Lynn for something I had done. I had been lying about my homework, gotten caught, and was grounded and sent to my room. While in my room, I started to think about all the times in the past Mom-Lynn had bought me clothes or taken me to the movies. I actually started to feel bad about being so rude to her all of the time. Although I hated to admit I was wrong, I wanted Mom-Lynn to know that I cared about her and her feelings. I was sorry, so I decided to apologize.

I left my room and walked down the hall. "Can I tell you something?" I asked Mom-Lynn.

"Yes," she said, glaring at me.

"I'm sorry for lying,"

"I know," she said icily, still glaring at me.

It was a disaster. I went back to my room, humiliated. I was angry with myself for actually feeling bad and doing something as stupid as apologizing. I had put aside my pride for no reason. I decided that I would not apologize again, and I would not let anyone make me feel guilty again. Now, three years later, I was still keeping this vow. I would not apologize, and I felt no need for atonement.

Although I hadn't been formally charged with breaking and entering and there was no court date pending, I wasn't out of the woods yet. I still had an appointment with a probation officer. My dad took me to the meeting, where the probation officer told me I had some choices. The county could reinstate my charges and I could go to juvenile hall, or I could go to a live-in group home. I chose the group home.

My dad took me to the group home and signed the necessary papers. By now I had found out that Gary's parents had also sent him to a group home far away, and I wasn't hoping to see him again.

Once inside the group home, the counselors showed me to my room and then introduced me to the other kids. With the exception of one boy, all the residents were girls. I was happy to find that I already knew one of the older girls. She was one of the girls who had kicked it with TDS back in "the day," and she became like a big sister to me. Her name was Kathy.

From the minute I walked into the group home, I had been looking for ways to run. It was a lockdown facility, but there were fieldtrips. However, the rules said that if I left, I would be reported to the police who would then take me to juvenile hall. That didn't faze me, however, because I wasn't planning on going home, and I didn't see how the police would find me without an address. Besides, Santa Clara county had a lot of crime; I figured the police had better things to do than actively look for a runaway. What *did* faze me was Kathy. She'd seen me looking around, taking in details, and had guessed my intentions.

"You better not take off," she'd tell me. "You're doing good in school, and the adults here are hella cool. This is a good chance for you." I'd think about what she'd said, and each time decide to stay another day. It wasn't so bad, and the field trips were cool.

One Saturday we took a trip to San Francisco. I loved it there. I loved the smells, the crowds, and the overall ambiance of the place. This was a city that seemed to be a whole world within itself. There were all kinds of people, and I liked just watching everybody. All these people with separate lives, their own stories, coming together in the same place, literally crossing paths amazed me.

Back at the group home, some of the girls were due to "graduate" soon. Kathy was one of them. When she left I was happy for her, but knew I would miss her. She had kind of kept me accountable.

A couple of days after she left, we had a field trip to one of the nearby parks. I was surprised to recognize the park; my friends and I smoked weed there back in "the day." I remembered how Mark's friend would drive, and we would always sit in the car in the same spot overlooking the park while we listened to music and smoked weed. The park had about three different parking lots, and I tried to remember which one it was as I reminisced. *The one at the top of the hill,* I remembered, glancing up. At the top of the hill I could see the parking lot, and there was a burgundy car in our spot! Freddy's car was burgundy. If this were Freddy and Mark, I'd seriously trip out. None of my old friends knew where I was. I started walking up the hill. I could hear beats! Bone Thugs! It *was* Freddy and Mark.

As I neared the car I could see them inside. "Whoa, it's Jasmyn!" Freddy said, as I stuck my head in the window.

"Where'd you come from?" Mark asked, surprised.

"I was staying at a group home," I explained, grinning. "We're on a field trip."

The boys laughed, surprised that I was staying anywhere.

"You like it there?" Mark asked.

"Naw," I said. "Let me get a ride."

"No way; I'm not getting in trouble," said Freddy.

Just then one of the group home counselors saw me and yelled for me to come down. When I didn't, he motioned to two of the other counselors, and they started up the hill. I had to think fast. I still had ninety dollars at juvenile hall that they had taken from me after my arrest. "I'll give you thirty bucks!" I said to Freddy.

"All right, get in!" He started the car. I got in the car and looked out the window. The counselors were running now, waving their arms and yelling. I couldn't hear what they were saying 'cause Freddy had turned up the beats as we peeled out of the parking lot. "Thanks, man," I said, laughing.

"No problem," said Freddy. "Where's my thirty bucks?"

"At the police station," I told him.

"What?"

"Don't trip," I laughed. "If you get me down there before the group home reports me, I can pick it up without getting arrested."

"Jasmyn, you're crazy," Freddy told me as we headed downtown.

I picked up the money without a problem and asked Freddy to drop me off at a strip mall near Gary's house where a lot of Gary's friends kicked it. There was a guy named Roy who worked at the McDonalds there, and I knew that he and his girlfriend would probably let me stay with them.

When I walked into the McDonalds, however, I was surprised at what Roy had to say. "Hey, Gary was in here a little while ago asking about you."

"Yeah, right; Gary's in a group home."

"Naw, he's been back for a week."

I went outside and walked around and soon found Gary. We were happy to see each other and it seemed like we had never been apart. We kicked it together all the time and slept in schools or at people's houses when Gary was kicked out of his parent's house, which was often.

One day we were all sitting at the park, bored and broke. Someone suggested robbing a house. I was hungry, so I agreed. Ross, Ruby, a guy named Sam, and I went to find one. The others stayed at the park, laughing. They didn't think we'd do it. We almost didn't.

The four of us walked for a while into a neighborhood we didn't recognize. It was the middle of the day and the whole street looked deserted. Everybody was at work. We picked a house and Ruby and I walked up and rang the doorbell. We wanted to make sure nobody was home. If someone had answered, we would've acted like we had the wrong house and left. Nobody answered.

The boys walked around to the back of the house. They were supposed to find a way in and then let us girls in through the front. We waited about five minutes and then the boys returned, not through the front door as planned, but through the yard. They'd been too scared to enter the house.

"Let's go," Ruby said, rolling her eyes, and all three of them started to leave.

"Hold up," I said, irritated. We'd already wasted a lot of time, and I didn't want to give up. I walked around to the back of the house and looked through the window. The house was obviously occupied by men. It was a mess, but there were three nice mountain bikes in the kitchen. I wanted one, and we could sell the others. I tried the windows, but they were all locked. I pulled the end of my flannel over my hand and plunged my fist through the window. The window didn't shatter, but the hole I'd made was large enough for me to unlock the window. I opened it and crawled through.

I only felt guilty for a moment. I vaguely believed in God, and it was even my habit to pray each night, copying a prayer I'd learned listening to Metellica's *Enter Sandman*. But my god was not the structured God of the bible, just a vague idea I had of someone powerful looking out for me. More real to me was my belief in strength, the need to take care of myself without showing weakness. I'd felt strong plunging my fist through a window when the older boys were too scared. I easily put my guilt aside.

I went into a bedroom and grabbed some socks for my hands so that I wouldn't leave fingerprints. Then I went and opened the door for my friends. They looked at me, surprised. I made myself a sandwich and grabbed a bike. Each of the boys grabbed one and we left through the front door.

We got back to the park and everybody gave us "props." (Props are a kind of congratulatory handshake showing proper respect for a job well done.) The story of what happened got around, and I often overheard my friends telling each other, "Jasmyn is *down!*" That meant fearless—ready for anything. I was proud of my reputation.

A couple of weeks later, after the money from the bikes was gone, I was walking around with Jessi. We were wired and she was asking me about the experience. We talked for a while, and Jessi was pretty admiring. "I want to rob a house," she said. I grinned. "Alright," I said, pointing to the house we happened to be passing. "How 'bout that one?"

"Are you serious?" she asked, wide-eyed, as we walked up and rang the doorbell.

"Yup," I said confidently when no one answered the door. "Wait here and I'll come and let you in."

I went around to the side of the house and found a small bathroom window that was unlocked. I'd thought a lot about the best way to "do" houses in the last couple of weeks and decided I'd acted foolishly the last time by breaking the window. That had made a lot of noise, and the owners of the house were sure to have reported a break-in to the police once they'd gotten home. I figured that the best thing to do was find houses with unlocked windows and then, once inside, take what I wanted and put everything else where it had been. I figured that if people didn't realize they had been robbed right away, they wouldn't report it and I would be a lot less likely to get caught. With these thoughts in mind, I put some socks over my hands and went and opened the door for Jessi.

"Grab some socks," I told her, pointing toward the bedroom. She went into the bedroom while I looked around the house and put the things I wanted into my backpack. After about thirty seconds she came out of the bedroom. "I don't like this, Jasmyn," she said shakily. "Let's go."

I wasn't leaving yet. "Wait outside if you want," I told her. "I'll be right out."

She went outside, but kept calling to me nervously. She was starting to make me mad. I decided to look through the bathroom for jewelry and then the master bedroom closet before I left. I didn't find much in the bathroom, and carefully put anything I didn't take back where I'd found it. As I started looking through the closet, Jessi became more nervous.

"Jasmyn, come on!" she yelled through the house. *Stupid bitch,* I thought, *she's going to call attention to us.*

"Hold *on!*" I hissed, as I pulled some shoeboxes down from the closet. I pulled off the lids, and there was nothing good in the first two. The third one was a different story. "DAMN!!" I yelled as I stared into the box at a big wad of cash. I picked it up and saw that it included more than a few hundred-dollar-bills.

"What'd you find?" yelled Jessi. I wished she'd stop yelling from the front porch.

"Four hundred bucks!" I told her, shoving four of the hundreds into one pocket and the rest of the wad into another. "I'll give you half if you chill out."

I put all the boxes back where I'd found them, closed the bathroom window, and left, locking the front door behind me. Once outside, Jessi and I were thrilled. I couldn't wait to count the money. I pulled the socks off my hands as we started walking and was about to tell Jessi to do the same, when I realized that her hands were bare.

"Where are the socks I told you to grab?" I asked her.

She opened her backpack and showed me the contents. It was full of socks.

"You didn't have any on your hands?" I asked.

"My hands?" she echoed, looking confused.

"Yeah," I told her, feeling just as confused. "We don't have gloves so we use socks in order to avoid leaving fingerprints." I saw a look of comprehension pass across her face. "Why did you *think* I told you to get socks?" I asked her.

"Well," she explained, "I thought you didn't have any 'cause you're home-less."

"No way!" I exclaimed, cracking up. This girl was *hilarious*. I gave her two hundred dollars and we walked over to McDonalds, where I went into the bathroom to count my money. Eleven hundred eighty-four dollars was left after I'd given Jessi her two hundred. Damn. I was rich. Life was good. I felt a pang of guilt as I wondered if the residents of the house had been saving up for something special, like a vacation. I quickly pushed it aside, figuring that they had a nice house with nice furniture and probably had a lot more money. Besides, I was in a great mood, and I didn't want to ruin it for myself by feeling guilty.

Now that I had money, I felt like I could do anything I wanted. I still called my parents periodically to let them know I was okay, but I didn't want to go home. I had more freedom than I'd ever had before. I also had power. My friends would come to me when they needed money for something and I would ask them why they needed it before deciding whether to grant or deny their request. I knew everybody's business and was able to make decisions that would affect other people. I could take care of myself.

I gave one of the older boys about eighty dollars to take some girl to his junior prom and asked him to hold the majority of my money for me since I didn't want to carry it around. He kept it for me without stealing any.

I gave Ross more money than anybody else. He was persuasive and cool to have around. He was also intelligent, so I had more respect for him than most of the other guys. One night I gave him two hundred dollars. One hundred was to buy a gun for me. He said he knew where to get one and I'd decided a gun would be useful to have while I was living on the streets. The other hundred was for him to buy himself some weed to sell, and he was going to pay me back out of his profit. He didn't end up making either purchase.

It was April 20, and everybody had big plans. Since "4:20" is the police code for "marijuana use in progress," April 20 is a pretty big unofficial holiday for a lot of people. Gary, some of his friends, and I were going to a rave. Ross and some of my other friends were busy stealing a car.

The rave was in Oakland and we took the light-rail. We got off at the wrong stop and never found it. Instead we spent the night walking around Oakland and running from the police. Though it was a long night for us, it was an even longer for our friends who'd stayed in San Jose.

They got caught with the stolen car, and Ross, who was driving, did not pull over for the police. The police chased them and arrested Ross at gunpoint. Since he had drugs on him, they confiscated his belongings, along with my two hundred dollars.

With Ross locked up, everybody was kind of subdued. Ruby, who was one of my good friends and Ross's girlfriend, was devastated. I was tired of everybody asking me for money and of being in San Jose. Gary was grounded and although that had never stopped him before, he wouldn't come out and kick it.

I was thinking of all these things one day when it started raining. It was cold, I was hungry, and I didn't have anywhere to go. I didn't have any money on me and the guy who was holding my money for me was at school, so I couldn't get any from him. I decided to do another house.

I walked around in the rain until I'd found a neighborhood that looked promising. Everybody seemed to be at work and the houses were upper-middle class. I choose one and went in through a back window. As soon as I got in, a dog started barking. Damn. I'd never even thought about what I'd do if the house had a dog. I dropped to one knee and held out my hand. The dog stopped barking while he sniffed my hand and I petted him. Animals had always liked me; after a moment, he licked my hand and wagged his tail.

After that, he followed me as I went from room to room, looking around. I went into an office and talked to him as I looked through the desk. I was glad for the diversion, because it kept my mind off my nervousness. I had never done a house by myself before and it meant there would be no one to warn me if someone unexpectedly came home. I found a hundred dollars in the desk, along with an extra car key. I put everything else back exactly where it had been, said goodbye to the dog, and left through the window. There were no cars outside, so I stuck the key in my pocket. I went to Burger King and got myself something to eat.

A couple of days later, Gary got kicked out of his house again. I told him about the car key, and we decided to go to the house that night while everybody was sleeping and take the car if it was there. It was.

We got in the car and Gary started it up. I didn't know how to drive. I felt a rush of adrenaline shoot through me as we backed out of the driveway and then—

"What happened?" I asked franticly as Gary tried to start the car again and again. It seemed to have broken down as soon as we'd backed out of the driveway. We were sitting in a stalled car we'd stolen, in the middle of the street, not even ten feet from the house we'd stolen it from!

"I don't know; let's go!" Gary said, and we got out of the car, leaving it in the street.

We slept at a school that night, trying to stay out of the rain. It was freezing and we didn't sleep well. The next morning we discussed what had happened. Although we'd hastily tried to wipe off fingerprints from the stalled car, we figured that we'd probably missed some and knew the police had a record of our prints from when we'd been booked at juvenile hall for breaking into the Amtrak station. We decided to leave town. I got my money, though there wasn't much left, and we took the Bart to San Francisco.

San Francisco was even better than I'd remembered. When we got there we took a bus to Pier 39. We were walking around looking at everything when we spotted some kids about our age who looked homeless. It was getting dark, so we decided to ask them if they knew of a place where it was cool to sleep.

Although we had been on the streets for a while, in San Jose Gary and I knew enough people that we had been able to take showers and do laundry almost every day. We must not have looked homeless because as we approached the group of kids, one of them asked if we had any spare change.

"Naw," said Gary. "We actually just got here from San Jose and were wondering if you knew of a cool place to sleep."

The kids invited us to go with them. They had just finished "spanging" (asking for spare change) and were about to buy some beer. They slept at Golden Gate Park, at the foot of Height Street. We went with them and soon knew dozens of the kids living on Height. Some of them had deemed themselves married and were recognized on the streets as husbands and wives. Street relationships are strong and grow more quickly than other relationships because the people involved are usually around each other constantly and almost immediately go through a lot together. Knowing someone on the streets for two weeks is about as intense as knowing someone off the streets for two years. After about two days, Gary and I felt completely at home on the streets of San Francisco.

During the day we would spange either right on Height or over at the pier until we had enough money for everybody to eat and ride the bus. We always did it with a smile and it never took long, especially for me. Men gave me money because they thought I was cute and women gave me money because I was young. It was a very winning combination. I also loved spanging. I would laugh and joke with the tourists as they walked by. San Francisco felt like a huge carnival to me, and for the tourists, giving money to the homeless was all part of the experience.

After spanging, Gary and I would break off and go shopping at the pier. We liked all of the little souvenir shops and since we didn't have much money, shopping meant simply taking whatever we wanted. We always ended up with more stuff than we needed and gave little souvenirs away to our friends.

One day we were shopping in a little corner shop near the pier. Gary took a few things, but I was bored with shoplifting and told him I wanted to leave. As we were stepping out of the shop, I caught a glimpse of a man in a tan trench coat standing outside as if waiting for something. I was suddenly scared, and, without knowing why, I stepped in front of Gary. At the same instant the man stepped toward us and reached his hand inside his coat. *Shit!* I thought. *He's going to shoot us!*

He pulled his hand out and I saw, with great relief, that he was holding a police badge. He was an undercover officer, not a psychopath, and instead of shooting us, he was merely arresting us for shoplifting. He took us around to the back of the shop and called for a uniformed officer to come and get us. While we were waiting, he tried to talk to us.

"You think he loves you?" he asked me, inclining his head toward Gary. "Look, you're getting arrested because of him."

"Thanks for your concern," I said sarcastically, "but I know what I'm doing."

"It doesn't look like it," he muttered.

Once we got to the station, Gary and I were separated and booked. I went to the girls' section and soon found out that whoever was on her best behavior would get the privilege of attending church the next day. I had never been to church before and didn't care about the ceremony. I did care that it would be co-ed; if I went, I would probably get to see Gary. I was on my best behavior and about a half hour before church started was informed that I'd be able to go. I was very excited. A few minutes later, however, a guard came to get me. My mom had come to pick me up and I was being released.

Once in the car, my mom noticed my bad mood.

"What's wrong?" she asked, unhappy about having to drive all the way to San Francisco to pick me up. "Did you want to *stay?*"

I was instantly contrite. My mom had driven a long way to pick me up. I apologized, and she asked where in San Jose I wanted to be dropped off. I asked her to drop me off at Ruby's, and I spent the night in her closet. The next day I said hi to all my friends and asked around about Gary. I finally found out from someone who knew his brother Jed that he had been sent back to his group home. I was confident that he would get out again and I decided to wait for him—in San Francisco.

By this time I was out of money, but that was no problem. I asked a friend for money to take the bus to downtown San Jose, where I spanged up enough bus money to get to the Bart station and then take the Bart back to 'Frisco.

Back in San Francisco, I had to reintroduce myself to everybody. Although I had only been gone a few days, on the streets Gary and I had been known as "Gary-and-Jasmyn-From-San Jose." We had been a kind of unit, and I was not immediately recognized without Gary.

I started hanging out with some guys we'd met named Jax and Noel, and the three of us immediately became really close. On the streets, I was usually the youngest, and most people treated me like a little sister. We slept in an abandoned building located right between Ocean Beach and the San Francisco Zoo, known as the "Haunted Squat." It was said to have been an old abandoned mental institution haunted by its old inhabitants. Most people were too scared to sleep there, but the three of us found it perfect.

We could chill at the beach as late as we wanted and then have somewhere to go within walking distance. In the mornings, we would hop the fence into the zoo and use the bathrooms to wash up. Sometimes we even took the time to look around at the animals. It was on one of those occasions that we met Lisa.

Lisa worked at one of the food stands inside the zoo, selling hot dogs and ice cream. Jax, who was very cute, told her we didn't have any money and asked for some food. She gave us all hot dogs and ice cream, and when she got off work, she took us to her parent's house to take showers. After that, she came down to the Height a couple of times each week to see if we needed anything. Her parents were obviously rich, and she seemed to feel bad that anyone should ever be hungry.

Eventually Jax and Noel started talking about going back to Arizona, where they were from. They wanted me to go with them. Although I loved them like brothers and really wanted to go, I still thought Gary would get out of his group home soon and knew he wouldn't be able to find me if I went to Arizona. I decided to stay.

On the day they were leaving they introduced me to their friend Jimmy and I started kicking it with him and his friends. He was a nineteen-year-old self-declared hippy from Seattle. We did drugs and went to parties, and I showed them the Haunted Squat.

Although San Francisco wasn't the same for me without Jax and Noel, I still considered it home, and there was a lot going on. There was the National Rainbow gathering being held soon in the Ozark Mountains of Missouri, and the Grateful Dead were about to start touring. I learned from Jimmy that a rainbow gathering was a huge gathering of hippies from all over the country. Money was not used inside the gathering; instead, things were purchased through barter and trade. I also found out that the Grateful Dead parking lot parties were even more fun than the concerts themselves. And Jimmy wanted to visit Seattle.

In San Francisco, a concert was being held in Golden Gate Park. There were going to be a few bands and thousands of people. It would be a great spanging opportunity, and we decided to spange up enough money to take the Greyhound to Seattle. We planned to stay there for a couple of weeks and then hitchhike to Missouri for the rainbow gathering, after which we would follow the Grateful Dead back to San Francisco. Since we would eventually be coming back and I didn't want to miss out on such great adventures, I decided to go.

15

Waiting for the Phone Call, Hoping It's Not the Morgue

Father's story

Jasmyn was gone. Life had to go on. I went to work, came home, and constantly rehashed the previous year, trying to figure out what I had done wrong. But we had another child to worry about. Joshua was only two and a half years younger than Jasmyn; and he was distraught over what was happening with his big sister.

Joshua was from the same parents, brought up in the same home, but he was completely different from his sister. He tried his best in school and did well. He took great pride in his accomplishments and was thrilled to come home and see the pride we had in his work and attitude. When he wanted something out of the ordinary, he was eager to do extra chores to earn a special treat. My wife and I made it a point to not let him get lost in our frustration over Jasmyn. When she was in our home, he felt like a second-class citizen. We spent so much time tiptoeing around Jasmyn that Joshua felt she was being rewarded for her lack of responsibility.

One day, Joshua talked to me about his confusion. "Dad, I don't understand something. Why doesn't Jasmyn have to go to school? It's not fair."

"Jasmyn is ruining her future. Is that what you want to do?"

"No, but it's still not fair. She runs away and does anything she wants without getting into trouble."

I tried again to explain, but he didn't get it. The next day I took him to work with me. My business was doing well, and my client list included many multi-millionaires who were building homes with more than ten thousand square feet and adding all the amenities. My business specialized in fun things like theater rooms and computer-controlled homes. We designed systems that controlled all the lights, security, heating and air, pools, and whatever a wealthy homebuilder could dream up. Our slogan was, "We are only limited by your budget," and we meant it.

Joshua and I visited a few mansions we had just completed. He was awed by the spectacle. The majority had grand marble entryways, huge theaters, game rooms, and extravagant pools with theme landscaping. I explained to him that the people who lived in these homes paid attention in school and worked hard. They went to college and got good jobs. Because of that, they were able to earn enough money to afford to live in these incredible mansions.

Next we took a ride over to the east side of town. This was a run down area with old tenement apartment tracts and decrepit homes. Many front yards were littered with old abandoned cars and piles of trash. It was an extreme example of a place where no one in his right mind would want to be caught anytime, day or night. I explained to Joshua that the people who lived here probably didn't finish high school or go to college. Like his sister, they decided it wasn't important to get a good education and a good job. "Jasmyn made a choice," I said. "You have the same choice. You can work hard in school for a few years and have it easy the rest of your life. Or you can not work hard for the next few years and struggle the rest of your life." He was quiet for a while on the way home. I didn't know what he really thought until he described the homes to his mom at dinner that night. Then I knew the day had left an impression.

Over the next eight months we received sporadic calls from Jasmyn. At first she was living with friends in San Francisco. I asked her how she was surviving. She told me they all got together and did some thing called "spanging." I learned from her this was a word derived from "begging for spare change." She said, "I'm fine, Dad. We make enough to eat, and we're saving up to travel."

"But living on the street is dangerous," I said. "We worry about you." I tried to convince her to come home, but she didn't care how worried we were.

"I can take care of myself," she said. "It's my life; I'm not asking you for anything, so why should you care? I just want to enjoy my life, and I like living on the street with my friends." At the end of each call, I always told her that I loved her no matter what she did, and she always had a place to live when she was ready to come home. She always said she loved me, too, and I could tell she meant it.

I was glad to know Jasmyn was all right, but it was hard to talk to her. Often after a call I would pull out an old home movie we made when she was six and her brother was four. It was a rainy afternoon in the country and the kids were bored, so I decided to make a movie with them. We called it CinderJasmyn, modeled after Cinderella. Jasmyn dressed up like a princess and Joshua dressed up like a knight. They were brought together by Casey (their dog) and Suitcase (their cat). Mom-Lynn was in the kitchen making a large dinner but participated in the movie as well. When I watched the movie, I longed for the days when Jasmyn was six and the epitome of a perfect child. I didn't pull this film out often because it sent me into a depression that was difficult to overcome. I needed to be strong for my son and my wife.

Daughter's story

My friends and I spanged enough money for three of us to take the bus to Seattle. There were six people going, so the other three would have to hitchhike. Since Jimmy was the one who had parents in Seattle and we were planning to stay with them, Jimmy was taking the bus. As the rest of us were discussing who else should get to ride the bus, Jimmy broke in. "Jasmyn's with me," he announced.

"What, are you guys together or something?" asked Debbie, one of the girls who was going with us, with narrowed eyes. She liked Jimmy, and "together" meant a couple.

I hadn't seen Gary in a couple of months and wasn't sure he was coming back. I looked at Jimmy and shrugged. Why not? Jimmy was okay.

So now that Jimmy was my boyfriend, we decided that Debbie would hitchhike with the two remaining guys and that the remaining girl would get to ride the bus. We thought that a girl should go with us because that would leave two guys and a girl, a safer hitchhiking combination than two girls and a guy, and I didn't like Debbie.

We purchased our tickets, but the bus didn't leave until the next morning. Jimmy knew a guy who owned a doughnut shop and would be there all night preparing doughnuts. We went over to his shop for the night, kicking it and helping the guy make doughnuts. It was a warm place to be but as soon as the sun came out our plans were almost ruined. The shop opened at five in the morning, and just as we were leaving, two police officers walked in.

As I walked out they looked me over and one of them stopped me. The mayor's thirteen-year-old daughter had just run away and every officer in the city wanted to be the one to find her. They thought I was her. I protested violently. Thirteen! Couldn't they tell I was fifteen?

They took me down to the police station, but Jimmy promised to wait for me at the bus station even if it meant missing the bus. Once there, they grabbed a "missing" poster of the mayor's daughter and realized I wasn't her. Her eyes were brown, while mine are green, and she was two inches shorter than I. They ran my name anyway in case I was a runaway; to my surprise, my name didn't come up. I realized with relief that my name must have been taken off runaway alert when I was released into parental custody after being arrested for shoplifting with Gary.

The police asked me for my parents' name and phone number. I gave them my mom's number but asked them not to call her. I pointed out that it was not yet six on a Saturday morning and said that my mom knew where I was. I told them that Jimmy was my cousin and was taking me to Seattle to visit my aunt. I showed them my bus ticket as proof. I said that Saturday was my mom's only morning to sleep in and she would be needlessly worried if she found out that I was in police custody instead of with my cousin who was supposed to be taking care of me. The officer's looked at each other, not sure what to do.

Finally, they decided to put the number I'd given them into the computer to see if it was really assigned to the names I'd given for parents. If it didn't match up, they would keep me. It did, and just to be extra sure, they asked my mom's address. I gave it and started complaining about how mad my parents would be if I missed my bus. Since all of my information added up, they believed my story. They drove me to the bus station.

I got there in time to catch the bus, and soon we were off to Seattle. Once there, we went to Jimmy's dad's house for a couple of days before meeting our friends. After we saw them, we went to Jimmy's mom's house, where we stayed for about a week. I loved being at her house. Jimmy had a little sister who was only a year older than me, and I spent most of the time we were there with her and her friends. They were all "good girls" and still had slumber parties and pillow fights. I hadn't done that in years and felt like a kid again.

Jimmy's mom let me call my dad from her house and I told him where I was and that I was okay. When he found out I was with a nineteen-year-old guy, he told me to be careful and asked me to come home. I didn't want to go home. At home I would just spend most of my time in my room, grounded. Compared with absolute freedom, it was a dull prospect. I couldn't imagine anything worse than sitting in my room while life passed me by, constantly trying to prove myself innocent of whatever my parents happened to suspect at the time. I reminded my dad that I never asked him for money or anything when I called and was taking care of myself. I only called him because he was my dad and I loved him. I didn't want him to worry.

After the week, Jimmy's mom's family was going out of town. His mom didn't want him at her house while they were gone, and made him promise that he wouldn't come over. It was a promise he didn't keep.

That night we were sleeping at a park in Seattle, and I kept overhearing people talking about going to a party with Jimmy. He hadn't said anything to me about it. "Are you going to a party?" I finally asked him.

"Um, no…" he said, "I'm *throwing* a party."

"Oh? Am I invited?"

"Well," said Jimmy, "I didn't think you'd want to come. It's at my Mom's house."

He was right. I didn't want to go. His mom trusted us, and while I didn't mind breaking promises to people who didn't trust me anyway, I did mind throwing away trust that was freely given. I tried talking Jimmy out of it, but he just rolled his eyes.

"Look, you don't have to come if you don't want to," he told me.

Although I didn't want to go, I wanted even less to stay on the streets of Seattle alone. I didn't know anybody in Seattle and didn't feel as comfortable there as I did in 'Frisco. I went to the party.

The next morning, a sheriff woke us up by pounding on the front door. Jimmy's mom had asked a neighbor to watch the house and call the police if anybody came over. We were arrested for breaking and entering.

Once at the station, they ran my name to see if I was a runaway. Of course, my name didn't come up, and after a few hours in a holding cell, they released all of us, without calling my parents. The charges had been dropped.

We stayed on the streets for a while and then the six of us started hitchhiking to Missouri. We hitched a ride with some people in a car and asked them to drop us at a truck stop. The truckers were better to hitch rides from because they were usually crossing two or three states at a time, and they had beds in their cabs so there was enough room for all of us. Besides, actually going up to someone and asking them personally for a ride was a lot more effective then sticking out a thumb while people drove by.

We were cautious about whom we accepted rides from and had a method that worked pretty well. The girls would walk up to a trucker and ask where he was headed. If he was planning on going the same way as we were, we would ask for a ride. Once he accepted, we would say we had to grab our stuff and then come back with both it and the boys. We figured that if the truckers didn't intend to harm us they would still give us a ride. There were only a few times when the truckers changed their minds once they saw the boys, and no one tried to hurt us. We hitched first east, toward Chicago, then south, toward the Ozarks. The trip took six days, and we met about twelve truckers.

Missouri was *hot.* I'd never experienced such humid heat before; it took a couple of days to get used to. A lot of the people at the Rainbow Gathering walked around completely naked. People had booths set up and they were trading weed and acid right in the open. There was a mud pit and a couple of food camps. The gathering was like a whole city of just hippies. Some people had tents, but it was so warm that most people slept right in the open.

I wasn't prone to nakedness, but it was so hot that I started wearing just big baggy overalls with a bra. At night there were huge campfires surrounded by a drum circle and singing. I was surprised to see so many little kids running around. There were whole families that lived in busses and just traveled around.

There were no bathrooms; instead there were big waste holes dug right into the ground. I was reluctant to squat over an open hole in the ground, so I didn't go to the bathroom for the whole time we were there—about a week. That wasn't too big a problem though, since I wasn't eating or drinking very much anyway. Most of the people were vegetarians, so the people who had volunteered to cook didn't cook any meat. The food was mass-produced and dishes were shared. One night some guys invited me to their camp. They were cooking for themselves and I ate a hamburger. It was the most food I ate in one sitting the whole time I was there.

For the most part, I was too busy to eat. I was meeting a lot of people and having tons of fun. I loved skinny-dipping in the ice-cold river water. On one of the last days we were there, it rained. Someone was trading a tent, and since I didn't have anything he wanted, he just gave it to me. I also found someone who was giving away puppies. I'd wanted a dog for a long time, so I got one. He was a cute little thing and I named him Doobie.

That night inside the tent, I noticed that my throat was hurting. I felt the side of my neck and was surprised to find it was swollen to the size of a golf ball. I was sick, but I thought I would get better if I just ignored the symptoms. I had been away from home for about eight months and hadn't been sick once.

When it was time to leave the gathering, it was easy to hitch a ride because so many other people were leaving, too. We got a ride with some girls, but as the morning dragged on I became sicker. I finally asked them to pull over so that I could throw up. I got out of the car, but only threw up a little. Afterwards I continued to dry heave. My body was trying to get rid of something, but there was no food in my stomach. As I was throwing up, Doobie wandered away into the bushes.

"Doobie," I called, surprised at how weak my voice sounded. I didn't really expect him to come back. I'd only had him a couple of days and didn't think he knew his name yet, and even if he did my voice had become so feeble that I doubted he could hear me.

I was wrong. As soon as I whispered his name a second time, he perked up his ears and came running back. He crawled onto my lap, licking my hand and whimpering. I smiled. He knew he was my dog.

I tried to get back into the car but could hardly stand up. The people we were with helped me into the car and took me to the hospital. Jimmy came in and waited with me while I was admitted. After that, he was going to leave, but he said he'd wire me money to get back to San Francisco once I was better.

"Wait!" I said, panicked. "Leave my dog!"

Jimmy said he'd keep him for me, but I doubted Jimmy and I would see each other again. I was surprised to find that I didn't care. I just wanted the dog. "Don't worry," he said, walking out.

"No," I yelled after him with all my energy, "you can't take him. I'll come out and get him!"

I got up and started detaching my I.V., but my movements were weak and slow. My body wasn't doing what I wanted it to do. A nurse came in and told me to lie down. I whispered that I would after I got my puppy. She informed me that my friends were already gone, and I slumped down in defeat.

After the doctor examined me, I found out I had pneumonia, strep throat, dehydration, and a form of hepatitis, probably from not going to the bathroom. But all I kept thinking about was how Jimmy had stolen *my* dog.

I decided that if I ever saw Jimmy again, I would kill him.

Father's story

A month passed before we had another call from Jasmyn. She was staying at someone's home in Seattle, Washington with a nice woman she and her friends had met. She just called to tell me she was fine and not to worry. I was glad, as always, to hear from her and find out she was still alive. I implored her to call more often. She said she would. After I hung up, I found I was furious with all these "helpful" people: the people on the streets in San Francisco who gave these kids money and this woman in Washington who let them stay at her home. Didn't they know they were enabling these kids to be runaways? If all these do-gooders would just stop, perhaps Jasmyn would be forced to come home. But it didn't help to spread the blame around. I continued to pray for the day when she would come home.

The days turned into weeks and the weeks turned into months. No word from Jasmyn. We were getting used to life without her. We were constantly worried and jumped at the sound of the phone.

Still, life went on. I continued to take my mental vacations by flying on instruments. Before long I had passed my written exam and flight proficiency test and received my instrument rating. I was flying so much that it became economically feasible to buy an aircraft of my own. I purchased a 1969 Mooney, a high-performance, four-seat aircraft that was very fast. Because my business had grown so much, we were covering a large geographical area, and the plane became a great asset to the business. For insurance purposes, I decided to obtain my commercial pilot rating. Compared to the instrument portion of my training, the commercial rating was a piece of cake; I completed all the required training and passed the proficiency check ride in a just two weekends.

I took my son flying with me often. I loved sharing my passion with him, and he was becoming quite the young pilot himself. I decided it would be a good idea to obtain a rating to fly multi-engine aircraft. I was flying clients to their beach homes on the coast to discuss the work they were contracting with my company. I was a member of a flying club that had many planes, both single and multi-engine, available to rent. I leased my Mooney back to the flying club, thus making it available to other pilots to fly and deferring the cost of ownership.

Since flying was so relaxing for me, I decided to become a flight instructor. I discussed my intentions with Lynn and my son; they were both very supportive. My wife knew that flying was an escape from the constant worry about Jasmyn. In fact, I can honestly say there has never been an idea or venture in my married life that my wife wasn't enthusiastic about. Her never-wavering support is probably the biggest reason for the majority of my successes. My son's reaction was typical for a young man of 12: "Cool."

It took a few more months of training, but in the end I obtained my goal; I was a flight instructor with multi-engine and instrument endorsements. As a result of this accomplishment, I received what I consider to this day to be one of the greatest compliments I could ever hope to receive. One night at dinner, Joshua was talking about the future. He said he wasn't really sure what he wanted to be when he grew up, but he knew he could be whatever he wanted.

Not being used to such an optimistic view of life from him, I said, "I agree. But what makes you think so?"

"Look at you, Dad," he said in a matter-of-fact way. "You decide you want to do something, you study and work really hard, and you do it. I'm just like you! I can do anything if I'm willing to work hard." As I write this I still get a chill thinking about that evening. The mistakes I made with my daughter were not repeated with my son. He had learned valuable lessons, not by lectures but by example. It remains one of my greatest achievements.

One day the phone rang again. We hadn't heard anything from Jasmyn in a long while and had adopted the attitude that no news was good news. My heart dropped when the man on the other end of the line asked if I was Jasmyn's father. It's amazing what can race through one's head in a nanosecond. This was the call I had feared for months; this man was going to tell me my daughter was dead. He continued, "This is Detective Johnson. I'm with the juvenile division in St. Louis, Missouri. We have Jasmyn here in the hospital. She's a pretty sick young lady."

I didn't know what to think. My first reaction was relief; she wasn't dead. I needed to calm down and listen. "Her friends brought her in, but they left. I'm going to give you a phone number for her doctor; he can tell you what's wrong with her. When she's released, I'll escort her to the airport and put her on a plane home. All you need to do is send a money order for the ticket."

"The money will be on the way this afternoon," I assured him. I thanked him and called the doctor. The doctor said Jasmyn was suffering from malnutrition and hepatitis as a result of the poor eating habits Jasmyn must have practiced the last few months. Although she was very sick, he assured me that with proper care and bed rest she would recover fully.

He gave me the number to Jasmyn's room and I called her next. She sounded weak and frail. I told her she needed to get better and come home. To my amazement, she said, "I can't come home. I have to find my friends and get my puppy back."

I was willing to tell her just about anything to get her home. I persuaded her that once she was better, we would get her another puppy. "What's really important is that you come home and get better. You could die from hepatitis." She finally agreed. She would be well enough to travel in a week.

Daughter's story

The next couple of weeks were kind of a blur. I spent most of my hospital time asleep, but I remember being angry that when I was awake, the doctor wouldn't let me have a cigarette.

Although I remember waking up at home, I don't remember the plane trip from the hospital or my arrival there. I vaguely remember waking up in my parents' house and wanting my dad. It seems that I was delirious for most of the first couple of days, which is probably why I don't remember much.

16

Back at Home

Father's story

Jasmyn's arrival back home was something I had been hoping for; and the approaching date filled me with anticipation. We had a game room with its own attached bath above the garage. We prepared for Jasmyn's arrival by setting this room up as a kind of studio apartment. Previously she had occupied a much smaller bedroom next to her brother's room. We wanted to make her feel really welcome.

I went to the airport to pick her up. The flight arrived and I watched as the people were herded off the aircraft. After five anxious minutes, I saw Jasmyn emerge from the cabin door. Although I was thrilled to see her, she looked terrible. Jasmyn had always been thin, but now she looked anorexic. She had lost so much weight that her face had a skeletal appearance. She stood five foot three inches tall and was, at the most, eighty-five pounds. She was carrying a beat up knapsack. I gave her a big hug to welcome her home. "How are you feeling?" I asked.

"Not very well," she answered.

"We'll get your luggage and go straight home."

"Dad, I don't have any luggage, except this." She pointed to the tiny knapsack.

I had planned to talk to her on the way home about where she'd been and what the future might hold, but as soon as she climbed into the passenger seat, she was fast asleep. I watched her sleep and thought how nice it was to have her back. At home, I helped Jasmyn up the stairs to her new room. She started crying because she felt so sick and said she just wanted to go to bed. Jasmyn had always been very modest about her body. She would get very upset if anyone saw her less than fully clothed, so I was stunned when she took off her shirt and pants in front of me and lay down on top of her bed clothed only in her undergarments.

I pulled the covers from underneath her and covered her up, wondering if her time on the road had caused her to abandon her inhibitions. I sat and stroked her hair, hoping this was not the case. I didn't know how she had survived the past several months without any money. This sudden willingness to remove her clothes with me in the room caused my imagination to suggest at least one possibility but I put the thought out of my mind and concentrated on how nice it was to have her back.

Now that Jasmyn was back, it was time to establish a plan of action. She needed to go to school and be normal again. All I had to do was go down to the corner magic potion store and buy some "good girl" dust to sprinkle about Jasmyn, and all would be fine. Since the "magic potion" store seemed to have closed before we could purchase the dust, we needed to come up with a plan. We had our household rules that we were unwilling to modify for the sake of our son. Jasmyn would be required to go to school. She would have to obey curfew hours. She would also have to pitch in with the household chores. As soon as she was well, we would sit down and explain these things to her.

Jasmyn slept through to the next day. When she awoke, she seemed to be recovering, and soon we fell back into the same old routine. Our household was filled with tension brought on by the constant fear that Jasmyn would take off again, and this time the call would be more devastating. Eventually, Jasmyn was well enough to go out. She wanted to see some of her old friends. We couldn't keep her a prisoner in the house, so we decided to let her go. I explained to Jasmyn that she needed to be home no later than ten o'clock. She agreed.

That night she returned about 1:30 a.m. Understandably, Lynn and I were furious. Jasmyn stated that she had missed the bus and could not get home at ten. As usual, it wasn't her fault. Lynn decided as a punishment, Jasmyn would have to stay home the following day and complete a list of required items. One of the items on the list was to listen to the Doctor Laura show on the radio and outline what was discussed. Jasmyn thought this was the stupidest thing she had ever heard, but she agreed. The next day we asked to see the outline. It was done but not to our satisfaction. Jasmyn had related everything that was discussed on the show to herself, adding phrases like

"This proves I'm a terrible person." Her intent was blatantly sarcastic, and she succeeded.

"Try again tomorrow," we said. She was furious and said she was going out. I responded with a flat "No." She said we couldn't keep her from going out.

I was sure we could. I sent her to her room and locked the door with a chair, determined not to let her run again. I knew she couldn't get out through the window because her room was on the second floor. I was wrong again. Things were much too quiet, so I went out in front of the house to see if she had somehow tried to escape. I found the screen to her window broken and tossed onto the front lawn. She had tossed her mattress out the window and slid down to the ground.

Quickly looking around, I spotted her walking a few blocks away and ran after her. As I got closer I called out her name. To my surprise, she stopped and turned. Seeing me, she sat down on the curb. "You can't keep running away," I said. "It's not fair to keep putting Lynn, Joshua, and me through the anxiety of wondering if you're alive or dead." After a few minutes, she decided to return home.

Daughter's story

Once I came home, my parents told me they expected me to follow the same rules as before. It was back to school, homework, and two to three hours of chores a day. The kids at school seemed incredibly young and sheltered, and I couldn't stand being there. I also hated being at home. The only reason I stayed was because I'd seen how worried my dad had been when I was sick and didn't want to put him through that again. He always seemed to be stressed, and Mom-Lynn always seemed angry. I felt like the smallest thing could set her off, so I tried to stay out of her way. She was determined to make me a moral person.

One day she decided that I should listen to the Doctor Laura show and write a page on three of the calls detailing what each call was about and what Doctor Laura's advice had been. Her intent was obviously to show me the error of my ways, and I felt like this was a personal attack on the ideas and system of morals I had formed for myself. I was not willing to denounce my own thinking, or even pretend to, and instead reacted with enough sarcasm to be obvious. If I *was* immoral, I planned to stay that way.

Mom-Lynn was angry when she read what I wrote and came up with another assignment. I was to write two lists. One list was to contain nice things she had done for me over the years that I was grateful for, and the other was to be a list of things I had done that were detrimental to my family. Each list was to have a minimum of ten items. I couldn't believe it! This *lady*, who wasn't even my mom, was deliberately trying to make *me* break down my own self-esteem. And if she insisted on pretending to be my mom, why was she demanding gratitude for things moms were supposed to do anyway?

I sat down with a piece of paper and went to work, being more sarcastic on this assignment than the last one. The list of things Lynn had done that I was grateful for contained things as petty as, "Smiled at me last week." The list of detrimental things I'd done to my family included things beyond my control such as, "I was born. Sorry." Also, since I knew Mom-Lynn would have to read the list when I was done, I took a small stab at revenge by making my writing as small as possible.

Mom-Lynn read the list and furiously demanded I do it again. I would not. I was not willing to pretend that I was a bad person. I wasn't. I was just a kid with too many parents. Mom-Lynn was acting like I *owed* her for letting me be a part of *her* family. But it had been *my* family first. I had never *asked* her to marry my dad and take over my life. Why should I be grateful that she had? Why should I even have to pretend to be? I didn't have to, and I wouldn't, no matter what she did or said.

When my dad came home, she showed him the list and informed him that I had refused to redo it. I heard them arguing and then they came and got me. Together they insisted I redo it. I looked at my dad, disbelieving. I was his daughter, yet he was letting this lady demand my gratitude that I'd been treated as a daughter in *his* household just because he'd happened to marry her? I felt my eyes filling with tears and stomped upstairs, not wanting to let them see me cry.

Forget this, I thought. I was only here because I was worried about my dad's feelings, but obviously he didn't care about mine. I dried my tears and started to go downstairs but the door was locked. I looked around. I couldn't go out the window because I was on the second floor. My gaze rested on the bed. If I threw the mattress down onto the driveway and landed on it, I could probably jump out the window without getting hurt. Feeling like McGyver, I tried it. The plan worked better than I'd expected. When I dropped the mattress, instead of landing flat on the driveway it landed on its side, leaning up against the house. I slid down onto the driveway. I was free.

I had only walked about a block when I heard my dad's voice behind me. "Jasmyn!" he yelled, running after me. I turned around and saw him. This was the man who had played ball with me and taught me how to change a tire and how to punch like a boy; the man who'd bought me a guitar when I was fourteen and given me my own phone line; the man I'd looked up to above anyone else as a little girl. He looked tired. He loved me enough to chase me. I remembered how he took me camping as a kid and knew that he must never have imagined that his little girl would put him through all that I had. I couldn't help feeling bad for him. I wouldn't run. I stopped on the sidewalk and waited for him to catch up. When he did, he started talking about how worried he was when I was gone. He said he always wondered if I was even alive, and he wished that I would stop running away.

I didn't want him to go through all of that, so, with a feeling of despondency, I promised not to run away again, but told him I wasn't willing to redo the list. I hated being at home, but it was a sacrifice I was willing to make if the only alternative was my dad's constant worry.

He brought me back home and things returned to a semblance of tense normality. After a couple of weeks I was allowed to go see my friends. I took the bus from Santa Clara, where we lived, to San Jose. I had agreed to be home by ten o'clock, but I left San Jose at eight, just to be on the safe side. The bus didn't come until eight-thirty, and I still had to change buses downtown, before the forty-five minute ride back to Santa Clara. I got to the downtown bus stop at about five after nine, and the bus schedule posted at the stop said the bus was to have arrived at 9:03. Since the buses were often a few minutes off schedule, I wasn't sure if I had just missed the bus or if it would be arriving at any moment. If the latter was true, I didn't want to risk leaving the stop to call my parents, because the next bus wasn't scheduled until 10:03, and I didn't want to be downtown that late.

After waiting about twenty minutes, I realized I had missed the bus and would now miss my curfew. A guy came and sat down at the bus stop and we started talking. After a while, he offered me a line. I hadn't done a line in a while, and I was cold and nervous about riding the bus and walking home by myself so late at night. I knew a line would make me feel invincible and would also help me to be alert for the fight that was sure to ensue as soon as I got home. Besides, I figured I wouldn't be able to go out for a long time anyway, so I might as well do something for myself while I had the chance. I gladly accepted. We ducked into a doorway that was out of the wind, and he chopped me a couple of lines on his credit card. I did them and he asked me for my phone number. I told him I didn't have a phone, but let him give me his number. I knew I wouldn't call.

The bus finally came and by the time I made it home, it was close to eleven. My parents were waiting up and were as angry as I'd expected. I explained that I had missed the bus.

"What time did you leave your friends?" Mom-Lynn asked.

"Eight o'clock," I said, and explained what had happened.

Her and my dad looked at each other. "We don't believe you," Mom-Lynn finally said.

"Yeah, I didn't expect you to," I shot back, shrugging my shoulders.

The conversation quickly escalated into a shouting match and ended in my being ordered to leave. On my way out the door, my dad stopped me.

"First give me your contact lenses," he said.

"What?" My contact lenses were prescription and I could barely see without them.

"You think you can take care of yourself and make your own rules, well, fine. I paid for your contact lenses, and I want them back," my dad said, trying to show me that I couldn't take care of myself. I could tell that he wanted me to ask to stay. Yeah, right. He'd told me to leave, and I wouldn't ask him to *let* me stay, especially when I was only there to prevent his apprehension in the first place.

"Naw," I said, "if I don't have my contacts, I won't be able to see, and then I won't be able to defend myself. Do you *want* me to get killed?" I asked him.

"Fine, Jasmyn," Mom-Lynn said, "If we let you keep your contacts will you leave *right now*?"

"Sure."

She glanced at my dad imploringly and he nodded. I walked out the door and didn't turn around as it slammed behind me. I felt relieved. I had wanted more than anything to be on my own again but had stayed because of my promise to my dad not to run away anymore. This was the first time he had ever kicked me out and by doing so he had given me *permission* to leave, releasing my from a promise that had made me feel trapped. I started to run. I wanted to be gone in case he changed his mind.

17

Heroin

Father's story

Jasmyn agreed to go to school and follow the house rules. The problem was, she had been on her own for so long she was no longer capable of coping within a structured environment. It wasn't long before she took off again. I can't say I was surprised. Life at our home was no picnic. Lynn and Jasmyn were constantly fighting over something. I was so concerned with the prospect of Jasmyn bolting again that I was hesitant to even try to discipline her. Jasmyn and Lynn both sensed this. They handled my tentativeness differently. Lynn stepped up her campaign to get me to control Jasmyn. Jasmyn wanted me to get Lynn off her back.

Other problems in our lives added to the turmoil. Lynn and I were still trying desperately to conceive a child; we were spending money we didn't have on specialists. The anxiety over not conceiving built every month and curtailed our ability to deal with Jasmyn. At the same time, our landlord called to tell us she had decided to sell the house we were renting. We could buy it at a ridiculously high price or move. We had no choice. Once again, we needed to move.

The housing market in the area was very hot. Rentals stayed listed for a matter of hours and homes for sale had prospective buyers forming lines on the day of an open house. The realtors would specify a time for receiving offers and the bidding war commenced. Lynn and I did not know where we would end up. Our financial situation did not add up to home ownership.

Lynn discussed the situation with her mother Esther. Esther told Lynn that she was tired of the upkeep owning a house presented, and she wanted to sell her home and move into a condominium. Esther's home was a four-bedroom, ranch-style house bordered in the back by a sound wall separating the property from a major freeway. Lynn came up with the idea of buying her mother's house. We could make the deal work financially by quick deeding the property over to us and refinancing at a later date. This was also a good alternative for Esther as she could sell the home to us without a realtor and without having to make the repairs a thirty-year-old home would require before sale. Her condo would not be ready for a few months, but she could live with us in the interim.

Lynn's solution was our only option. We moved once again. Joshua had just graduated from middle school and would start high school the following autumn. He was concerned and needed some stability in his life. We promised him we would not move again until he graduated. We had moved five times in the previous six years. We settled into our new home.

A month later, we received a call from the juvenile authorities in Los Angeles County. Jasmyn had been arrested along with half a dozen others on a beach in L.A. They were all under the influence of heroin. The officer wanted to know what we wanted them to do with her. They could have her sent home immediately since she didn't have any criminal history.

I honestly didn't know what to say. I asked how long they could keep her locked up. The answer was a few weeks, until the arraignment. I decided a few weeks in lock up might do her some good and the officer agreed. I spoke to Jasmyn and told her she was really in trouble this time. Because the charge was for heroin, there wasn't much I could do. Jasmyn said it was the first time she ever did heroin. She just wanted to try it. She didn't like it and wouldn't try it again. According to her, it was no big deal. The officer had confirmed Jasmyn had no track marks (needle scars) and that she was probably telling the truth about this being her first time. Thank God she got caught. Her one experience with heroin was not pleasant enough to repeat. Four weeks later she was released and sent home.

Daughter's Story

After being kicked out, I stayed with my friends in San Jose for a few days before going back to San Francisco. 'Frisco was a better place to be than San Jose if one was homeless, and I considered it home. I was also hoping to see Jimmy so I could get revenge for when he'd taken my puppy. Homeless people are usually pretty mobile, and although street families are very close-knit, they are constantly traveling and changing. There were a lot of different people living on Height Street when I returned, and I made all new friends.

I still loved spanging and was pretty good at it. I noticed that although tourists didn't hesitate to give *me* money, the older people who lived on the streets had a much harder time. Instead of giving them money, people usually suggested that they get jobs, and a lot of them had health problems or drug addictions that they were unable to tend to. I realized that I wouldn't be young and cute forever; I started thinking that I should have a back-up plan in case I ever tired of the streets. Although the idea of a backup plan seemed sensible, I felt no urgency to implement it. I was still young and enjoying my freedom.

In the mornings when I woke up, the first thing I would do was to spange up enough money for breakfast and then walk up Height street until I saw something that looked good to eat. One morning as I was walking down the street in search of my breakfast, I passed an older man who was confined to a wheelchair. He looked like a veteran and since that wasn't unusual, I probably wouldn't have noticed him if he hadn't spoken to me.

"You got any spare change?" he asked me in a gruff voice.

I looked at him and considered. I had been spanging for about an hour and had a pocketful of change, but I was hungry. Besides, homeless people didn't spange *each other*. But since I'd been gone for a while and had just taken a shower the day before, it was possible he didn't realize I was homeless.

"What's it for?" I finally asked him, narrowing my eyes. I wasn't about to forgo my breakfast just so that some old guy could buy beer.

"Coffee," he answered immediately, rubbing his hands together. It *was* cold out, and I knew that I could get money a lot easier and quicker than he could. I gave him four dollars of my change, keeping about three for myself, without telling him I was homeless, and continued walking down the street. About three minutes later I walked by again, this time on the opposite side of the street, and saw the man drinking a steaming cup of coffee. He didn't see me and I smiled, surprised that he had actually spent the money on coffee.

The next morning I passed him in the same spot and again gave him about half of my change. This little ritual continued for about a week before I was found out. One morning I passed the guy as usual and he asked me for change. I had gotten into the habit of spanging a few extra dollars so this guy could have his coffee. Today, however, he wasn't alone, and the guy he was with recognized me.

"She's homeless, too," he informed his friend when he asked me for change.

"No, she's not," the man in the wheelchair argued. "She gives me change every morning."

His friend laughed. "Tell 'im, Jasmyn."

"Yup," I said lightly, "guilty as charged."

"Then why did you keep giving *me* money?" asked the first guy.

I shrugged and grinned. "Because you kept *asking*!"

The two men laughed. "You're such an angel, Jasmyn!" said the one who had recognized me. After that the story got around among the older adults on the streets that I was a sweetheart, and everybody seemed to know who I was. The guy in the wheelchair didn't ask me for money again, but soon I was spanging for somebody else.

I met Nick, Ryan, and Star at a park one day. Ryan and Star were a couple, and Nick was their friend. The three had been roommates before they'd lost their apartment, and now they traveled around and lived out of Ryan's car. Star was 19 and the boys were 23. I started kicking it with them all of the time and it soon became apparent why they'd lost their apartment. They were addicted to heroin.

They usually woke up in the morning too sick to care about anything else but getting well. "Sick" meant their bodies needed heroin in order to function normally. When they shot up, they didn't even get high. They just got back to the point of normal functioning, or being "well." The normalcy would only last until the fix wore off and then they'd need more to avoid getting sick again. When they were well, they were really nice and cool to be with. When they weren't, though, they were snappy and irritable and their speech was mumbled and slow. Since I didn't like it when they were like that, and most people wouldn't give them money because they *looked* like they'd spend it on drugs, I soon started spanging money for their morning fix.

I'd get up in the morning and spange up twenty or thirty dollars for them; then while they went to buy the heroin, I would stay wherever I was and spange up enough money so I could eat. Then they would come and get me, having already shot up, and be their cool, normal selves.

I didn't understand why someone would do a drug to the point that it didn't even make them high anymore, and being a heroin addict, or any kind of addict for that matter, wasn't appealing to me. But I did want to try every drug at least *once*, just so I would know what things were like, and I soon started hinting to my friends that I wanted to try it.

The hints didn't work, and I so finally just told Nick, who for some reason had decided he was responsible for me, that I wanted to try it.

"No," he said, "I'm not going to let you become addicted, like we all are."

"I won't become addicted," I insisted, "I just want to try it *once*."

"No, if you try it once, you'll probably become addicted."

"Well, if it's *that* great," I continued, "then I *definitely* want to try it."

"It's not that great!" he said, almost yelling by now.

"Then I won't get addicted!" I snapped back, matching his tone. He wasn't my boyfriend, and I had no idea why he insisted on acting like my guardian.

"Fine!" he said, throwing up his hands in exasperation, "Think what you want, but *I'm* not going to be the one to give it to you."

Damn. Where else did he think I could get it? *I* didn't have any heroin connections. The next day I decided to ask Ryan. I waited until he was alone and then approached him. His answer surprised and frustrated me.

"Nope," he told me, "I wouldn't let you even if I wanted to, which I don't—Nick asked me not to."

I decided to drop the subject, but only for the time being. Trying every drug at least once was the closest thing I had to a goal. Well, that and making sure I had good karma. Since living in San Francisco and hitchhiking around with hippies, I had started to believe in karma, the idea that whatever one did, good or bad, would be paid back tenfold. Or threefold—it depended on who was explaining it at the time.

A couple of days later we decided to go to Ventura, where the Grateful Dead was currently stopped on their tour. It was nice not having to hitchhike, since Ryan had a car, and we stopped on the way to spend the night in a motel. Star and I weren't sure how, but the guys had come up with a few hundred dollars before we'd left.

Once in the motel, I again broached the subject of my trying heroin. I was met with the same refusal as before, but this time I persisted.

"Look, I'm only going to try it *once*! I don't have an addictive personality! Plus, I *paid* for you guys to do it for weeks!" I yelled after about twenty minutes of argument.

"Fine," Nick relented, "but only this once. And don't let me ever hear about you trying it again."

I fought down the urge to sarcastically snap "Or what?" and instead, smiling sweetly, said, "Thanks!"

In San Francisco, there was an organization that passed out hygienic supplies and clean hypodermic needles to people on the streets. I still had a couple of unopened needles that I had taken once to use as weapons in a pinch. I grabbed one out of my backpack and handed it to Nick. I watched him cook up the drugs, a mixture of heroin and cocaine, and pull them up into the needle.

Since I had never shot up before, Nick would do it for me. He wrapped a belt around my upper arm and I watched the needle pierce my skin and felt my whole arm burn as the drugs disappeared into my arm.

"I don't feel anything, but my arm's numb," I told the others, feeling disappointed. "Is that all that's supposed to happen?"

"*What?*" Nick said, grabbing my arm and looking at it. "Damn, I missed the vein!"

"What does that mean?" I asked, feeling anxious. I wasn't ready to die.

"I think you'll be fine, but let's just wait awhile and see," Ryan said. After awhile my arm started feeling normal and I wanted to try again. This time Star did it and she hit the vein. I felt the effects of the drugs immediately. My body felt warm, as if I was wrapped up in soft cozy blankets, and while I was still conscious of reality, I felt like I was floating. I also felt totally content and happy. I eventually fell asleep and woke up feeling fine but a little disappointed that I'd slept off so much of such a great high. Still, I wouldn't try it again. Heroin was nice, but not worth the desperate lifestyle that had ensnared my friends so deeply.

We left the motel and drove the rest of the way to Ventura, where we spent all day and most of the night at the parking lot party, doing drugs and meeting people. Someone gave me a ticket to go into the concert, but I gave it away. I was having too much fun in the parking lot, and besides, I didn't like the Grateful Dead's music.

Afterward we all met back at Ryan's car, and he drove over to a campground so that we could go to sleep. Since the office was closed, there was no way to pay for a campsite, but we stayed there anyway. We slept in the car, Star and I in the backseat and the guys in the front, and the next morning I woke up to a sheriff pounding on the passenger seat window of the car.

Nick was sleeping in the passenger seat, and since the pounding hadn't woken him up, Ryan leaned over him and rolled down the window. The sheriff started talking about giving us a ticket for staying at the campsite and then stopped, noticing a syringe on the windshield in front of the passenger seat. He asked if any of us had shot up that morning, and we all said we hadn't. At the sheriff's insistence, Ryan tried to wake up Nick. He wasn't waking up. The sheriff pushed up the sleeve of Nick's short sleeve T-shirt. There was a rubber medical band still wrapped around his arm. The sheriff radioed for help and within minutes there were ambulances and fire trucks all over the place. Nick had overdosed.

One of the officers on the scene checked our arms for track-marks. Ryan and Star both had them, and they were both arrested. The one time I'd shot up hadn't left a mark and so I didn't have any, but the officer seemed reluctant to let me go, especially once he found out I was sixteen.

"What's that?" he asked, pointing to a freckle on my wrist.

"It's a *freckle*," I said, rolling my eyes. "That's why it's brown."

"Well, better safe than sorry," he commented, placing me under arrest.

When he got into the car he explained to me that since this was a drug case, the first place he was taking me was to the hospital where I would undergo a drug test.

"How's Nick?" I asked.

"He's alive," the sheriff replied, glancing in the rearview mirror.

Relieved, I turned my thoughts to myself. "I'm not taking a drug test," I informed the officer.

He didn't answer, and soon we arrived at the hospital. He waited outside the room, leaving me with a female nurse, who told me to go into the bathroom and pee in a cup. "Well, actually," I said respectfully, "I already told the officer that I wouldn't."

"You have to," she stated. I sighed. I didn't *have* to do anything, but I didn't feel like arguing with her.

"I don't need to go," I said. She told me to go and get a drink out of the water fountain and then wait a while. I went to the water fountain but just let the water run over my lips, without drinking any. I knew I had done heroin, but I didn't know how long it would stay in my system. I figured the more time it had to get out of my system, the better my chances of not being convicted of whatever they were planning to charge me with. I would not be taking a drug test today.

After a couple hours of walking back and forth to the water fountain, the officer knocked on the door and asked us what was taking so long. When the nurse told him that I wouldn't take the test, he informed me that we weren't leaving until I did and left the room. Fine, I thought, I'd just wait him out. It wasn't like I was in a hurry to get to juvenile hall. After about another hour the nurse came back in. The cup was still empty and she was getting frustrated.

"If you don't go now, I'll have to use a catheter," she warned ominously.

"What's that?" I asked, interested. I loved to learn new things.

"A catheter is a tube that is inserted into your bladder in order to empty it," she explained. Then, just in case I wasn't yet scared, she added, "It hurts."

"I'm not taking the test."

I was wearing overalls, and she took a step toward me and reached for one of the straps as if she was going to take them off of me. I pushed her hand away. Did she think I was stupid? "I *know* I'm a minor," I told her, "and a catheter is a form of medical treatment. You can't give medical treatment to a minor without signed parental consent."

She went outside and a few minutes later came back with the sheriff. He handcuffed me again and we left. "Sorry, that took so long," I told him, "but I *did* tell you before we got there that I wouldn't take the test."

Once we got to the station, I gave the officers my parents' information and was booked and taken to juvenile hall. I had a cell to myself, which would've been cool except that newcomers weren't allowed to come out of their cells until they'd had a medical examination in order to make sure they didn't have any contagious illnesses. It was Friday night and the lady that did the intake exams had already left. She didn't work on weekends and had Monday off. With the exception of being allowed to talk to my public defender in the visitor's area, I wasn't allowed out of my cell for the first four days.

When I talked to my public defender, I found out that I would have to take a drug test. I was being charged for being under the influence of heroin. I told her that there might be heroin in my system, but found out that since I was being charged by Ventura county, the state would have to show that I'd done heroin within the county.

The next day I got my examination and took a drug test. As I'd suspected, there was barely any heroin in my system. I would contest my charges, but the arraignment wouldn't take place for another three weeks. My case was dismissed eventually since the amount of heroin in my system was too small to show that I'd done the drug recently, but I'd spent about 28 days in juvenile hall.

The time didn't seem too bad. The floor I was assigned to was co-ed, and I made a lot of friends. It seemed kind of like a summer camp where you couldn't smoke and had to go to bed at nine o'clock. We even got to read all the time and play basketball every day. Still, I was happy to be released. I *really* wanted a cigarette.

18

Job Corps

Father's story

When Jasmyn was released from juvenile hall, she came back to our home. Despite the many fights and the tension created by having Jasmyn around, Lynn and I were thrilled to have her back again. I wanted all three of us to make plans for the future. Jasmyn seemed to be tiring of the homeless life-style. She came up with the idea of checking out the Job Corps, which is a government program to help young adults learn job skills. Lynn and I secretly dreamed of how wonderful it would be if Jasmyn could get into such a program. I scheduled an appointment for her interview and, a few days later, we went downtown to meet the Job Corps counselor. She told us all about the program. Jasmyn didn't appear too enthusiastic but I could tell she was intrigued.

Job Corps was a live-in program. They offered classes to obtain a GED high school diploma. They also had advanced schools located around the country for other specialties. The counselor explained that the rules were not to be broken. Curfews were strictly enforced. Any deviation from the rules could and would result in Jasmyn's termination from the program. I cringed. Jasmyn always had a problem with curfews. Actually, Jasmyn had a problem with rules of any kind.

After the interview I asked Jasmyn what she thought. She replied it sounded pretty cool. I asked her about the rules. She said they wouldn't be a problem. I wasn't so sure. Perhaps she could do OK. After all, these weren't rules and restrictions placed on her by her parents. These were the terms she needed to respect so she could live on her own. Without being too preachy, I tried to gently impress upon her the importance of not screwing up. The next week, she was off to Job Corps.

Daughter's story

Job Corps was great. I was hungry for knowledge and happy to be doing something positive on my own. I didn't mind the rules because they didn't come with all the tension that accompanied rules at home. They were clear-cut and the same for everybody, and I didn't have to worry about the particular mood of the authorities. Besides, I'd always lived by rules, and had a set of my own that I followed, including

Never hitchhike by yourself.

Never call the police.

Don't let people see you cry.

Make sure you're in control of yourself.

Don't steal from people you know.

Never sell your body.

This last was kind of a privilege for me, which a lot of girls on the streets didn't have. A lot of them spent much of their lives feeling desperate; since they had nowhere to go, they would do anything for a couple of dollars. Even though I didn't choose to go home, just the knowledge that I *could,* if I had to, had been enough to keep me from feeling desperate enough to do anything that I didn't want to do or that I considered dangerous.

I remember one day in San Francisco when I hadn't eaten all day, something happened to confirm that my decision to stick to this rule was a good one. I was standing on the street spanging when a man who must have been in his early thirties offered me ten dollars to chill with him in his hot tub for a while.

"Ummm, I'm only fifteen," I'd told him, wondering if he was a sicko.

"That's okay," he'd said. "I'm not asking for anything sexual; I just want some company."

Ten dollars seemed like a lot of money right then, but I knew it wouldn't do me much good if I were too dead to spend it.

"Naw," I'd said snidely, feeling perfectly safe on the crowded street. "I'd rather just stand here and ask people for quarters."

He walked away, but a few minutes later, he drove by in his car to ask me if I was sure.

"*Positive!*" I assured him.

About five minutes later, I'd asked an old lady for a quarter and she'd stopped.

"For what?" she'd asked.

"I'm trying to get up enough money for a burrito," I'd said. "Even a dime or a nickel would help."

She'd looked at me for a long time, must've been a full thirty seconds at least, before she'd reached into her purse and handed me what I though was a dollar. "Thanks!" I'd said as she walked away. Then I looked at what she'd given me. It was a ten. Thinking she'd made a mistake and not wanting to take advantage of someone who was trying to help me, I ran after her and told her she'd given me a ten-dollar bill instead of a one-dollar bill.

"I know," she'd told me. "Go get something to eat." I grinned. If I had broken my rule I probably would have ended up dead trying to earn ten dollars.

My plan at Job Corps was to get an education so that I would be qualified for *something* and then go back to the streets of San Francisco. That way, when I *did* get tired of being on the streets, I would have an alternative and not be stuck as so many others were. My goal was to build myself a safety net, not get a job and an apartment, which seemed to be everybody else's goal. As I'd tried to explain to my dad once, stable housing and a good job seemed like a lot of unnecessary responsibility. I didn't want to be tied down. I'd thought about it a lot and saw no point in working my butt off all day so I could go home, watch T.V., and go to sleep at night, just to do the same thing again the next day.

On my first day on campus, I left my purse in the orientation room. I went back to get it but the door was locked. I looked around, not sure what to do. I didn't remember where the office was. Just then a tall blond guy with long hair and a leather jacket walked up to me. He grinned, revealing a dimple on his cheek and even, white teeth. "What's wrong?" he asked me.

"With what?" I asked, staring up into blue eyes.

"Did you *lose* something?" he asked, laughing.

"Oh. My purse," I explained sheepishly. "I left it in there."

"'Kay, wait right here" he told me, walking away and reappearing a few minutes later with a man who let me in to get my purse.

"Thanks," I said after the man left.

"Anytime. And my name's Jaxon," he said over his shoulder as he walked away.

I smiled. I was going to like it here.

I met my roommates and we went to our dorm. The housing was four girls to a room, and they put newcomers together. The four of us were an odd assortment. There was Lalie, a black girl; myself, a white girl; and Yvonne and Shorty, who were Mexican girls from rival gangs. Within a few days, the four of us were the best of friends.

I met a lot of people within the first couple of days and soon had a huge group of friends, mostly guys. Besides my roommates, and the few girls I had been friends with over the years, I didn't trust females. I found them whiney, competitive, and usually empty headed.

By the end of the first week, Jaxon was my boyfriend. He was 21 and more mature than the boys I was used to going out with. I liked being with him and had respect for him. Since everybody was living on the same campus, friendships and relationships developed quickly. I think I was a little different than what Jaxon was used to as well. He was cute and kind and a lot of the girls on campus were interested in him. Most of them tried to be whatever they thought he wanted so that he would be interested in them. I wouldn't change for anybody.

One morning I had just finished putting my makeup on and was coming out of my dorm when I saw Jaxon. I smiled and walked up to him.

"You know," he said, taking my hand, "I really don't like makeup that much."

"Great," I said, brightly, "then you won't wear any!"

He laughed and put his arm around my shoulder.

In class we were supposed to make a collage representing who we were. I put pairs of eyes all over mine, a pack of cigarettes, a guitar, and books. When the teacher asked what the eyes were for I explained that eyes represented who I was because I could use them to take in information. I wanted to learn as much as possible, and I loved observing people and figuring out who they were and why they did the things that they did. I was excited about choosing a trade. I knew I could excel in whatever I chose, and getting my GED didn't seem like a bad idea either. I felt optimistic, popular, and completely at home.

As part of our intake assessment we all had to get a physical during our first week on campus. The physical consisted of a check-up and tests for sexually transmitted diseases. I had lost my virginity when I was 14 and had had a lot of sexual partners since then, so when I found out we would be tested for HIV, I was scared. What if I had it? Did I really want to know? I didn't, but not taking the test wasn't an option if I wanted to stay at Job Corps. Suddenly karma didn't seem strong enough to protect me, so I decided to make a deal with God.

That night, as I went to sleep, I prayed in the only way I knew how. I recited the prayer I'd learned listening to Metallica when I was younger. "Before I lay me down to sleep, I pray the Lord my soul to keep, and if I die before I wake, I pray to you my soul to take." I figured that that was my entrance to God's ear and now that I had his attention, I continued, "Thank you God, for my family and friends. Please make sure I don't have AIDS. If you do, I promise I'll never have unprotected sex again, and I'll pray *every* night, for the rest of my life. I won't forget. I promise. Please, please, please. Amen."

We took the tests and a couple of days later they brought us all in for the results. "Jasmyn," The lady announced, summoning me into the office. Damn. Why was *I* first? My last name started with a K. Shouldn't they be doing it alphabetically? This must mean I had it and she had to tell me. I was first so that she could get it over with. I rose slowly and followed her into a room. She shut the door and told me to have a seat. I did, feeling like she was about to hand me a death sentence.

She opened my file and sighed. She looked at me and back at the file. "What?" I finally asked, unable to stand it any longer.

"I see that you're sixteen and sexually active," she told me.

"Yes." I said, wishing she'd just get on with it. I'd answered all these questions before I'd taken the test.

"Well," she said, "your results are negative."

My heart leaped and my eyes filled with tears. Negative meant bad. But wait, people who had HIV were HIV positive, right? I was confused.

"So that means…"

"You don't have HIV," she said.

Yes! Why hadn't she just said that in the first place?

I walked out of the office with a big grin on my face.

"Jasmyn's obviously alright," someone said.

I hadn't told anybody how worried I'd been, so Jaxon was pretty startled when I ran up to him, threw my arms around him, and said happily, "I don't have AIDS!"

"Well," he said, bemused, "I'm certainly glad to hear *that.*"

At the Job Corps we were allowed to leave campus on Tuesdays as long as we were back by the ten o'clock curfew and overnight on weekends. On Tuesdays, we usually went to drink by the river. On the weekends a lot of people went home. Sometimes I went home and sometimes I stayed on campus with some of my friends, coming and going as we pleased.

After about two weeks, I brought Jaxon home for dinner to meet my parents. I told them he was nineteen and they seemed to like him. Later that day he told me he was going home to see his mom during the next weekend and asked me to come. I wasn't sure if I wanted to spend a whole weekend with his mom, whom I'd never met, so I told him I'd think about it. Instead, I decided to stay on campus that weekend.

He left on Friday and one of my friends asked me to go drinking with him and some other people. He and four girls that I didn't know very well were going, so I said no, but at the last minute I decided to go. My roommates had gone out to dinner, I hadn't wanted to join them, and I didn't have anything better to do.

On the way to the spot where we were going to drink, one of the girls invited a guy I didn't know. He came along and we all started drinking. We had some rum, mad dog 20/20, beer, and something I had never tried before, Goldslogger. I liked the little golden specks in it and drank a lot of it, chasing it with the mad dog.

It got dark, and the guy I didn't know asked me if I wanted to take a walk with him. Since the girls chattering was bothering me I agreed, but when I stood up I was surprised to find that I could hardly walk. I hadn't thought I was all that drunk, but after a couple of steps I had to sit back down. I wanted to go to sleep. It was getting late, and I heard the girls start to leave. They were only a couple of yards away, with only a bush separating them from my sight. I started to call out for them to wait up but suddenly this guy's tongue was in my mouth and his hands were up my shirt. "Stop," I said, pushing him away. "I'm with Jaxon." What was this guy doing? *Everybody* knew that I was with Jaxon.

I started to sit up, but he pushed me back down and stuck his tongue in my mouth again, telling me it was okay and that Jaxon wouldn't know. I told him *I* would know and tried to push him off, but my movements were slow; I was too drunk to fight very effectively. The other people were gone now, and he started to pull off my shorts. I tried to pull them back up, but he got them away from me. I told him to stop, but he kept ignoring me and I finally stopped trying to push him away, knowing he'd probably be done soon anyway. He was.

He got up and walked away, and I sat up, still too drunk to do much else. Except cry. Why was I crying? I *never* cried. I didn't think I was hurt. Why was I being such a baby? I groped around for my shorts and finally put them on. I tried to think straight. I had to get back to Job Corps. If I missed curfew, I might be terminated.

The river was behind a restaurant and I decided to use their bathroom to wash my face. I didn't want people to see that I'd been crying. I entered the restaurant and was walking toward the back, where the bathrooms were located, when I heard my name.

"Jasmyn! *What* happened to you?" It was Yvonne. I looked over and saw her sitting in a booth with Shorty and some other people. As soon as I saw my friends, I started crying again. What did she mean what happened? I looked down at myself. I was filthy; my shirt, shorts, and legs were covered with mud. Yvonne and Shorty excused themselves and walked me to the bathroom.

"What happened?" Shorty asked.

"Nothing…" I said, angrily choking back sobs. I didn't even know why I was crying. "I mean, this guy had sex with me, but…" "What do you mean 'had sex with you'?" asked Yvonne.

"Well, I didn't want to and he did and he wouldn't listen and I shouldn't have drank so much and I need to wash my face!" I said.

"Jasmyn, you were raped," Shorty said.

Raped? I splashed water on my face. I just hadn't been taking care of myself as well as I should have. Since I hadn't wanted to have sex I should've been sober enough to fight off unwanted advances. I'd gotten too drunk. I had to sober up. This was serious. People who were raped were victims. I hated that word. I didn't want to be considered a *victim.*

"I wasn't *raped,*" I said, "I just didn't want to have sex. It's not like he hit me or had a gun or a knife or anything."

Yvonne and Shorty exchanged glances and helped me wash up. Then they called the shuttle that would bring us back to Job Corps. Once in the shuttle, the driver asked why I was so dirty. Shorty told him, amid my protests. He said he would have Job Corps staff call the police once we got back to campus.

"No!" I exclaimed. I didn't want to talk to the police. I was fine.

"We're mandated reporters," the shuttle driver informed me.

I wasn't sure what that meant, but I didn't like the sound of it. I started crying again and hated myself for my weakness. How many people would see me cry tonight?

Plenty, it seemed. Once we got back to campus, the police came in and started questioning me. I didn't want to answer any questions; I just wanted to go to bed. I was in the admin office and the police told me I couldn't leave until I answered their questions. They said they'd already arrested someone and asked if I would identify him. I wouldn't. They told me he was being held in the orientation room. The orientation room consisted of three walls that were solid, and the fourth, facing out toward the common area, was a huge window made completely out of glass.

"What do you want to know?" I asked angrily, thinking that everyone on campus must know what was going on.

"What happened?" After much prodding I gave them a detailed, factual account of everything that happened. I left out my feelings and never once said the word "rape." I informed them that I didn't want to press charges and they said I didn't have a choice. I was a minor, and Job Corps could press charges on my behalf without my permission. Also, since I was sixteen and he was twenty-four, the district attorney could charge him with statutory rape.

Next, instead of being allowed to go to bed as I'd been promised, I was taken to the hospital for a thorough examination and had my clothes taken away from me as evidence. My parents were waiting at the hospital and they took me home. I was finally allowed to go to bed.

I spent the weekend at my parents' house and went back to Job Corps on Sunday. I had been worried about being terminated since I'd told the police I'd been drinking in front of Job Corps staff, and Job Corps had a strict no tolerance policy concerning drugs and alcohol. Under the circumstances, I was informed that I was not to be terminated. I was, however, "strongly advised" to stay in my dorm all day Sunday. Everybody on campus knew I had "accused" someone who was well liked of rape and there were mixed feelings about it, resulting in a huge scandal on campus.

Sunday night, Jaxon appeared at my window. "I just heard," he said, leaning through the window and hugging me. "I'm sorry."

"It's okay," I told him. "It's not your fault." Damn, he didn't have to treat me as if I was damaged. He hugged me again and said he'd see me the next day. He could get terminated for being at my window, but he'd just wanted to make sure I was okay.

Monday morning, I did my make-up and hair carefully before I ventured out of my dorm for classes. I knew everybody would be looking at me and talking about me, so I wanted to appear confident. The place where I had felt so at home only a few short days before suddenly felt foreign to me. At barely sixteen, I was the youngest one on campus, but suddenly I was the center of gossip and speculation.

The student body was divided in their belief of what had happened. The people who believed I was raped treated me as if I was broken and went out of their way to ask me if I was okay. The people who believed I had falsely accused someone of rape glared at me and whispered to each other when I walked by. I would've been hard pressed to decide which treatment I liked less. Even the teachers and authorities seemed to have different opinions. Some of them went out of their way to be nice to me, while others gave me tight little smiles or even glared at me.

Jaxon still treated me as if I was fragile, and I started to avoid him. Only Yvonne and Shorty seemed to treat me normally. After the first couple of days, the group of people that believed I was raped seemed to shrink. I wasn't sure why, and although I didn't really care, I found out anyway. I was in line in the crowded cafeteria when a girl I'd seen a couple of times around campus decided to confront me.

"Why are you out here?" she demanded loudly. "If I was raped and I was you, I'd be in my room crying, not out here acting like everything was normal!"

"*If* you were *me,*" I started, and then paused to look her up and down contemptuously, "—and you're *not*—you would hold your head up *no matter what!*" It was the closest I ever came to explaining my motives or feelings to anybody.

After that I refused to talk about it, and no one else on campus said anything about it to me directly, but now I had a better understanding of what was going on. I wasn't acting like a victim, so I must be lying. I was supposed to be devastated and broken inside. But why? It wasn't as if I'd been a virgin. I'd had sex before. Heck, I'd even had sex when I hadn't wanted to just because there were times when it had seemed an easier thing to do than make excuses.

The only difference was that this time I'd *verbalized* my desire for the other party to stop. He hadn't, but it was just one more time of having sex when I didn't want to. Why should I be devastated this time when I hadn't been all the other times? The aftermath was far more traumatic than the event itself, and I wasn't going to let people's expectations or condemnations get me down. Not visibly at least.

Even my parents didn't understand why I seemed to be doing so well, or why I wouldn't testify. I told them I didn't want to talk about it. I didn't want to testify because testifying meant going in front of people and saying what was *done* to me, as if I were too weak to have prevented it. I didn't like to admit weakness and didn't feel I should have to. Besides, the guy being accused hadn't beaten me up or anything. He'd just had sex with me. I wasn't pregnant, didn't have any diseases, and didn't feel dead inside, as I imagined I would if I had been the victim of a rapist, and so I didn't see why he should go to jail. But he *had* ignored me numerous times when I'd told him to stop and even tried to push him away. I wouldn't testify, but I wouldn't try to protect him from his own choices either.

I was not allowed to leave campus the following Tuesday but did anyway. In spite of my successful attempts to *appear* immune to the hostility directed toward me, inside it was having an effect. I had to get away for a while. I went to my mom's house for dinner, and she gave me some cough medicine because I was coming down with a cough.

When I got back to campus, I was called to the office. My departure had been discovered, and I was to be given an alcohol test. It came up positive. I was being terminated.

When my dad came to pick me up, I told him that I hadn't been drinking and wasn't sure why the test had been positive. He was skeptical until the next day, when I remembered that my mom had given me cough syrup, which probably had alcohol in it. He called my mom and asked her if she had given me any medicine, and she confirmed that she had. She checked the label. It wasn't alcohol free.

My dad called Job Corps and explained what had happened. I had been doing well, and they agreed not to terminate me, as long as I was willing to be transferred. They didn't want me back on their campus. He agreed. I was to be transferred to San Diego.

Father's story

With Jasmyn safe at Job Corps, Lynn and I could stop our constant worrying for the first time in years. Joshua started high school and decided to try out for the football team. He had made many new friends over the summer and had no problem acclimating to his new school.

Jasmyn was doing very well in Job Corps. She was excited about her high scores on aptitude tests. She took her pre-tests for her GED and passed them all with top scores. Her counselor told her she was defiantly college bound. I experienced the same proud feeling I remembered from long ago when Jasmyn was six and we were told she should be in the gifted and talented program. Jasmyn came home on weekends and lived at the dorm on the Job Corps campus during the week. There was still some tension when she was around. However, it was not as bad as before. We all knew she was going back to the campus on Sunday night. It was hard to believe, but it seemed Jasmyn was growing up. Lynn and I continued to go to fertility specialists; our inability to conceive was particularly difficult. Lynn has three sisters and two brothers. It seemed that every time we talked to anyone in the family, another sibling was pregnant. During the years Lynn and I struggled with infertility, twelve nieces and nephews were born.

We decided to explore other alternatives such as foster parenting and adoption program. We learned that the cost of private adoption was approximately $25,000, and we considered putting the cost on credit cards. Then we checked out the programs offered by social services. In California, contrary to popular belief, it is not easy to become a foster parent; Lynn and I were impressed with the requirements. We would have to take classes in parenting and then continuing education. We decided to enroll in the foster parent class.

At the same time, we met one of the nicest people on this planet. His name was Hale, and he was the social worker assigned to Lynn and me. He would help us navigate through the maze of social services. Hale expedited our enrollment in class and checked back with us to see how things were progressing.

The first class was an orientation. One of the speakers was a pediatrician who was confined to a wheelchair. He told us about the special needs the children in the system would most likely have. Then he did the most extraordinary thing; he wrote his pager number on the chalkboard and told the entire class of more than forty people to call him anytime with any questions or concerns. These people were blowing our preconceived notion of government employees out of the water! We looked forward to the subsequent classes and started rethinking our opinions about adopting through social services.

Jasmyn took to Job Corps with a renewed sense of optimism. She called us often to tell us all about her progress. Then came a bombshell. About two months into the program, we got a call from the local police department. Jasmyn had been raped. It was a Saturday night; according to the officer on the phone, she had been out partying with friends and was raped in the park. She was at the hospital. We jumped in the car and sped off to be with her. I was furious. As a father of a teenage daughter, rape is one of the words I hoped I would never hear. I wanted to kill this person who violated my little girl. No, killing was too good. I wanted to torture this monster and then slowly watch him die.

When we arrived at the hospital, an officer met us in the corridor. He told me that they already had the rapist in custody. I was relieved, but my anger did not subside. I asked where my daughter was. I was led to a very small examining room. Inside was Jasmyn, dressed in a hospital gown and with her knees pulled up to her chest, sitting on an examination table. I went to her and put my arms around her. I asked her what had happened; in true Jasmyn form she said, "Nothing."

The police wanted her to give a statement, but she refused. Jasmyn hated the police. She had spent the past few years avoiding them and could not comprehend the fact that they wanted to help her. I pleaded with her to cooperate to no avail. The police informed us that since she was a minor and the rapist was over 21, he could and would be charged without Jasmyn's consent or testimony. Eventually we were allowed to take her home.

Once home, I had hoped we could get Jasmyn to talk about her ordeal. Not only did she not want to talk about it, she seemed unaffected. The next day she was ready to go back to Job Corps right on schedule. Lynn and I wondered privately if she had been raped at all, but all I had heard and seen about rape on television taught me that there was no standard response by the victim. I decided to watch my daughter closely and to be there when she needed me.

The next weekend Jasmyn returned home. I asked her how things were going. She replied that people at Job Corps were being mean to her. Since the guy whom the cops had arrested was also from Job Corps, the place as divided into two groups: those who believed her and those who didn't. Jasmyn said it was no big deal, but I was concerned. This incident could trigger behavior that would get her thrown out of the program. She had been doing so well and was truly proud of her accomplishments. I didn't want to see that destroyed. I tried to get Jasmyn to talk about what was going on, but she shut down. Not wanting things to escalate into a blow-up, I let it go. Eden was coming to pick her up. We would talk further next week.

Then on Monday, Jasmyn called; she was being expelled from the program. Apparently she had failed a drug test. I didn't see how this was possible since she was with me and then Eden the entire weekend. Jasmyn asked if I would come and pick her up. I did and she explained what had happened. She was feeling ill and her mom had given her some medicine. It showed up on the drug screen. I asked Jasmyn if she had explained this to the staff at Job Corps. She did, but they didn't believe her. Jasmyn thought they wanted her out because of the rift developing on campus over the rape. She was dejected and ready to give up.

I believe one of the reasons Jasmyn found herself in the life predicaments she kept getting into was the fact that I was always there to bail her out. However, in this case she had done nothing wrong; in fact, she was the victim of a horrendous crime. I was not willing to stand by and watch this opportunity be taken away from her.

I called the local Job Corps office and spoke to the administrator. She explained that policy was set and there was nothing to be done. I asked if there was any consideration of the fact that this sixteen-year-old girl had been raped by another one of the Job Corps residents just the week before. "Yes," she said. "That situation has caused a lot of turmoil on campus; even the staff is divided about what really happened."

That was the wrong thing to tell me! I realized I was getting nowhere with this person and went to work on the problem. After a few phone calls, I found the number of the chief administrator of the program in Washington, D.C. I called and explained to an office worker what had happened to my daughter; she transferred me to the politician in charge. After making noises about going to the press with my daughter's story, he decided Jasmyn would be allowed to continue in the program. She would be transferred to San Diego and given a fresh start. Jasmyn was thrilled with the news.

19

San Diego

Daughter's story

The San Diego Job Corps wasn't taking new people for two weeks, and I stayed with my parents while I was waiting. At one point I called Jessi, just to see how all my old friends were.

"Did you hear about Gary?" she asked me.

My heart leaped. I hadn't heard anything from or about Gary since we'd gotten arrested in San Francisco. I compared all guys to him, and besides Jaxon, no one measured up. "What about him?"

"He got in a huge car accident just a couple of days ago. He was on a field-trip with his group home, and now he's in the hospital."

I got off the phone, shaking, and called his parents' house. They weren't home. If he was in the hospital, they were probably with him. My parents got the newspaper and I looked through all of them for the past week, trying to find news of a big crash involving a group home. I didn't find anything and hoped that meant Jessi was wrong, but I still wasn't sure by the time I left for San Diego

The San Diego Job Corps was a lot different from the one in San Jose, and I liked it less. My roommates were nice, but nothing like Yvonne or Shorty. I made friends quickly, and with the exception of one Mexican girl named Nina, avoided female friends at all cost. I wouldn't go anywhere unless guys were going, because I didn't trust girls to have my back if there was trouble. We were only allowed to leave on the weekends, so we tried to make the most of them. We went to Tijuana most weekends, where the legal drinking age was eighteen, but they didn't bother to card females so it really didn't matter that I was sixteen.

A couple of weeks after I arrived, a new group arrived. When I met them, one of the guys, Robert, made a sarcastic comment about something. I laughed and made one back, and soon we were best friends. Robert sold crank, so he was a pretty convenient best friend. We did everything together, and he kicked me down whenever I wanted at no cost from his personal stash. Eventually he said he liked me as more than a friend. I told him that I didn't like him as anything more than a friend, so our relationship stayed about the same for a while.

Then, on one trip to Tijuana, we got really drunk and ended up messing around. The next day, he thought it meant we were together, and since I didn't want to hurt his feelings, we became a couple. I started spending weekends at his house with his family. I didn't mind being his girlfriend. Since we were friends, I liked to spend time with him, but since I wasn't at all attracted to him, I wouldn't sleep with him unless I got drunk first. He either didn't notice or didn't care.

After a couple of months, I flew home to visit my parents. They had recently moved into a new house that I hadn't seen yet. When I decided to go see Yvonne and Shorty, my dad asked me to be home by eleven and I agreed. I had a great time with my friends and then started home. I got off the bus at 10:20 and started to go to my dad's house, but I couldn't find it. I had made a wrong turn somewhere and was lost and didn't remember their phone number. I wasn't worried about getting in trouble, since I didn't even live with them, but I needed to get home before eleven so that they wouldn't be worried.

A car pulled up next to me as I was walking around and the driver asked if I needed a ride. There were three guys inside who looked to be in their early twenties, and I almost refused. But I *knew* I'd gotten off at the right bus stop and figured if they would just drive me around for a few minutes, I would be able to recognize my parents' house. I accepted the ride.

Once in the car one of the guys asked my name and age and I told him. As I was explaining that I was lost, I noticed that the driver was getting on the freeway. "Hey!" I protested. "What are you doing?"

"Shut up," said the guy in the backseat, holding my arm tightly. The driver pulled into a clearing that seemed to be in the middle of nowhere. I had no idea where we were. While his friend held me down, he climbed into the backseat and yanked down my pants. I managed to kick him in the face before he pulled off my shoe and sat on my legs. I was relieved when he pulled out a condom, and I stopped fighting. I didn't want to cause him to rip it or anything, because I didn't want him to do anything to me without one. I wasn't going to get pregnant or get AIDS, and if I could just chill out for a minute I figured I would probably be okay.

When he was done, he pulled me out of the car by my hair. "You want your dick sucked?" he asked one of his friends.

"I'd bite," I warned. At the same time his friend said, "No, dude, she's only sixteen."

"I don't care if she's twelve," the driver said, pulling off my other shoe and throwing both of them, one at a time, as far as he could into a field.

"No, let's go," said the guy who seemed concerned about my age. They got in the car and left. Relieved, I tried to straighten myself out as best as I could before going into the field in search of my shoes. I could only find one of them.

I went out to the street and looked around. It was pretty late and the streets were empty. I had no idea where I was. I decided to find a payphone. I would call my mom and ask her to come and pick me up.

After walking for what seemed like a long time, I still hadn't seen any payphones. As I approached a stoplight, I noticed that there was a car stopped there, headed in the opposite direction I was. It looked like a police car! I decided to flag it down, tell them I was lost, and ask them to take me to my mom's. Worried that the light would change before they'd see me, I ran into the middle of the street, waving my arms. It worked; they pulled up to me and stopped.

"Are you trying to kill yourself?" one of the officers asked me.

"No," I explained. "I was trying to get you to stop. I was coming home from a friend's house and I got lost. I was wondering if you could take me home."

"Were you raped?" he asked, looking at me strangely.

I looked down at myself and for the first time noticed that my hand and arm were all scraped up and realized how strange I probably looked walking around in my socks and carrying only one shoe.

"Oh, no; I was drunk earlier," I lied, "and I fell down walking across the field, so I took my shoes off and I must have dropped one of them." I knew my explanation didn't make any sense but was hoping this would encourage the officers to bring me home and let my parents deal with me. I wasn't going to say anything about what had happened. I knew how the San Jose police dealt with rape.

"Maybe she'd feel more comfortable talking to a woman," the officer said to his partner, and they drove me to a Safeway parking lot. Once there, they radioed for backup and asked that a female officer be sent. It took a long time for her to get there, and once she did the three of them had a private talk while I waited in the back of the car.

Finally she opened the door and looked at me. "What happened?"

I repeated the story about being drunk and falling and said that since I'd been so drunk, I'd probably gotten off at the wrong bus stop and now I just needed them to take me home so my parents wouldn't be worried.

"Why did you take off your shoes?" she asked me.

"Because they kept getting stuck in the mud," I explained, "and that's why I fell."

Finally, she squatted down so that we were at the same eye level. "If you were raped," she told me, talking softly, "you need to tell us so that we can help you."

"If I had been, I'd want help, so I'd tell you," I said, looking into her eyes. "But I wasn't raped."

She sighed and turned to the officers, "If she says she wasn't, I guess there's nothing we can do about it."

The officers agreed to take me home and I asked them to take me to my dad's. Explaining that I was visiting from San Diego and that my dad had just moved, I gave them the major cross streets near him and asked them to drive me around in that area until I recognized his house. They drove me around for about ten minutes, and when I still couldn't find it, I gave them directions to my mom's.

It was late when we got there, and my mom found my dad's number and called him to tell him I was safe. I talked to him and explained that I had gotten lost and was relieved that he didn't seem mad. I told my mom the same story I'd told the police to explain why I was all dirty and then went and took a shower. When I came out of the bathroom, my mom was still up. She made me some coffee and listened while I talked excitedly about how well I was doing at Job Corps and how fun it had been to see Yvonne and Shorty again. After about forty-five minutes, she set up a bed for me and we said goodnight. I was home safely and no one was mad at me. I went to bed in a great mood.

The rest of my visit was uneventful and I was soon back at Job Corps.

I was doing well there and had decided to take auto mechanics because it was such a hands on trade. I was progressing faster even than the boys in the class. Since I couldn't take my GED test until I was seventeen, the plan was to let me learn my trade first and then enroll me in the GED preparation classes.

Robert and I were doing crank everyday, and it seemed normal to me. One Monday, however, after we'd returned from a weekend at his house, he handed me a bag with enough powder in it for at least a couple of rails. I took it back to my dorm and cut a line. Before I could do it, a thought popped into my mind. *What if I'm pregnant?* The thought surprised me. My period wasn't due for another couple of weeks, and my last one had been right on time. And although Robert and I had been having sex for at least four months, I'd never before wondered if I was pregnant. Why would I suddenly think of that now?

I wasn't sure, but I decided to be safe. I scooped the line back into the bag and hid it in my locker. I would do it when I had my period and was sure I wasn't pregnant. Even though I was used to doing the drug every day, the thought of a couple of weeks without it didn't bother me. I did it because I liked it, not because I needed it.

I didn't say anything to Robert about being pregnant because I wasn't sure; I wasn't the kind of girl who told people she was pregnant every five minutes just to get attention. When Robert handed me another bag a couple of days later I just said, "No thanks, I still have some from last time." He looked surprised but didn't comment on it.

My period didn't come and I went to the Job Corps medical office and asked for a pregnancy test. The results came back positive, and I found out that I was pregnant the day before my seventeenth birthday. I wouldn't be going back to the streets.

The woman who gave me the results immediately started talking about abortion arrangements. I told her I'd consider it so that she'd stop trying to convince me and let me leave the office. I didn't intend to have an abortion. It was true that I was young and didn't know anything about how to raise a child, but I *did* know that actively killing it certainly seemed like a step in the wrong direction.

I told Robert that I was pregnant and he seemed happy. I wasn't surprised since he thought he loved me. Now I just had to tell my parents.

I told my mom first and asked her not to tell my dad. I'd decided not to tell him until I was three months pregnant. I thought he'd want me to have an abortion and at three months it would be too late. Although I'd never planned on having a baby, I was already fiercely protective of this one.

The next time I talked to my dad, he was in a great mood. I talked a little about how I was doing and then said, "Guess what? I quit smoking!"

He'd wanted me to quit smoking since I'd started and was really happy. "I'm so proud of you!" he exclaimed. His obvious enthusiasm made me feel bad about lying to him, even by omission. I decided to tell him even though it would probably lead to an argument.

"Well," I said, "You're not going to be in a minute," I started.

"Why?" he cut in. "You're not pregnant, are you?"

"Uh, actually, I am," I said, then held my breath.

He was silent for an instant and then said, "I'm going to be a grandpa?" He sounded...happy! "Yeah," I said, relieved. I was glad I'd told him. I'd been really stressed wondering what he'd say and had been anticipating an argument that now, it seemed, wasn't going to take place.

We talked for a few more minutes and then got off the phone. I felt like a huge weight had been lifted off my shoulders.

Father's story

Jasmyn was doing extremely well in San Diego. She decided to check out other programs and opportunities the program offered. She informed Lynn and me that she had decided to become a certified diesel mechanic. My initial response was to laugh. Jasmyn was five-foot three-inches tall and weighed ninety-five pounds soaking wet. The mental picture of her changing a tire on an eighteen-wheeler cracked me up.

Lynn and I continued the process to adopt a child. We attended classes twice a week to learn about the special needs an at-risk child would have. The further we progressed in our education, the more thankful I was that Jasmyn had finally straightened her life out and was going to be OK. One of my major fears had been a teenage pregnancy. I don't know why I thought Jasmyn had dodged that bullet. She was about to turn seventeen and she was making plans for her future. I was not naive enough to actually believe she wasn't sexually active, but somehow I convinced myself that she wasn't.

The illusion was shattered with her next phone call. I was thrilled as always to hear her voice, especially now, because I loved hearing about her successes in class and listening to her future plans. Diesel mechanic still cracks me up! This call started the same as all the others. "Hi dad, how are you?"

"Fine honey; what's new?" Jasmyn had some great news. She had decided to quit smoking. I was ecstatic. I had been trying to get her to quit for years. I told her how proud I was.

Her response was unexpected. She said something like, "Well, you won't be in a minute."

In an instant, I knew why she'd quit smoking. I blurted out, "You're not pregnant are you?"

"Yes."

I had one of those episodes that you hear about on talk shows. In a matter of a few seconds, hours of thoughts raced through my mind. Jasmyn had always done the opposite of any advice I gave her. She was obviously excited with the prospect of having a baby. I had been unable to control her or influence her decisions in the past. She was seventeen now—an adult, in her view. If I flipped out and started ranting and raving, this could be the last conversation we would have for a long while. I didn't want that to happen. All I could think of was, "Be supportive." There was plenty of time for the details later.

I mustered up all the happiness I could project in my voice and said, "I'm going to be a grandpa?" I could hear the relief in Jasmyn's reply.

"You're not mad at me are you, Daddy?" We talked for a few more minutes and ended the conversation with our normal "I love you" good-byes. From the tone in Jasmyn's voice, I could tell I had made the right decision.

I was then faced with the prospect of telling Lynn the "good news." I had watched her turmoil of late with each pregnancy announcement from our family and friends. I could almost hear her "I told you so" ringing in my ears as I approached her.

As anticipated, Lynn was devastated. She had predicted Jasmyn would end up pregnant, and that is exactly what happened. Between fits of uncontrollable crying, Lynn tried to verbalize her feelings. "What were we going to do now? Why didn't you listen to me when I told you this would happen? It's not fair. What is she going to do?"

Lynn seemed to think that my failure to act on her prediction of Jasmyn's pregnancy added to the cause of the pregnancy. I couldn't see this connection. While Lynn's predictions were accurate, Jasmyn had always done what Jasmyn wanted to do. She did not accept our interventions. Therapy had failed. Incentives to award success had failed. And now, Job Corps had failed.

Jasmyn was continuing her downward spiral. We could extend a hand for her to grab onto and pull herself out, but we could not make her grasp it.

20

Bad News Boyfriend

Father's story

As anticipated, Jasmyn was not allowed to stay in Job Corps. She moved into her boyfriend's parents' home. She had told us that her boyfriend, Robert, was also in Job Corps, but we knew nothing else about him. I had hoped that since he was in a program that encouraged young adults to learn a skill and be self-sufficient, he might be, at the very least, a positive in Jasmyn's life.

I didn't hear from Jasmyn for about a month and then she called again. Apparently, Robert had had a fight with his father that nearly came to blows. They could not live there anymore. They had decided to move to the Bay Area. Jasmyn would be home in a few days. I broke the news to Lynn and waited for Jasmyn's arrival. Lynn and I were anxious, to say the least. Jasmyn had been a source of frustration and constant anxiety for the past few years. Our household was peaceful and relaxed when she was not there. We hoped this would not change with her return, but we both knew better.

Jasmyn and Robert showed up on our doorstep a few days later. She was already showing signs of pregnancy. She introduced us to Robert. Robert was almost six feet tall but walked hunched over, so he seemed much shorter. He wore his hair in a very short crew cut, and his face was scarred from a past case of bad acne. He wore baggy pants and an old, dirty tee shirt.

We shook hands and introduced ourselves. I didn't like him from the first. We all sat down around the kitchen table to get acquainted. I asked Robert how he came to be in Job Corps. He told us a bizarre story about his days as a drug dealer. He said one day he was walking down the street with more than a million dollars in a bag from dealing drugs. He decided he didn't want to be a drug dealer anymore, so he walked up to a dirty homeless man and handed him the bag full of money. Then he joined the Job Corps.

Needless to say, this was the most ridiculous thing I had ever heard. The really strange part was that when Robert told these wild tales, and there were many more to come, he really believed what he was saying was true. He was the first pathological liar I had ever met.

It was getting late, so we all decided to go to bed and talk further in the morning. Jasmyn would stay in her old room; Robert could sleep on the couch in the garage. Although she was already pregnant, in our home she was an unmarried teenage girl, and we wouldn't let her share a room with a boy. That was not the message we wanted to send to Joshua.

The next day, I asked Jasmyn to call her grandmother, my mother, to tell her she was safe. When Jasmyn announced she was pregnant, her grandmother offered to let her and Robert come and stay with her until they got their feet on the ground. She lived in a small two-bedroom apartment about two hours from our home. I had a very bad feeling about this idea, but we had adopted a "Jasmyn is an adult" attitude and saw no point in trying to intervene. The next day, after borrowing bus fare from me, Jasmyn and Robert were off to see her grandma.

Daughter's story (Age 17)

Since Job Corps wasn't set up for pregnancy, I would have to leave. Although I wouldn't be able to take diesel mechanics as I'd planned, I had already completed my auto mechanic classes. One of the counselors arranged for me to take my GED test, but explained that I wouldn't have time to stay and take the preparation classes. They arranged for me to take the next test scheduled, figuring that I probably wouldn't pass without preparation, but I definitely wouldn't pass without taking the test at all. I wasn't worried. Even though I'd dropped out of school when I was fourteen, I still read a lot. How hard could it be?

While I was waiting for the test, I was still getting up every morning to do my chores. I experienced daily morning sickness, throwing up many times throughout each day. I already loved my baby but hated being pregnant.

During the beginning of my pregnancy, the smell of cigarette smoke made me nauseous. Robert always smelled like cigarette smoke, and so it wasn't long until even the thought of Robert made me feel like throwing up.

Pregnant women often experience moodiness, and I was no exception. I had never been overemotional (I considered showing emotion a weakness), but during pregnancy everything was a catastrophe. My whole pregnancy was a series of major ups and downs. Since every day I experienced many tragedies and triumphs, the few days I spent at Job Corps awaiting the GED test felt like months.

When I finally got to take the test, I was surprised by how easy it was. I had heard that it was extremely hard, and I knew a lot of people who had spent months preparing for it and still failed. The counselors had also told me I probably wouldn't pass, and although I didn't believe them, I expected it to be somewhat difficult. In taking the test, I would have to prove I had an education equivalent to four years of high school when I'd actually only had one year.

The scores came back; I had passed with flying colors. Not only had I earned my GED, my score was high enough to qualify me for entrance into a four-year university if I ever wanted to go to college. I didn't plan on going to college anytime soon but was happy with my scores. They made me feel smart.

Job Corps gave out a biweekly allowance of twenty dollars, and when I went to pick up my check I was surprised to find out that Job Corps staff had been talking about me. "Name and ID?" asked the lady passing out checks.

"Jasmyn Klarfeld," I supplied, handing her my ID. She looked at it and then looked up at me in surprise. "Hey, you're that young girl who scored so high on her GED test without studying, huh?" she asked.

"Umm, I *guess*," I said, trying to act bored. But I was pleased. It was kind of cool to be recognized for something positive.

Robert had completed his mechanics program and left Job Corps on the same day I did. We moved in with his parents.

Living with his parents was hard. His whole family lived there, and I felt like an outsider. They had a lot of animals and the house was filled with fleas. They all smoked inside the house, and I hated the stench. I knew that smoke was bad for the baby, so I spent most of my time alone in Robert's room with the window open.

It was during this time that I saw how Robert had been raised and watched his true personality emerge. His family fought constantly, their fights going beyond yelling and screaming and often coming to blows. Robert would easily become uncontrollable and defensive and was not above pulling knives on family members. This way of life was foreign to me; throughout all of the places I'd gone and lived, I'd never seen a family to whom violence was the norm. I didn't know how to react to it and felt sorry for Robert. When he was uncontrollable, I was the only one who could calm him down. Once calm, he would cry and say he hated his family. I was glad that I could calm him and felt that since I was the only one he responded to, he was now my responsibility.

I also saw his total lack of personal responsibility. He would steal cigarettes from his family members and then lie about it. Even when caught and confronted with the item, he would continue to lie. If anyone pushed, he would fly into a defensive rage and accuse his family of setting him up, claiming that *they* were the ones lying.

After about five months of constant fighting, his family got tired of the situation and informed us that we would have to leave. His dad drove us to the Greyhound station where I called my dad. He said that we could all talk about things when we got to San Jose.

Back in my parents' house, Robert and I were expected to sleep in separate rooms. I would get my old room and he would have to sleep on a couch in the garage. I felt bad for Robert because I remembered how awkward I had felt around his family and thought he must feel even worse since he had to sleep in the garage. I thought it was a pretty stupid arrangement since I was already pregnant. However, my parents were adamant on this point because we were not married, and although I argued a little I was relieved to have my own space again and to be in a non-violent environment.

After the first night, my dad told me to call my grandma because she had been worried about me. I called and talked to her for a while and she invited Robert and me to come stay with her. I agreed, and before the week was over we were moving on.

Brief Retrospect

Like many of my parents "stupid" decisions, the decision to house Robert and me separately was a smart one. My parents had taught me certain things while growing up, and I knew that they did not condone sex outside of marriage. If they had thrown away those values and teachings simply because I had gotten pregnant, showing that they didn't live by what they taught me, I might have never gone back.

By sticking to the example they had tried to provide for me, even when it seemed ineffective, my dad and step-mom were setting a strong foundation that I would later be able to fall back on in my adult life. Their moral constancy was like an anchor to me. I was able to drift but stay afloat. Without an anchor, I might have been lost in the ocean of life.

Father's Story

Jasmyn and Robert lived at her grandmother's house for the next few months. They both looked for work. Jasmyn landed a job at a coffee shop, but Robert was less successful. In his eyes, everyone was against him and nothing was his fault. In spite of Robert's less than sterling employment record, they decided to enlist Grandma's help in securing an apartment in the complex she lived in.

When Jasmyn told me the news, I was concerned. She was getting closer to her delivery date. After the baby was born, she would have to rely solely on Robert for support. Her grandmother was nearby, but the relationship was growing strained, and her grandmother's health was deteriorating. Lynn and I suggested they move back to the Bay Area. After all, Jasmyn had two sets of parents and several friends, all within close proximity. The employment opportunities were much greater in the larger city so Robert would have a better chance of landing and keeping a good job.

After thinking about it and talking to Eden, Jasmyn decided to move back. Eden was a property manager and located an apartment in the seedy part of town. The apartment was a small studio with a tiny kitchen area and a bathroom with a total of no more than 500 square feet of living space. They didn't have the money for a deposit or rent, so I loaned it to them. I was apposed to giving them so much help, but I saw no alternative.

Lynn went to garage sales with Jasmyn and purchased some used furniture and household goods. Eden went to the grocery store and stocked them up with household supplies. All that was left was to find Robert a job.

Lynn's father, Arthur, was an entrepreneur. He used to own a heating and air-conditioning business and now was heavily into real estate. Although he didn't have to work installing residential systems, he enjoyed being in the game. Arthur always had a few jobs lined up and was continuously looking for help. He also enjoyed taking any individual who was willing to learn and teaching him the sheet metal business from the ground up. In a few short months, he could give Robert the training he needed for a real career with the potential of making a comfortable living. He offered Robert a job.

Arthur always said that anyone working with him got good pay, a full day's work, lunch, and a lecture. Robert had an opportunity to learn while making a good wage; all Arthur asked in return was an honest day's work.

Things went well for a few days. Arthur picked up Robert at the apartment and dropped him off at the end of the day. One day they went to lunch; while Arthur paid for lunch, Robert decided to buy a pack of cigarettes. Arthur was surprised to see Robert pull a wad of twenty-dollar bills out of his pocket and peel one off to pay for the smokes. After lunch they returned to the day's jobsite, an upscale home in a very nice neighborhood.

About mid-afternoon, the homeowner, an old friend of Arthur's, approached him with a concern. "Arthur" he said, "I'm sure I had four hundred dollars in my top dresser drawer this morning. Now the money is gone." He had known Arthur for years and was not implying he had taken the money but wondered about his helper.

Arthur was embarrassed and enraged. He pulled out his wallet and said "I'm so sorry!" offered to give his old friend the four hundred dollars. The homeowner refused, saying Arthur shouldn't have to incur the loss. He knew he didn't take the money. Arthur insisted and gave the money back to the homeowner. He apologized for the intrusion and told his friend he would be back the next day. He needed to have serious words with his helper.

Back in the truck, Arthur confronted Robert. Robert denied any knowledge of the money. He told Arthur to go ahead and search him. He emptied his pockets—nothing there. He must have stashed the bills in his socks or underwear while the homeowner questioned Arthur. Arthur told Robert he had seen the wad of twenties at the lunch counter, but Robert again denied having any money.

Arthur took Robert home and that was the last time they worked together. I wasn't told the reason until months later. After I heard the story, I asked Jasmyn what Robert had told her. He said her grandfather fired him after an argument, nothing more. Jasmyn also remembered Robert having a large amount of money that night, all twenties. There was no doubt he was the perpetrator.

Since Robert lost his job with Arthur, I decided to give him a job with my company. In retrospect, I wish I had known why Arthur stopped using him, but I wasn't told of the missing money. My business catered almost exclusively to the very rich.

I gave Robert a job as a helper, but after working with him for a few days, I had enough. He was by far the laziest person I had ever employed. One day, I was on top of a ladder aligning a big screen TV projector. I sent Robert out to the truck to get a tool. Twenty minutes later, he hadn't returned. I went looking for him and found him asleep in the front seat of the truck. That was his last day working for me.

Months later when Arthur told me his story, I wondered how many of my clients fell victim to Robert. Thinking back to the few days he worked with me, I can recall him disappearing for ten minutes at a time and emerging from a bedroom where we were not working. I hope he didn't find anything worth stealing, but I fear he did. Besides the violation of the trust clients placed in my company, he was risking the reputation I had worked so hard to obtain. I couldn't risk having him work for us any longer.

Over the next few months, Robert continued to look for work, get hired, and usually within days, get fired. He came to me occasionally to borrow money for groceries and rent. I continued to lend them money, knowing the baby would be born soon. As the delivery day approached, I didn't want my daughter stressed out over the possibility of being homeless.

Robert eventually landed a job working at a local tire shop. In Job Corps, he had trained in auto mechanics. The establishment wasn't far from the apartment so he could get to and from work on his own. After a few months, the job would offer benefits for his family. Jasmyn was excited about the prospect of Robert finally finding a long-term job.

I checked in with Jasmyn often as her due date approached. She was huge and had trouble functioning day to day while waiting for labor to begin. I always asked how Robert was doing. One day she told me that Robert was fired from his job.

"What happened?" I asked.

"It wasn't his fault," she said. Someone had been stealing change out of the customers' cars while they were having tires put on or brakes repaired. "Robert is the newest employee, so they blamed him and let him go as an example to the other workers."

Poor Robert—always the victim. The next time he came over he told Lynn and me that his father worked in the government and had a team of lawyers at his disposal. He would sue them for millions. The lawyers would get right on the case. After they left, Lynn and I talked about how ridiculous his stories were. How could Jasmyn stand it? I swore I caught her rolling her eyes every time he started with another wild tale. I guess love really is blind, and, in Jasmyn's case, deaf as well.

Daughter's Story (Age 17)

Life at my grandma's was slow, but seeing her again was good. She was thrilled to have us there and to be close to me during my pregnancy. I was growing bigger everyday and felt like a whale. I thought the pregnancy would never end. Robert looked for jobs, but even when he got hired, he wasn't able to keep anything for long. One of my grandma's friends was looking for a counter-person for her coffee shop and I got the job. I had to leave the house at four-thirty in the morning to be at the coffee shop, which was hard because of my pregnancy, but we needed the money to get our own place, so I kept the job.

My grandma seemed to really like Robert and asked him why he didn't marry me. He truthfully told her that he'd asked me many times but that I'd repeatedly refused. After that, she often tried to talk me into marrying him. Although I felt responsible for Robert, I didn't have a lot of respect for him and knew I'd never want to marry him. I was getting tired of my grandma's overt "hints."

We welcomed the opportunity to move into our own apartment. We would barely have enough money for rent on my salary, but Robert said he would try harder to find a job before the baby was born. I didn't believe he would be able to support both of us—or even himself—without my help, but I decided to just worry about things one day at a time.

The apartment was only days away from being ours when my dad convinced me that I should consider the possibility of moving back to the Bay Area before the baby was born. "Just come up for a visit," he suggested. "You can look for apartments here, and if you don't find anything, you can take the one near your grandma. But at least here you would be near your family and your friends to help you once you have a baby."

His advice seemed sensible and I took it. We moved back to the Bay Area, this time into a small studio apartment my mom had helped us find. I liked being so close to my family and all my old friends, but things between Robert and me were becoming increasingly strained. He didn't seem to understand the need to go to work every day, so he kept losing jobs. He would leave the apartment every morning as if he were going to work, but in reality he was spending the little money we did have on drugs. Most of the time, we barely had any food in the house.

Concerned, my family started casually bringing food over when they came to visit. My mom had a key to the apartment since she was the apartment manager, and sometimes I would come home from somewhere to find my refrigerator stocked. My step-mom would bring over fully cooked meals like whole lasagnas, claiming she had "accidentally made too much."

The gestures were more than welcome since I knew that the baby needed nutrients, but Robert would come home high and eat all the food. I ate as little as I felt was necessary to keep the baby healthy, not knowing when we would have more groceries.

Somehow we always scrounged enough money to pay rent, Robert saying that he had earned it or borrowed it from a friend. I later found out that he had been borrowing money from *my* parents behind my back, which was something I had clearly told him I wasn't willing to do. My parents hadn't realized that I didn't know this was going on, and they gave the money thinking that I had asked Robert to borrow it. They had been loaning him money for groceries as well. Since we never had money for groceries, I concluded that Robert had been spending the grocery money on drugs when he was supposed to have been at work. I was furious when I found out how much money we owed my parents.

I spent my time at home during the day trying to get the apartment ready for the baby and reading every book I could get my hands on about infant care and child development. I must have read over a hundred books on that subject alone during my pregnancy. Before the baby was even born, I already knew which parenting theories I agreed with, which ones I thought were preposterous, and which values I planned to teach my son. About three o'clock every afternoon, I would look out the apartment window and enviously watch the high school kids walking home from school, trying to remember how it felt not to have to worry about bills, eviction, and how I was going to scrape together dinner that night.

I hadn't been that carefree since I was fourteen. At seventeen, I felt decades older than any of those kids on their way home to parents and homework. They looked skinny and happy, swinging their backpacks carelessly in the warm California sun. By contrast I felt ugly, my own body swollen with pregnancy. To try to make myself feel better (younger), I decided to call some of the people I used to hang out with during my carefree days. I called Sara first and was surprised to find out that both she and Ruby were pregnant. All of our babies were due within the same month. She also mentioned that Gary had been asking about me, and I called him next. He was thrilled to hear from me and asked for my phone number. Robert and I couldn't afford a phone, so I had to walk to a payphone about a mile away from our apartment to make my calls. I told Gary I didn't have a number, but promised I'd call him again.

It was a promise I intended to keep. I hadn't seen Gary since we'd been arrested in San Francisco over two years before. Since that time, I'd compared all the guys I'd met to him, and no one really measured up—definitely not Robert. My favorite thing about Gary had been his honesty. He'd been willing to tell the truth even when it got him into trouble or caused someone to be mad at him. Robert lied about everything; whether he needed to or not. I couldn't break up with Robert, though. Not only would he not be able to support himself if I did, but my son wouldn't have a father. But I would still keep in touch with Gary. I wasn't planning on marrying Robert, and maybe someday, after my son grew up, Gary and I would get back together.

Talking to some of my old friends made me feel more confident, and I decided to confront Robert about the lies I had previously just ignored. When I confronted him with all the facts and asked him what was really going on with his jobs, and what had really happened to the money he'd been borrowing from my parents, he got extremely defensive. For someone who'd had so much daily practice at the art of lying, he was surprisingly bad at it. He couldn't keep his stories straight, and the longer he talked, the more implausible his scenarios became. Although in the past I would have just dropped the subject at this point, this time I was determined to get to the bottom of it. The baby was due soon, and our money couldn't just keep disappearing. I decided to push it.

The conversation quickly turned from a discussion about his stories not adding up into a heated argument about why I never believed what he said. His face turned red, and he pushed it into my face, yelling and screaming. As I had done with others in the past, I forced myself to remain calm and detached while he lost control emotionally. Keeping a tight reign on my own emotions was my way of maintaining control of situations. I waited for him to stop screaming and pause for breath, and when he did I coolly said, "Will you move your face, please? Your breath smells."

There was a slight pause, and then he screamed again and pushed me, hard, against the wall. My control snapped.

"You pushed me!" I screamed. "*Nobody* pushes *me,* you stupid jerk! I'm leaving!" I started for the door of the apartment. I was almost there when he grabbed my arm.

"Wait," he said, "I'm sorry, baby. I just got so mad that I didn't know what I was doing. I am *so* sorry."

"Get your hand *off* me," I said, jerking my arm away and opening the apartment door.

As I started to step outside, he grabbed my shoulder, yanked me back inside, and slammed the door shut. "Just *listen* to me!" he screamed.

I can't believe I'm in this situation, I thought, noticing a vein popping out of the side of his neck, beneath his red, swollen face. Only trashy people lost control and had violent fights at full volume, right? *I* wasn't trashy. Why was this happening?

"Okay," I said, wanting him to shut up so that the neighbors wouldn't hear, "I will listen for *one* minute. But when the minute is up, you will let me go for a walk, *by myself,* so that I can think."

"Will you come back?" he asked.

"Sure," I said, thinking that I really wouldn't. "You're wasting your minute."

"I really am sorry," he said. "I just lost control. I never should have done that and it won't happen ever again. I love you more than anything in the world. You're the first person who's ever been there for me in my whole life. You're my best friend. I'd just die if you left, babe."

"Great," I said, just wanting to get out of there. "*Now* can I go on my walk?"

"I guess," he said, moving away from the door.

Finally, I was out of there. I wasn't sure where I was going. It was dark and cold, but I didn't notice. I had a ton of angry energy, and at first I just walked and thought.

I should have made *him* leave. I was the one who was pregnant. *Now* where was I supposed to go? I couldn't go to my family and ask for a place to stay. They would've wanted to know why I needed somewhere to stay when the father of my baby and I had a perfectly good apartment. I couldn't just say, "He pushed me," like some kind of whiney little victim, like I was weak and needed protection or something. Yeah, right. I could take care of myself.

But that *was* pretty weak of me to start yelling right along with him. I couldn't believe I'd acted that way. I hated people who couldn't control themselves. I felt embarrassed and trashy. I couldn't just go back to our apartment and act like everything was normal.

I decided to stay gone as long as possible to make him think I'd left him. Then when I got back, he'd be so relieved that I hadn't, he would never do this again. He'd see that even though this was normal behavior in *his* family, it wasn't the way that *I* was willing to live. Plus, I reasoned, I couldn't just take a baby away from its father. That wouldn't be fair to the baby. I had to make every effort to make this thing work.

I must have walked around for a few hours, although my mind was racing so fast that it didn't seem to be that long at all. When I got back to the apartment, my feet and back were killing me, and it was after midnight.

Robert was curled up on the couch, holding one of my sweatshirts and crying. "I thought you weren't coming back," he said. I looked around. He had cleaned the whole apartment while I was gone.

"Well, I'm back, but you better never do that again," I said. "I'm not the kind of person who just gets pushed around."

He apologized again, and I went to bed. As I dozed off, I realized that he never had told me what had happened to our money.

21

It's a Boy

Father's story

A few months after arriving back in San Jose, the baby was born. He was the cutest thing. He had long little fingers and gigantic feet just like his grandpa. Jasmyn came through the delivery very well. We all visited her in the hospital and took turns holding him. Jasmyn decided to call him Elijah. As I held Elijah, I couldn't believe I was a grandfather at age 39. As wrong as I thought her getting pregnant was, the blessing of a newborn is a great eraser of doubt. He was perfect in everyway. Jasmyn and Robert decided not to have the baby circumcised because Robert was under the delusion that he was one quarter American Indian and the tribal chiefs would be disappointed. Jasmyn agreed, not wanting the baby subjected to the pain of the procedure. I disagreed strongly, but it wasn't my call and not a battle I thought worth fighting. I didn't want my daughter to have to choose sides.

After a day in the hospital, Jasmyn and Elijah were released and on their way home. The girls had set up a crib for the baby in the studio apartment and divided the one room into two. While Jasmyn was in the hospital, Lynn went over to her apartment and completely cleaned and prepared for the arrival of the baby. Jasmyn arrived home to a cozy nest to start her role as Mom. Robert eventually went back to looking for a job he could hold. According to him, the lawyers were hard at work suing the tire store.

Daughter's story (Age 17)

Things went smoothly for a while after the pushing incident, but soon there were more blow-ups. Anytime Robert did anything violent, he would be immediately sorry afterwards. He would cry, beg me not to leave him, write me love letters, and clean or cook for the next few days in order to prove his undying love.

I was growing increasingly uncomfortable from the pregnancy. And although I was getting tired of pretending to my family and friends that everything was great between Robert and me, I didn't feel like there was anything else I could do. Asking for help would be weak. It would turn me into a victim. Better to keep handling things myself.

My due date was approaching, and I was enormously excited about the baby. I sang songs to my belly every day (I'd read that the baby could hear my voice in uterus), and read him Dr. Seuss books to give him an early start in literature. I had a doctor's appointment on my due date but missed it because I went into labor.

Robert had to go downstairs to use a neighbor's phone to call my mom, who came over right away. We had already decided that she and Robert would be in the delivery room with me. My labor went smoothly, and I delivered an extremely healthy baby boy.

From reading all the pregnancy books, I knew that most of the time newborn babies look kind of shriveled up and their heads tend to be somewhat pointy from going through delivery. So I expected him to look kind of weird at first. But when they placed Elijah in my arms after delivery, I saw that my expectations had been unfounded. They had handed me a *perfect* baby. I was now a mother.

A wave of the most potent love I have ever felt washed over me the second I saw him. It caught me completely off guard. I had expected to love my baby, but I hadn't even known a love like this could ever exist. I was absolutely enchanted. Everything about this little human was wonderful, new, and miraculous to me, from his little lips and toes to his tiny fingernails. Even his newborn cries brought instant, undiluted joy to my heart. Such a deep, full sound. The moments when I first met my little boy and discovered what it felt like to love so completely, unconditionally, and without expectation, remain to this day the happiest in my life.

I had planned to breastfeed Elijah, but after the first time I put him to my breast, the plan changed. He sucked so hard that it left my nipple irritated and blistered for over a month. The enthusiasm he displayed at this first feeding turned out to prophetic. I would soon find out that Elijah approached almost everything with extreme adamancy.

Father's story

A few more months passed. Lynn and I had completed our parenting classes and were now certified foster parents. As soon as we completed the curriculum, we got a call from our social worker about a baby boy who was available; the selection board had chosen us for placement. We were thrilled. It had been hard watching Jasmyn take Elijah home knowing how much Lynn yearned for a child; now the day was finally upon us. We met with the worker and found out the baby was six weeks old and had been in the system for all but the first two weeks of his life. The mother had given up all parental rights. The father was incarcerated and might be interested in trying to get custody, but the worker felt he didn't have much chance.

The worker stressed the risks involved. He explained that the baby had been exposed in-uterus to drugs and suggested we think it over and get back to him. But we didn't need to think it over; we had been preparing for this moment for the past year. We told him we would love to have this child. He made a few calls and arranged for the baby's social worker to bring him over the next day to introduce us. We were thrilled.

The next day we met Leslie for the first time. What an ugly baby! (Just kidding). He was the cutest little thing. He had big fat cheeks, and even at six weeks old he had the biggest smile I have ever seen on a newborn. He was already giggling and had his own personality. I know it sounds hokey, but we loved him from the minute we saw him. Our first visit was to be just that, a visit, but Lynn, in a way only she could pull off, convinced the social worker to leave the baby with us. The worker watched us feed him and interact. It was obvious he was in loving hands. Our son was home.

I took a few days off from work and Lynn and I began our new roles as parents of a newborn. After almost twenty years of watching friends and relatives with their newborns, it was pure joy to watch Lynn. She would look at Leslie and break into tears. Life was good, indeed.

Meanwhile, Robert had landed a new job as a door-to-door vacuum cleaner salesman. I won't mention the brand name but it was a very well known national brand. He was very excited about the prospects of the sales pitch he received. The vacuum cleaners would sell themselves, and after only a few days, the employer told him he was manager material. He would soon be earning trips to Hawaii as reward bonuses. The money would be rolling in.

He went to work every day and came home early evening every night. The only problem was there was no paycheck.

He insisted that the managers were ripping him off. He would have to put his father's team of lawyers to work again. Rent was due and there was no money. Once again I was being asked for a loan. I was tired of the game. I asked Robert what had happened to the commission checks he was expecting. He said the office wasn't returning his calls. I offered to call them on his behalf. I had been in business for myself for years and never had a problem collecting what was owed. Jasmyn thought this was a great idea and convinced Robert to let me help. He gave me the phone number to the office.

The next day, I talked to the district manager on the first call. I explained who I was and why I was calling. The gentlemen explained to me that Robert seemed to be a nice young man at first, but after a few days, he stopped showing up for work. He had made no sales and was due no money. He thought he had potential but had no use for someone as unreliable as Robert. I was not surprised; in fact, I had expected to hear this type of story. Robert was a loser with a capital "L." I didn't know how long it would take for Jasmyn to see this. I hoped it would be soon. I was getting tired of paying their rent.

Daughter's story

My mom drove us home from the hospital, and when we walked in I was amazed. The apartment had been completely cleaned and reorganized. It looked beautiful. I later found out that Mom-Lynn and one of her sisters had spent hours redoing it while I was in the hospital. I loved how it looked and was thrilled to be able to bring my new son home to such a wonderful start.

Robert had calmed down and was going to work every day. Everything was great until the rent was due. Robert didn't have any money.

"What do you mean?" I asked him. "How could you not have money when you've been working? What happened to your paycheck?"

He said something vague about the company not paying him but said he could borrow rent money from a friend at work. (I later found out he borrowed it from my dad, again).

"Why don't you get a different job?" I asked him. "You *know* we have to pay rent."

"Jobs aren't that easy to get," he said. I gave him a Look. "Fine," he said. "If they're that easy, then *you* go get one."

"Fine!" I replied. "Watch the baby. I'll be right back."

I left the apartment and rode the bus until I saw a storefront with a help-wanted sign on the window. I got out and went inside. "I noticed you had a help-wanted sign on the window," I said to the guy at the counter.

"Sure," he said, handing me an application. "Fill this out."

I sat down and filled it out, using my parents' phone number as my contact number. I went back to the counter and handed the application back to the guy. He said he'd give it to the manager.

"Is the manager here right now?" I asked. It couldn't hurt to introduce myself.

"Hi," I said to the manager when he came out. "I'm handing in an application and wanted to introduce myself while I was here. Do you have any questions for me?"

"Sure," he said, shaking my hand. "Do you have time for an interview?"

The interview took about ten minutes. I got the job.

I got on the bus and went home, feeling smug.

"I got one," I said to Robert casually as I entered the apartment.

"One what?" he asked.

"A job," I said, grinning.

I went to work the next day. My son was only three weeks old, and I wasn't supposed to be on my feet so often, but I knew I couldn't count on Robert to take care of our financial needs. If I wanted Elijah to have a home, diapers, and formula, I would have to be the one to provide it.

After a couple of months, my manager decided to hire some extra help. I suggested Robert, and, knowing the manager probably wouldn't want to hire an employee's boyfriend, I told him Robert was my roommate. I told him that I was a single mom and that Robert took care of the baby while I worked, but would probably be willing to work whatever shifts I wasn't working. The manager hired Robert but fired him after only a month.

It was hard taking care of Elijah, working, keeping the house clean, and keeping all the laundry done at the same time, so sometimes my parents helped me with laundry. By this time, Elijah was about three months old.

One time, when my dad brought the laundry over, Robert asked to go down to his car and use his car phone. My dad tossed him the keys and stayed upstairs to talk to me while Robert was using the phone. When Robert came back, I told my dad that I had to work at five and needed to start getting ready. He kissed the baby and left.

About five minutes later, he was back. "What's up, Dad?" I asked.

"*Give* it back!" he said to Robert, without even answering me.

I looked at Robert, who apparently knew what was going on. "What?"

"My five dollars!" my dad replied, looking very angry.

"I don't have your five dollars."

"It was there before you went down to use the phone, and now it isn't. Give it back."

"I don't know what you're talking about, dude."

"Forget it," my dad said in exasperation. "You're pathetic. Don't ever come to my house again. I don't want to see you any more." He walked out, leaving Robert and me alone. I checked on Elijah, who was sleeping, before I addressed Robert.

"You stole his money!" It was a statement, not a question. I knew how Robert was. But I still couldn't believe he'd stolen from my dad when he'd helped us so much.

"No, I didn't!" he insisted. "You can even search me!"

I decided to call his bluff. I searched him. Nothing. But I *knew* he had taken the money. Where could it be? Robert himself answered my question shortly.

"*See?*" he said, walking over to the garbage can and starting to pull up on the sides of the bag. "I don't know *why* you never believe me."

"What are you doing?"

"Taking out the garbage."

Wait a minute. Robert was *volunteering* to take out the garbage? Something was wrong here. With the exception of right after a major blowout, this was a guy who *never* voluntarily did any work. I practically had to beg him to help with the dishes after dinner, and even then he'd only wash one cup or plate before claiming to need a twenty-minute break. I realized Robert must have put the five dollars in the garbage can while I'd been checking on Elijah.

Knowing Robert would never admit to this willingly, I decided to check for myself. "You're right, babe," I said, walking over to him. "I should have believed you. I'll take out the garbage while you sit down and relax."

"That's okay." He said, pulling the bag out of my reach. "I don't mind."

After a few minutes of us both insisting that we would just *love* to take out the garbage, I was able to convince Robert that it would be my way of apologizing for not trusting him. Not wanting to lose his stolen five dollars but seeing no other option, Robert handed over the bag reluctantly.

Once outside the apartment, I opened the bag with the unpleasant intention of digging through it for the five dollars. I didn't have to. The bill was right on top, underneath a napkin. I put the money into my pocket, shaking my head.

Now I would have to break up with Robert, I thought, as I brought the bag to the dumpster. How could I stay with someone who stole from everybody around him, including my family? People would start to think I was like that, too. But I couldn't just take a baby away from his father. What if Elijah grew up to resent me? We'd just have to work something out.

I went back upstairs and into the apartment. Robert was sitting on the couch, watching cartoons.

"What's this?" I asked, turning off the T.V. and holding up the five dollars.

"Uh, money?" supplied Robert, trying to appear unconcerned.

"Uh, *yeah*, "I said sarcastically, "I found it in the garbage can. I wonder *how* it got *there!*"

"Maybe one of us accidentally threw it away," he suggested.

"It's the five dollars you *just stole* from my dad!" I yelled, feeling like an idiot for even having to state something so obvious.

"I didn't steal anything from your dad!" he yelled back. "He's just saying that because he doesn't like me! I can't believe you'd believe *him* over *me!*"

"You know what," I said tiredly, not wanting to fight, "it doesn't matter anyway. I'm done with this."

"You mean you're breaking up with me?"

"Yeah."

"You can't do that!" he screamed, grabbing my hair and yanking me into the bathroom. "You can't take my son away from me!"

"I'm not taking him away from you," I explained. "You can still watch him while I work, and you can visit him whenever you want."

"I'm NOT you're friggen babysitter!" he yelled, pushing me into the bathtub and jumping on top of me. "You want to break up with *me*? You want to escape? FINE! I'LL HELP YOU!" He wrapped his hands around my throat and squeezed.

I tried to pry his hands loose, but it wasn't working. He was too strong and completely out of control. I couldn't breathe. Just as everything started to turn fuzzy and black around the edges, I heard Elijah start to cry. His cries seemed faint and unreal.

Please God, I thought, *let the baby be okay.*

Suddenly, I was at a fair. I could feel a warm breeze and hear laughter and carnival music playing in the background. Then, just as suddenly, I was lying on my bathroom floor, my senses overwhelmed by noise and Robert's big, angry red face looming above me. He was yelling something about "pretending to pass out" and Elijah was screaming. I felt disoriented and wasn't sure how I'd gotten from the tub to the floor.

Robert yanked me up by my arms, still yelling, and flung me onto our bed, which was located directly across from the bathroom. I wasn't sure anymore what he was mad about. I felt confused, and my brain didn't seem to be connecting things properly. Everything seemed hazy. Neither my thoughts nor the sounds around me made proper sense.

"HEY!" sounded another voice from near the apartment door. It sounded like my dad. But what was he doing here?

"Get the baby and go outside," he said in my direction. In a daze, I went over and picked up Elijah, who stopped crying immediately. I went outside, and sat down on the bottom step to wait for my dad. It was quiet, and my perceptions began to resume their normal focus. I felt guilty about taking Elijah when I'd just said Robert would still be able to watch him while I worked and embarrassed that my dad had seen what had happened.

After a few minutes, my dad came out of the apartment, followed by Robert, who was yelling and crying about my taking the baby. "I'm sorry," I said. "We'll talk about it later."

"Stay away from Jasmyn and Elijah," my dad warned Robert, who started screaming again at full volume about blowing up my parents' house.

We got in my dad's car and left. As we were driving to his house, my dad explained that after leaving my apartment, he worried that I would think I was included when he'd told Robert he wasn't welcome at my parents' house. So, since he'd known I was supposed to start my shift at five, he'd gone to my workplace to wait outside for me to arrive, so that he could let me know he hadn't been mad at me, just at Robert about the five dollars. When I didn't arrive, he'd gone inside to talk to my manager who told him I'd never been late for work before. Concerned, he went back to my apartment to check on me.

Remembering what had started the fight in the first place, I silently handed my dad his five dollars. I knew the money didn't matter to him, but I was too embarrassed to talk about anything, and that was my way of telling him that I knew he was right in his accusation of Robert.

Father's story

Despite the fact that I despised helping Robert, I helped Jasmyn whenever I could. I took her to the doctor for Elijah's well baby appointments and for her postnatal care. When I dropped her off at home I always slipped her a twenty or more. Lynn helped out as much as she could with laundry and groceries. On one such occasion Jasmyn was visiting our home. Elijah and Leslie lay on a blanket and looked at each other. Lynn did a load of Jasmyn's laundry and I put it in the car. Jasmyn had to work that afternoon and wanted to go home and get ready, so I said I would take her and Elijah home.

When I started the drive to Jasmyn's apartment, I remember thinking I should grab a bite to eat before going back home. I checked my pockets and was glad to find a single five-dollar bill. I wouldn't have to stop for cash before driving through somewhere for lunch. I threw the five spot up onto the dashboard of the car. When we arrived at Jasmyn's, I got out of the car and carried the baby up the stairs to the second floor apartment. Robert was home and asked to use my mobile phone. I tossed him the keys to the car. After getting the baby settled, I said good-bye to Jasmyn.

As I headed out the driveway, I started thinking about lunch again. I decided where I would go and headed in that general direction, but when I approached the fast food restaurant and reached for the five-dollar bill, it was gone. I pulled over and checked under the front seat. Nothing there. But it had to be there; I had locked the car at Jasmyn's.

I retraced my steps, and the little light went on above my head. Robert. He went out to the car to use the phone. I gave him the keys. He relocked the car and returned the keys. He took the money. That little bastard. After I had paid his rent, fed his child, and done everything I could do for him short of changing his diapers, he had the stones to steal from me that blatantly. I was beyond enraged. I swung the car around and headed back to Jasmyn's apartment. I banged on the door. Jasmyn opened the door and I walked by her and confronted Robert. "Where is it?" I screamed.

"Where is what?"

"You know, you scum," I replied. "The money you stole from my car! I know you took it, so don't deny it. It was there when I locked the door to bring Elijah up here and was gone after you used the phone. Be a man and admit you took it."

He just looked at me like a deer in the headlights. Then he said, "I don't know anything about a five-dollar bill."

Unbelievable! I never said "five-dollar bill." I said "money." At that point, I lost my last shred of control. I screamed at him. "Listen, you piece of shit. I've been paying your rent for months. I've given you a job and fed your family, and you pay me back by stealing from me? I'm done with you. Stay out of my house and out of my face. I can't stand the sight of you!" I stormed out. As I passed Jasmyn I told her she and Elijah were always welcome in my home but she should keep Robert away from me.

I went to the bank and got some cash. I had to calm down. I couldn't believe this guy. I could care less about the five dollars, but when would it stop? Little did I know I was about to find out.

A few hours later I clamed down and wanted to assure Jasmyn I was not angry with her. I knew she had to go to work so I went by to wait for her. She didn't show up. Concerned, I decided to go to the apartment and make sure she was all right. When I arrived I started up the stairs and heard a blood-curdling scream. It was Jasmyn. I ran up the stairs, four at a time. I didn't bother to knock. I threw the door open just in time to see Robert back hand Jasmyn across the face and throw her across the room. I ran to him and pinned him against the wall. I yelled at Jasmyn to grab the baby and get in the car.

Robert started half screaming, half sobbing, "Don't you take my baby." I told him to shut up and made sure Jasmyn was safely out of the apartment with the baby before I turned him loose. I wanted to kill him but knew it would land me in jail. I just looked at him and said in a low voice, "Stay away from my daughter and my grandson." I guess from the look in my eye or the vein popping out of the side of my neck, he decided not to answer.

I started down the stairs. When I reached the bottom, he came out the door and yelled, "If you take my son, I'll blow up your house and kill you and your bitch step-wife!" I'm not making this up. He actually said step-wife! I looked at him and said, "What did you say?" He threatened to kill my wife and me again. That was all I needed to hear. I got in the car and dialed 911 on the cell phone. I told the operator what had happened and described the death threats. I made it very clear I took these threats seriously and feared for my life as well as my family. An hour later, Robert was arrested.

When we arrived at my house, Lynn and I calmed Jasmyn down. I asked her what had happened. She said after I left she asked Robert if he took the money. He denied it and suggested she search him. (Sound familiar?) She didn't find any money on him. Then she told us the story about the garbage. She went out to the trash and looked into the bag. Sure enough, there was the five-dollar bill.

She went back into the house and asked Robert again if he had stolen the money. He replied he hadn't; she had searched him and he couldn't understand why didn't she believe him. She held up the dirty five-dollar bill and said, "This is why." At that point he attacked her. By luck or fate, you decide, but that was the very minute I was pulling up outside. After meeting with the police and filing a formal complaint, we decided we would talk further in the morning. Jasmyn and Elijah would stay with us for a while.

22

Three Lousy Rules

Father's story

Later that evening, Lynn and I discussed the situation and what we should or should not do. We decided we needed a plan. First, we would obtain a restraining order against Robert to keep him away from our home. After speaking with the police, we thought Robert would be in custody for quite some time, but we didn't want to take any chances. Next, we needed to figure out how to best help Jasmyn and little Elijah. With Robert gone, Jasmyn would have to support herself. We didn't realize it then, but we were about to repeat the same mistake concerning Jasmyn that we had been making for years. Lynn and I were strategizing to come up with a plan to solve Jasmyn's dilemma. She didn't ask for help. We didn't ask her if she needed our advice. We just took over.

We decided that since Lynn was a stay-at-home, full-time mom, she could take care of Elijah along with Leslie during the day. Jasmyn could move in with us rent-free. We would take care of all her expenses—food, transportation, clothing—whatever she needed. In return, Jasmyn needed to agree to a few unbreakable rules. First, break it off with Robert. I personally thought this to be a no-brainer since he was beating her silly. Second, go to school full time. Third, don't get pregnant again. That was it. We didn't want to impose a long list of rules on Jasmyn. These were the minimum we could live with. We went to sleep feeling much better with our plan of action in place.

The next morning we sat down at the kitchen table with Jasmyn. She was extremely quiet. No doubt she was wondering what she would do to survive with Elijah. Lynn and I were sure she would be thrilled with our proposal. I started by telling her how happy we were that the baby and her were safe. Robert could have done some serious damage if I hadn't come looking for her. I explained the plan to Jasmyn. Jasmyn listened intently. She showed no emotion or reaction. It was like she was waiting for the price of entry to be revealed.

I explained the three requirements for being at our house, but to my amazement, Jasmyn balked at getting rid of Robert. I've seen many TV shows on battered women who returned over and over to the abusive man. I never understood why. I still don't, even when it was right in front of me. My daughter wasn't stupid. This guy was in the process of beating the living hell out of her and threatening her parents' lives. The very next day she was ready to forgive and forget. I felt the hairs on the back of my neck stand up as my muscles tensed. How could I protect her if she couldn't see the reality of the situation she was in?

She didn't even want to sign a restraining order against Robert. Did he have to kill someone, most likely her, before she was convinced? I was at a loss. I decided I was too upset to continue the discussion. I didn't want to get into a debate or confrontation with my daughter. She knew the location of all my buttons and could play a symphony of frustration on them at will. I got up and walked away from the table. In my absence, Lynn explained the danger Jasmyn was in from Robert. Jasmyn said she had to think about what she wanted to do. We left it at that for the day.

Over the next few days, the tension inside our household took on a life of its own. Jasmyn was irritable and moping around. Joshua was not at all happy his sister was back home. She was once again the center of attention. It didn't take long before the two were bickering and shouting at each other. Joshua's chores included keeping the kitchen clean. Jasmyn had a terrible habit of leaving anything and everything she used right where she finished with it. This now included half-empty baby bottles and dirty diapers. Joshua didn't want to clean up after Jasmyn and didn't mind verbalizing his resentment. I tried to explain to him that his sister needed our help and support. "I know it's hard on you, Joshua, but I need you to pitch in and help."

His response was predictable. "You always take her side!" I knew he was right this time, but I dreaded talking to Jasmyn about cleaning up.

Daughter's story

I was back at my parents' house for the first time in years, and it felt strange and embarrassing. Unlike most seventeen-year-olds living in their parents' household, I didn't feel like I had a natural right to be there. The situation felt tense to me. Despite my parents' efforts to be supportive, I felt like an unwelcome guest. I didn't like being around people who knew what had happened between Robert and me, and I was nervous knowing that my parents would bring up the subject.

They eventually did and issued an invitation for Elijah and me to stay with them. They said that they would pay for me to go to school full time and watch Elijah during the day. It was a tempting offer. I'd always wanted to be a lawyer, and it seemed I might now get the chance to do so. The catch was I couldn't see Robert anymore.

"What do you mean by 'not see'?" I asked.

They were confused by my hesitation, and I explained to them that while I didn't want Robert to be my boyfriend, I firmly believed that children had the right to have a relationship with both of their parents. I couldn't agree to completely stop seeing Robert, because I had to bring Elijah to see him. My step-mom tried to explain to me that Robert's violence had lost him the right to see Elijah. Her argument didn't seem valid to me, because I wasn't concerned with whether or not Robert had rights—only with maintaining Elijah's right to a relationship with his father.

What I wasn't considering at this time, but would later come to understand, is that although children *do* have a right to a relationship with both their mother and their father, they also have a right to be emotionally and physically safe. Ideally, children should be able to have relationships with both parents *and* be safe. If their relationship rights and their safety rights start to conflict, however, it is the parental relationship that needs to be sacrificed, *not* the right to physical and emotional safety.

After a few days my parents and I came to a compromise. I could bring Elijah to see Robert, but Robert was not to come to the house and I would not see him socially.

This decided, I enrolled in school and started taking pre-law courses.

Things were slightly better between Mom-Lynn and me than before. Although I was always tense, waiting for a blow up, we seemed to have a little bit more in common now. She and my dad had just adopted a little boy named Leslie who happened to be the same age as Elijah. Many times Mom-Lynn and I found ourselves up together in the middle of the night, groggily feeding our infant sons. During the day, we would put Elijah and Leslie on the same blanket facing each other, and share delight whenever the two baby boys seemed to notice each other.

My parents didn't live far from Gary, and he and I started hanging out again. He'd come over to my house to talk, or I'd go over to his, usually bringing Elijah along. I didn't do much else socially, as I didn't want to ask my parents to baby-sit unless absolutely necessary. I didn't want to be the kind of mom who forced others to raise her child. Eventually though, my parents started offering to watch Elijah once in a while as I was preparing to go over to Gary's.

Although Gary and I hadn't seen each other in about two years, we almost immediately got back together. We hadn't ever broken up willingly and had missed each other often during our time apart.

Robert and I had arranged to meet about once a week in a public place so that he could see Elijah, though he only showed up sporadically. He had lost the apartment because he couldn't pay the rent and was now homeless. He was in and out of jail, and when he did manage to show up at the designated meeting place, he spent more time trying to talk me into getting back with him than actually visiting Elijah. Most of the time he was obviously on drugs and was easily irritated by the baby, once even snapping at him to "shut up" when he cried. Fortunately, his sporadic visits kept tapering off until Elijah was about six months old, when he stopped showing up altogether.

When Gary and I had been back together for about a month, my parents sat me down and said that they were concerned I would get pregnant again. They wanted me to go on birth control, but said it had to be the kind that would be inserted into my body, blocking my cervix. I didn't mind going on birth control, but I didn't want anything inserted into my body. I said that I would take the pills. My parents said this was not an acceptable option. It turned out to be a moot point.

When I went in to get a physical and talk to the doctor about birth control, I found out I was already a month pregnant. I was devastated. I had just turned eighteen, and Elijah was only six months old. How would I raise two babies? Although the thought of raising two children was a scary prospect, even scarier was the thought of telling my parents. I knew they would be disappointed and probably kick me out. I was almost finished with my first quarter in college and was getting all A's. I knew I had thrown away an opportunity.

Before I told my parents, I decided to tell Gary. I paged him, but when he called me back and I said I needed to talk to him right away, he said that he had some "stuff" going on and couldn't come by that day. We arranged to meet the next day, but he never showed up.

Furious, I called him. "Look," I yelled into the phone, "I told you this is really important. I'm *not* dealing with it by myself!"

"Damn!" he said back. "Chill out. I can't come over today. My parents are out of town and I'm throwing a party."

After about ten minutes of arguing, we agreed that he would send a friend over to bring me to his house. When I got there, I wordlessly handed him the results of my pregnancy test.

"What's this?" he asked.

"Read it."

He did, and his reaction surprised me. "I *knew* it!" he said with a sigh.

"What do you mean, 'you knew it'?" "Well, you told me a couple of days ago that it was extremely important and you had to talk to me. This is the only thing I could think of that could be that important. That's why I haven't wanted to talk to you. If I was going to be a dad, I wanted a couple more days of just being a kid before I had to get used to the idea."

His explanation didn't make me feel any better. If he'd known it was something like this, he should have shouldered his part of the burden right away instead of just leaving me to deal with it on my own. That would have been the mature thing to do. But *was* he mature? I realized I had gotten back together with him strictly based on the quality of the relationship we'd had when we were fifteen. Now, three years later, we really didn't know each other at all. I'd had a baby since then, gotten my GED, held a job, and had my own apartment. Gary still didn't have any responsibilities, lived with his parents, and spent his time partying with friends. He'd never experienced living as an adult. Thinking about this, I realized we didn't have anything in common. I'd moved on, and he'd kept the mentality of a fifteen year old. Unfortunately, I realized all these things too late.

"Okay," I said now, sitting on his driveway as he smoked a cigarette, Elijah slept in his carrier, and his friends got drunk inside the house. "We've got to talk about abortion or adoption or something, because there is no way I can raise *two* babies by myself."

"You won't raise them by yourself; I'll help you," he said.

"Whatever," I said, not having seriously considered the idea of abortion anyway. And I couldn't put the baby up for adoption. What if someday my child came looking for me and discovered that I'd kept Elijah but given him up? What if my future child thought I didn't love him or her as much as I loved Elijah? "How are you going to help?" I challenged Gary. "I'm going to get kicked out of my parents' house as soon as I tell them. Are *you* going to find us a place to live?"

"No, but I'll talk to my parents as soon as they get back into town."

"Great," I said sarcastically, waving away the cigarette Gary was offering me. "I can't smoke. I'm *pregnant* remember?"

It turned out that Gary's parents found out the very next day. Gary told his brother Jed, who announced to their parents over the phone that Gary had something big he needed to talk to them about. They insisted on talking to Gary, who glared at Jed as he handed over the phone with a grin.

"Can I just tell you when you get home?" I heard him asking as I took Elijah upstairs to change his diaper. I didn't really want to hear the conversation. After Elijah was changed, I took him outside to feed him. After a few minutes, Gary came out but didn't say anything.

"Did you tell them?" I finally asked. He had, and they'd been relieved. They'd thought he had been going to say he had AIDS. A pregnancy was almost good news in comparison to the blow they had anticipated. Gary said I should wait until his parents got home, since they wanted to talk to both of us, and then we could figure out what to do if I got kicked out.

I was still going to school and getting A's, but I had strong morning sickness and would sometimes miss whole classes because I was in the bathroom throwing up. If I started throwing up before I got to school, I would go over to Gary's instead and sleep until I was no longer nauseated. Then I would ride the bus to school to turn in my class work before returning to my parent's house.

During this time, my step-dad, Raul, had a stroke. He was in intensive care, and I visited the hospital. He was sleeping when I went to see him, so Elijah and I sat with my mom for a while. She didn't know what was going to happen and was scared. We talked for a while and I left.

A few days later, Gary's parents got home. I went over and talked to them, telling them that I'd probably get kicked out when I told my parents that I was pregnant. They didn't believe that would happen, but assured me that Elijah and I could stay with them if it did. Even though I was relieved that we'd have a place to stay, I wasn't thrilled with the prospect of living at Gary's house. I didn't know Gary's parents very well, but I did know what they thought of me. They were very religious and had always thought I was a bad influence on Gary. I decided to tell my parents that night.

I knew that they would be extremely mad, and rightfully so. Not wanting to come from a defensive position, I planned to sit them both down together and start by explaining that I understood that I was the one who was in the wrong, and that I was sorry. I wanted to thank them for all that they'd done for me up to this point and make sure that they knew that I understood I was wrong and was willing to deal with the consequences. It didn't quite work out that way.

"What are you doing tonight?" I asked my step-mom that afternoon after I'd put Elijah down for a nap.

"I'm not sure. Why?"

"Well, I wanted to talk to you and Dad tonight, and I was wondering if you were available."

"What do you need to talk to us about?"

"Well, I really would rather talk to you together," I insisted nervously. This wasn't how this was supposed to go.

She started guessing at what it was. "Are you going to tell us you want to quit school?"

"No, but I—"

"Oh, Jasmyn, you're going to move in with Gary! Is that it?" She interrupted, already looking disappointed.

"Well, that's not really up to me," I stammered, "but I really just want to talk to you both at the same—"

"You're pregnant! Is that it?" Damn! I just looked at her. When she stared back silently, unrelenting, I braced myself for an explosion and nodded.

"*Damn it!*" She screamed at the top of her lungs, alternately yelling and sobbing at the same time. "*How could you?* You don't deserve it! *Two* kids, Jasmyn?"

I was thankful that Elijah was sleeping as Mom-Lynn continued to yell and Leslie began to cry. She picked him up and continued to scream at me. Her noise mixed in with his, until I could barely understand her words. This was what I had been trying to avoid. She didn't need to spend hours screaming at me, trying to convey how wrong I was. I already *knew.* There was no way that she could possibly make me feel any worse than I already felt. The tirade was just causing unnecessary turmoil for her.

"Go to your room until your father gets home!" she finally shrieked. "I don't even want to look at you right now!"

I went into my room and shut the door, relieved that it was finally over. Elijah was still asleep, and I sank down onto my bed.

Father's story

The conflicts continued over the next few months. Jasmyn had moved back in with us but still had not agreed to our terms. For our part, we didn't give her an ultimatum. It was a touch-and-go situation. Jasmyn and Joshua continued to bicker like only siblings can. The house was noisy but settling back into a family routine.

Jasmyn started asking Lynn and me to baby-sit so she could go out with her old friends. Robert was being held on a felony charge for threatening to blow up our house. She had been to the county jail to see him at least once that I knew of. I thought if she went out with other people, perhaps she would get over Robert the slug, so we agreed to watch Elijah. After we agreed the first time, she asked more often. It occurred to me that she was taking advantage of the situation; after three months with us, she hadn't agreed to stop seeing Robert or registered for the next semester at school. Lynn wanted her to get on some sort of birth control. Jasmyn apposed the idea, claiming she wasn't having sex. About the time we decided to get tough and insist that she make some decisions, the bombshell dropped. Jasmyn was pregnant again.

I was at work when Jasmyn came home to find Lynn in the kitchen feeding Leslie. We had asked Jasmyn to help out more around the house, and she was trying. She walked over to the sink and started on the morning dishes. Lynn asked her if she had registered for school yet. Jasmyn replied no. Lynn told her she needed to get it done or find another place to live; it was that simple. It was OK if she had decided not to attend college, but she couldn't live at our house unless she did.

Jasmyn said she needed to talk to Lynn and me together. Lynn pressed her but Jasmyn refused and insisted she needed to talk to both of us together. Then a thought shouted in Lynn's head. "You're pregnant again, aren't you?" Jasmyn nodded. Lynn lost control and started screaming at her. "I thought you said you weren't having sex! How could you do this to your son? Don't you have any morals at all?" Jasmyn wasn't going to stick around and listen to Lynn scream at her. She grabbed Elijah and headed out the door.

Shortly thereafter, I came home and found Lynn sobbing. "What's wrong?" I asked.

"Jasmyn's pregnant again." I couldn't believe my ears. How could she? She swore she wasn't having sex. All I could think of was, "Three lousy rules. She couldn't live by three lousy rules."

I had never given much thought to if I was for or against abortion. Suddenly my mind was made up. She would have an abortion or get out of my house. Three lousy rules. I took her being pregnant as a personal slap in my face. I was done trying to make things easy on her. At the peak of my initial reaction to the news, Jasmyn came home. She was with a woman named Judy. I found out later that Judy was the baby's grandmother. As soon as Jasmyn walked in, I started ranting. "How could you? What are you, a slut? Can't you keep your legs shut for more than five minutes?" Then I told her, "You have two choices, get an abortion or get the hell out of my house."

She screamed back at me, "I don't believe in abortion!"

"Don't believe in abortion," I yelled. "You sure believe in being a slut! What's it going to be like around here on Father's day? A line of twenty guys at the door to pick up their kids? Forget it! Get an abortion or get out!" She decided to leave. I was furious. I followed her to her room and grabbed a huge pile of clothes off the floor. I carried the clothes out into the front yard and threw them on the driveway, screaming at her all the while.

Finally, she was about to leave with Judy and placed Elijah and his car seat in Judy's car. I calmly walked over and took Elijah out of the car seat. Judy looked at me and said, "You're not taking that baby."

If looks could kill, my return glare would have killed her instantly. I didn't reply. Fighting back the tears, I hugged and kissed Elijah. I told him I loved him and put him back in the car seat. I looked at Jasmyn and said, "I hope you realize what you're doing to this baby." Then I turned and walked back into my house.

Daughter's story (Age 18)

Lynn must have called my dad at work because he arrived home much earlier than usual. He yelled at me for a while and ended with an ultimatum: I could get an abortion or move out. I had until four o'clock to decide. If I hadn't committed to an abortion by then, I needed to take all my stuff and leave. I looked at the clock; it was two-thirty.

Telling my parents I needed to take a walk, I grabbed Elijah and walked out the door. It took me less than a minute to decide against abortion. I loved Elijah so much. What if he hadn't gotten a chance to grow up because I'd aborted him? It wasn't the baby's fault that I was so young. I couldn't kill it. I'd just have to figure something out.

I walked over to a convenience store and called Gary from a payphone. When I told him I was about to be kicked out, he told me his mom would come pick me up. I walked the short distance back to my parents' house and told my dad I wasn't having an abortion. He was furious. He followed me as I went to get some clothes, yelling at me and throwing my things onto the front lawn. Finally, Gary's mom Judy arrived and I put Elijah into his car seat as I went to get the rest of my things.

Besides my own belongings, I also had a ton of baby clothes and equipment. It took a while to get everything into Judy's car. When we were finally ready to leave, my dad kissed Elijah good-bye and said something about him deserving better.

When we arrived at Gary's, he was getting ready for work. He had a part time job, working about four hours a day at a grocery store. He glanced at me and said hi, and then headed upstairs. "Wait," his mom told him. "Come give your girlfriend some support." My eyes widened with embarrassment. This was weird.

With his mom watching, Gary reluctantly walked over and squeezed my hand. "Are you okay?" "Fine," I muttered, resisting the urge to pull my hand away. As soon as it seemed polite, I mumbled something about unloading the car and feeding the baby, ending the uncomfortable moment.

Aside from all of the things I had brought from my parents' house, I also had a whole storage unit filled with furniture and other household goods left over from my apartment. I had been paying for the unit out of some money I'd saved up when I'd been working, but I'd be paying rent for Elijah and me at Gary's house, and I was running out of money.

I had some friends help me unload everything from the storage unit and had a garage sale in front of Gary's house. Selling all of my belongings left me with barely enough money to cover the cost of closing out the storage unit.

During this confusing couple of weeks, I didn't call my mom at all. I hadn't talked to her since the one time I'd visited the hospital, and didn't want to add stress to her situation with details of my own. She didn't know that I was pregnant or that I was living at Gary's. I found out from an aunt that Raul had had surgery and was now at home recovering.

23

She's On Her Own

Father's story

Over the next several months I didn't speak at length to Jasmyn. She was living with her new boyfriend's family, although we soon learned that her new boyfriend wasn't new at all. She was back with Gary. This was the kid that Jasmyn was seeing prior to Job Corps. It seemed like decades earlier, but in reality, it was only a few years.

Apparently they had kept in touch, and as soon as Robert was out of the picture they were back together. Gary was another one in Jasmyn's group of friends who lived at home, couldn't hold a job and took drugs. I couldn't stand that they were together again. What made things much worse was the fact that they were going to have a baby together. I wasn't thrilled with the prospect of another go-nowhere guy being associated with my family.

Even worse, I couldn't believe I had a seventeen-year-old daughter who had a newborn and was pregnant again. I dreaded the question from friends, family members, and acquaintances, "How's your daughter doing?" It was embarrassing to have a daughter who appeared so promiscuous. It reflected on my parenting skills and my morals, but I honestly had no idea why Jasmyn acted the way she did.

Lynn and I visited our family therapist often. Although his opinions were insightful, his words did not change the situation I found my family experiencing. Therapy helps many people; I'm just not one of them. Lynn had a hard time with this. It bothered me when the therapist gave an explanation for a behavior that was exactly the same as what I had expressed to Lynn weeks earlier, she accepted the analysis from him. But when I voiced the same opinion, she rejected it.

I decided I did not want my lack of a current relationship with Jasmyn to affect the bond that Lynn and I had developed with Elijah. Lynn called Jasmyn every few weeks and arranged for Elijah to visit us often. Elijah and Leslie were getting older and loved to play together. Occasionally, I would see Jasmyn when I picked up or dropped off Elijah. She was getting bigger and starting to look pregnant. We would exchange greetings and instructions about the baby, but that was about it.

I agonized over whether or not I was doing the right thing. I decided that this was the best course of action. Every time I had stepped in to help in the past, I was hurt and disappointed. I wasn't going down that road again. Jasmyn was an adult now and had to live her own life, including taking responsibility for her actions and decisions. This newly adopted attitude was to be tested the next time we spoke to Jasmyn.

Daughter's story

After I had lived at Gary's about a month, things settled down a little bit, so I decided to call my mom to say hi and find out how Raul was. Gary was always at work or out smoking weed with his friends, and I seldom saw him. My dad and step-mom apparently weren't talking to me, and I felt isolated living in a new environment with people I didn't know very well. Although I felt guilty about not calling my mom sooner, I was looking forward to talking to someone familiar. The conversation didn't go as I'd hoped.

"You're just *now* calling me?" My mom was angry. "I'm sorry," I said. "I've had a lot going on."

"Well, you know what?" She brushed off my apology. "Out of this *whole family* you are the *only one* who hasn't been there for me while Raul has been sick. Besides that one time coming to the hospital, I *can't believe* my own daughter was the only one who didn't bother to call or visit! No matter how busy anyone is, it takes less then thirty seconds to make a phone call!"

"I'm *sorry*," I repeated, blinking back the tears. "I'm barely eighteen, I have a baby, I was in school, I'm pregnant again, I got kicked out of dad's house, *and* I had to sell all of my stuff. On most days I don't even have time to take a shower. I finally got moved in and got everything sold, and Elijah is sleeping right now, so I'm calling you *now*. This is *really* the first thirty seconds of free-time I've had this month!"

"God bless it, Jasmyn! You're pregnant again?" she asked after a few brief moments of silence.

"Yeah," I mumbled. "I'm living at Gary's."

"Well," she finally said, "you still should have found time to pick up the phone. I'm you're mom, and I needed you. I thought we were closer than that. I don't see how I can forgive you for this."

Not sure how to respond to this, I finally settled for a non-committal answer. "Umm, okay."

We talked for a couple more uncomfortable minutes and finally got off the phone. I wondered if she would ever talk to me again. Of course, she did, but the closeness we had once shared was gone.

After this draining conversation, I lay back on Gary's bed, guilt ridden and exhausted. (Gary and I were sharing his room. Elijah had his own room directly across the hall.) "What's wrong?" Gary's brother Jed asked, popping his head into the room. Since Gary was hardly ever home, and I felt uncomfortable around his parents, Jed was the only one I ever really talked to during the early months of this pregnancy. I told him about the conversation with my mom. He hugged me and asked if I was mad at her.

"Nah," I answered, "I *should* have called." Just then, Elijah woke up from his nap and started to cry. "I'll get him," Jed offered, giving me time to compose myself.

This pregnancy was a difficult time for me. Gary was controlling and jealous, not wanting me to go out without him unless it was absolutely necessary. When I was able to leave the house alone, it was usually just to take the bus to a doctor's appointment. On many occasions I would arrive home from the appointments to find Gary suspicious and angry, waiting to question me about whether I'd talked to or looked at any guys.

I dealt with this loss of freedom by acting aloof, coldly commenting that Gary was simply insecure. These mini-inquisitions would usually blow up into arguments that were never fully resolved.

As my pregnancy progressed, I developed morning sickness slightly worse than during my first pregnancy. It was worse early in the mornings than at any other time of day. Often, when Elijah woke up for his six o' clock feeding, I would get his bottle and then have to lay him on the bathroom floor while I repeatedly threw up. This would usually last from about half an hour to forty-five minutes, during which time my infant son would scream for his bottle, waking everyone in the house. On mornings like this, I felt guilty for throwing up while my son was left hungry, and everyone else in the house, including Gary, was angry at being woken up.

I finally came up with a solution that seemed to work for everybody. Since Jed didn't have a job and was low on money, I offered him one hundred dollars a month to get up with Elijah for his first morning feeding. This worked well for me, because if I slept until eight o'clock, I usually didn't get morning sickness, and Elijah got to eat during his first feeding instead of lying on the floor crying.

Because I wasn't talking to any of my family, and Gary made it extremely hard to talk to my friends, I quickly drifted apart from everyone I'd been close to before the pregnancy. My resentment for Gary grew with every passing day as our fights grew more frequent. Gary didn't hesitate to call me horrible, humiliating names, an occurrence that seemed to be commonplace within his family. Whenever we argued, his mother supported him one hundred percent. While she sometimes conceded that he was being unreasonable, she felt that I should just put up with it. I should ignore the names and the insults because answering back would only exacerbate the problem.

Not having anyone else to turn to, I started confiding in Jed more and more. I would have been embarrassed to broadcast my problems to anyone else, but it wasn't embarrassing to talk to Jed because he lived in the same house and already knew what was going on.

Besides fighting with Gary and feeling constantly at odds with his parents because they supported his behavior, I was beginning to see that Gary's parents—his mother in particular—were hoping to have a lot more control of my unborn baby's upbringing than one would expect in a normal grandparent-grandchild relationship. It started innocently enough, with Gary's dad commenting one day that none of his grandchildren had ever used a pacifier. I felt he was telling me this because Elijah used a pacifier, and he wanted me to understand that he didn't want this new baby to have one.

"Well," I answered, "I'll just have to see what's right for this new baby when it gets here."

"No grandchild of mine has ever used a pacifier," he repeated.

Not wanting to be disrespectful, I stayed silent.

A few days afterward, Gary's mom and I had a similar conversation, this time about what type of bottles the baby should use when I finished breastfeeding.

"I think we should use those newer bottles," Judy suggested. "You know, the ones with the little bags that have nipples shaped more like the mother's natural nipples."

"I know what you mean," I said. "I'm actually not very comfortable with that kind. I've heard the bags can be a choking hazard and that it's harder to tell exactly how much the baby's actually eating than with the traditional bottle."

"Well, but the newer kind is easier for the baby to use, and they don't take in as much air because the bag squeezes it out."

"That's okay," I explained. "I used the regular kind for Elijah, and he was fine with it. And besides, the air isn't a problem as long as the baby is burped often enough. I don't mind doing that at all. Plus, with the kind I already have, I don't have to worry about buying new bags all the time."

The conversation lasted about twenty minutes, and didn't end until I finally just said I appreciated her points but had decided to use the same bottles I already had for Elijah. "If they don't work for the new baby, then I'll consider a different kind," I stated, "but I'm sure they'll be fine."

A few days later, Judy came home from the store with about ten of the kind of bottles I'd clearly said I didn't want to use. Not wanting to appear ungrateful that she'd bought my child something, I thanked her for the gift and made no comment. These were only a few of the issues regarding the children that Gary's parents and I disagreed on.

Gary's mom didn't think I should allow my parents to see Elijah.

"I wouldn't allow those people to see my kids if they'd kicked me out like that," she told me forcefully one day after Mom-Lynn had called asking if she could take Elijah for the day. I was surprised and offended. I hated when people used kids to get back at people they were mad at. It only hurt the kids.

"Well, no matter how we feel about each other at the moment," I fired back, "'those people' love Elijah, and I will not keep him away from people who love him and deprive him of having a family just because I'm angry at someone. They can see him whenever they want—and the new baby, too, if they want!"

My unwillingness to use my children to reward or punish those who loved them was one of the few positions I was extremely vocal and unyielding about while living at Gary's. And although she didn't agree with my position, Judy would later benefit from it, as Gary seemed to have no scruples about using the unborn baby in this way. ("Fine!" he'd screamed at his parents on more than one occasion when he was angry with them, "then you'll NEVER see the baby once it's born!") I would later reassure Judy that I would always make sure my children got to see their family, as long as it wasn't physically or emotionally detrimental to them.

Both Gary and I wanted to know whether the baby was a boy or a girl. We'd talked about names, and the deal was that if it was a boy, Gary would get to pick the name, and if it was a girl, I would. We found out during an ultrasound that it would be a girl, and I decided on the name Dawn. We were all looking forward to meeting her, but as soon as we told Gary's parents it was going to be a girl, my apprehensive feelings about their level of involvement got stronger.

"I've always wanted another daughter!" Judy commented more than once. She also commented to a few of Gary's friends that if I couldn't take care of Dawn, she would be happy to raise her. This bothered me a lot. Dawn was MY daughter, and I had every intention of raising her myself. My discomfort finally rose to the point that I asked Gary to talk to his mom. I told him that I really appreciated his mom letting Elijah and me live there, but that I WAS paying rent and felt that she should respect my wishes and decisions regarding Dawn. He agreed that she did seem overly involved but said that he really couldn't do anything about it. Finally he agreed to talk to her, but nothing changed.

Frustrated, I confided in Jed, and he and I started spending more time together. Gary was often out with friends, but he didn't want me to see my friends, so I would be left in the house, hanging out with Jed. We would talk, take care of Elijah, or watch movies in Gary's room. Jed and I had jokingly flirted back and forth for as long as I'd known him, but we'd never really spent time alone together before, and it was surprising to find out we had so much to talk about. He was often at odds with his family, and I often overheard him defending me to his brother or parents.

I was touched that he'd say nice things about me when he didn't know I was listening. Gary was just the opposite. One day I'd walked into the kitchen at his house to warm a bottle for Elijah and found him and his mom already there. Gary had been eating cake frosting straight out of the container with his fingers.

"Yuck," I'd commented. "How can you eat frosting by itself? That's disgusting!"

Gary froze and looked over at his mom, who was glaring at him. Then he gave her a sheepish look, and they both burst out laughing.

"What's so funny?" I'd asked. "Well," Judy explained, "last week I was planning on baking a cake, but when I started I noticed that someone had eaten all the frosting. Gary told me that you'd been craving it, but asked me not to say anything to you because you'd be embarrassed." She looked at Gary. "It was really you!" She exclaimed, playfully throwing a washcloth at him. They both laughed, but I was furious! I'd already felt uncomfortable enough in their house without Gary telling his parents that I'd done something so inconsiderate. What other rude things had Gary told his parents I'd done?

Being pregnant also enhanced my emotions, which were all over the place. I seemed to overreact to everything, whether it was a good or bad reaction. While I was overly angry with Gary for lying about me, I was also overly appreciative whenever Jed defended me. I felt like he was the only one who really understood what I was going through.

One night, while Gary was with his friends and his parents were out, I put Elijah to bed and went downstairs to do the dishes. Jed came down to help me, and we started play fighting and just goofing around. Jed got me in a headlock, and I spun around to get out of it, leaving us face to face. We both froze, but after a moment I laughed, and we returned to the dishes. A few nights later, however, we kissed, and after that we were together whenever we could be. I was glad, because at last there was something in my life I could control. Gary didn't want me to see my friends, and I wasn't really speaking to my family, but this thing with Jed made me feel like I had some semblance of a social life within the house. Since Gary didn't know about it, he couldn't stop it. It was my secret and it belonged to me. Although having someone to chill with and talk to made me feel a little less isolated, it didn't solve all my problems.

I was running out of money and decided to get a job to continue paying rent and to make sure we would be able to buy diapers and other necessities for Dawn when she arrived. Gary was no longer working and agreed to watch Elijah. I was only about four months pregnant at the time and not yet showing.

I got hired in a restaurant during my first day of searching for a job and went to work the next day. It was hard work; my employers didn't know I was pregnant, and the job required me to be on my feet constantly. One day, during my first week at my new job, I was interrupted by a phone call from the hospital. Ten-month-old Elijah had had a seizure.

I started to rush out of the restaurant toward the bus stop, crying, when one of the waitresses stopped me and offered to give me a ride. I got into her car and we started out for the hospital. Everything seemed to be moving excruciatingly slow. I felt like I was in a horrible dream. I had to get to Elijah, wanted to move fast, but the rest of the world was in slow motion. Finally, after what seemed like hours (but in reality must have been about five minutes), we arrived at the hospital.

I rushed into the emergency room and somehow located Elijah. My little baby looked so weak and fragile. He was awake, but he had an I.V. going into his arm that was bothering him. Picking him up, I saw that he had little red dots all over his face and body, which the doctor later said could have been from loss of oxygen during the seizure.

He was in the hospital for three days for observation. The doctors took fluid from his spine to test for meningitis. At some point, various members of my family arrived, held Elijah, and encouraged me to eat and drink. I wasn't hungry or thirsty and didn't want to leave Elijah's bedside for any reason. My mom finally brought me a sandwich, reminded me that I was pregnant, and encouraged me to eat a few bites.

Elijah didn't have meningitis; he had a bad case of the flu, but there was nothing else wrong with him. The doctor said that the seizure had probably resulted from his temperature rising at a much faster rate then his body was used to. He was released, but his development seemed to have regressed. He seemed less active than he had before the seizure and had lost a lot of weight during his three days in the hospital.

I was happy to have him home but worried about him most of the time. I hated to go to work and worried about whether Gary was looking after him properly. Although Gary had stayed with me at Elijah's bedside during most of the hospital stay, Elijah didn't seem to want to be near him and cried when I left for work. I started noticing bruises on his face and head, which I questioned Gary about. He said he wasn't sure how Elijah was getting the bruises, but that they could be from Elijah throwing fits and throwing himself around when he was angry. Although the explanation seemed plausible since Elijah was prone to thrashing, back-arching fits at times, I didn't think he should be allowed to hurt himself, and felt he wouldn't if he was being sufficiently supervised. I asked Gary to watch him more closely, but I continued to notice new bruises. I quit my job so I could be home with him.

Still needing money to pay for rent, I applied for welfare, telling myself it was only temporary. Shortly afterward, Gary got re-hired at the grocery store he'd been working at when I'd moved in, leaving Jed and me more time alone together. Although Gary and I had agreed to save some money to get our own apartment, Gary refused to actually save any of his paycheck. His money almost always disappeared immediately after he got it, being spent on fast food and marijuana, a fact that wasn't missed by his parents. They saw his using drugs as a problem, but they seemed to hold ME responsible for solving it.

"Jasmyn!" Gary's dad had said one day, catching me on the way up the stairs. "I know Gary is using drugs. If he doesn't straighten out, you guys are going to be out of here!" His angry voice rose steadily as he continued, "He needs to stop the drugs, stop being with his friends all the time, start saving money, and become responsible." He went on to give me a list of all the things Gary owed him and Judy money for. After he was done, I continued upstairs, speechless.

What did his dad think I could do about Gary's behavior? Gary was *his* son! Why should I get yelled at for what HE was doing? He was seventeen years old. I was only eighteen myself. I wasn't his mom. Did his parents think that I should continue raising him where they'd left off? I already had a child and was about to have a second one. I wasn't about to raise Gary as well!

Still, although he wasn't contributing to anything financially, I was happy he had a job because it got him out of the house more often. When he was home, we'd get into screaming arguments, and he'd even pushed me a few times—once when I'd been holding Elijah. I wanted to break up with him, but I was pregnant and had nowhere to go. I hated my life and my uncontrollable mood swings; I missed my friends and family, and I hated living at Gary's. Jed and Elijah were the only enjoyable things in my days. And then Jed left.

His sister was in the military and needed someone to look after her kids while she worked. She lived in another state and flew Jed out to become her live-in nanny. Once he was gone, life in the house felt even more unbearable. I had nobody to laugh with, joke around with, or confide in after arguments. Gary was constantly suspicious and constantly hounded me about whether I was cheating on him.

"How could I, even if I wanted to?" I screamed at him in frustration one day. "I never even get to leave this house!"

He seemed to think about that, and realized I'd only had a chance to have contact with one person during the time I'd been living at his house. Jed. "You messed with him, huh?" he asked me constantly. "I know you did. He told me before he left!" I knew this wasn't true and constantly denied it. I knew if he found out, I'd get kicked out and have nowhere to go.

Eventually though, I stopped caring about getting kicked out. I HATED life at Gary's. Why should I care if I got kicked out? Wouldn't that be better for Elijah anyway? At least then he wouldn't have to listen to our arguments all the time. I decided that the next time Gary asked if I'd messed with Jed, I'd tell him the truth.

The opportunity presented itself a couple of nights after I'd made my decision. Gary and I had gone to the movies, and we arrived home in a pretty good mood.

"The movie was good," I said, after checking on Elijah, who was in bed for the night. Gary's parents had been babysitting and were now in bed as well.

"Yeah," answered Gary. "Uh, Jasmyn…you did sleep with Jed, huh?"

I looked at him, considering. If I said no, things would go on as they were. I would live here in this house, feeling like an outsider. Gary would be gone most of the time, and when he wasn't he would question me, scream at my, push me around, and call me names. He'd spend all his money, and we'd never have enough for an apartment from my money alone. The kids would grow up here. This would be our life. They'd think it was normal for men to act the way that Gary did.

If I said yes, however, it'd be done. Gary would yell and scream, and I'd get kicked out. I wouldn't have to feel bad about breaking up with Dawn's dad because he'd be the one to break up with me. The kids and I would have a better life. I didn't know where we would go, but anywhere would be better than here. I took a deep breath.

"Yeah," I said softly.

"What?" Gary exclaimed.

I knew that he'd heard me, so I stayed silent, waiting for his reaction.

When it came, it was pretty much what I'd expected. He started yelling, screaming, and calling me names.

"Shhhhh," I said. "You're gonna wake up your parents."

Too late. His mom was already out of her room.

"What's going on?" she asked, looking from me to a now crying Gary.

"She slept with Jed!" Gary yelled, pointing at me in a way that would have been comical in other circumstances.

His mom gasped and started to say something but was cut off by Gary. "I need a cigarette!" he declared, checking his pockets. He didn't have any, and must have seen this as an opportunity since he didn't have any money, either. "Jasmyn," he announced, "c'mon; you're gonna buy me a pack of cigarettes!"

We walked to the store, which was about a mile away, while Gary continued to alternately question and yell at me. I bought him his cigarettes and let him vent, wondering what would happen next. When we got back to his house, it was almost one o'clock in the morning, and I could hear Judy crying in her room.

The next morning, Gary's parents informed me that Elijah and I would have to leave. I wasn't surprised and felt thankful that Gary's parents were willing to let me stay a week so that I could find another place to go.

Most of the local shelters were full, but I was finally able to get a spot in a shelter for women and children. I packed up our things, and Judy drove us over. When we arrived, one of the counselors asked me a bunch of questions and led me to one of the rooms. It was a small room, with cement walls and a tile floor. It reminded me of a hospital room. Before leaving, the counselor told me that I would be sharing the room with another girl and her daughter. I nodded and sat down on the bed, holding Elijah, and absently rubbing my slightly protruding stomach. "Well, guys, "I murmured, looking around the room, "looks like we've got a new home."

24

Women's Shelter

Father's Story

Jasmyn was no longer living at Gary's. Something happened and she was kicked out. She was now almost seven months pregnant. In my heart, I wanted to track her down and bring her home. I had to remind myself of my decision to stop trying to run her life. Jasmyn was living in a facility for homeless mothers in a very rough part of downtown. Jasmyn called to see if she could come over and visit. I wanted to see her and where she was living, so I agreed to go pick her and Elijah up. I drove downtown and found my way to the address she had given me. The facility looked like a cross between a school and a jail. I walked into the lobby and spoke to the attendant manning the lobby office. He picked up a phone and told someone to tell Jasmyn she had a visitor.

I could not go into the facility as it was for residents only. I sat down in the lobby and took in the surroundings. There were informative posters on all the walls. The message was mostly drug related with a few targeting abused mothers and one about prenatal care. There was another handwritten sign pertaining to house rules. No drugs. No visitors inside the facility. All residents subject to search. Outside doors lock at 10 P.M. NO EXCEPTIONS. No weapons allowed. The furniture was old, worn, and dingy. As I waited a young girl was buzzed through the security door with a little girl, maybe two-years-old, in tow. She gave me a disapproving look. I said hi and smiled at the little girl. The girl asked whom I was there for.

"Jasmyn," I said. "She's my daughter."

The hard look she had greeted me with instantly faded and was replaced by a big smile. "Oh, she'll be out in a minute," she said and headed out the main door.

As I sat there waiting, I remembered a similar encounter a few months earlier. Jasmyn and I went to the bank to open a checking account. We had Elijah with us. We walked in and were directed to the new account area. We sat down at a desk and waited for what seemed a very long time. Finally, an older woman sat down behind the desk and gave us a very disapproving look. "What can I do for you?" she said curtly. I explained that we wanted to open a checking account.

Another nasty glare from this woman. "Under what name?" she asked. Jasmyn gave her name and date of birth.

The woman, looking at me with disgust, said to Jasmyn, "You will need a co-signer."

"I'll co-sign," I answered.

"And who are you?" she asked.

"I'm her father." Talk about an immediate attitude change. I could actually see this woman's hate for me melt away. She was now smiling and going out of her way to help us. This same scene played out every time Jasmyn and I went anywhere together. As a defense mechanism, I started having stupid conversations wherever we went so I could make sure people heard Jasmyn call me "Dad" as soon as possible. I resented Jasmyn for putting me in this situation.

Jasmyn came out through the security door with Elijah in a stroller. I was glad she was able to find a place to live. I had stayed out of it and she handled the situation on her own. On the way home I asked what had happened at Gary's. She said they had a fight and she got kicked out. That's all the information she wanted to give. I wondered what the arrangement would be once the new baby was born. We would find out soon enough.

Daughter's story (Age 18)

I was glad to have found a place to stay, but life in the shelter was not ideal. There were a ton of kids, and most had unstable backgrounds and parents who were unable or unwilling to discipline them. The rule was that the parents were not allowed to spank or yell at their kids, and most of the parents there didn't seem to know any alternative ways of discipline. The result was chaotic.

There was one little boy, age three, who always used to run up to the babies and try to choke them from behind while they were eating or playing.

His mom would just sit on the couch, watching T.V., and not do anything about it. After he'd done this to Elijah, I started staying in my room with him except for meals or mandatory meetings. On these occasions, I would hold Elijah in my lap rather than letting him play or sit in a highchair.

It was after one of these mandatory meetings that I made a careless mistake that would change my outlook on life forever.

I'd just gotten my welfare check and cashed it with plans to pay my rent at the shelter and then do some Christmas shopping. I'd put the money in my wallet, but after the meeting I'd forgotten my wallet on the couch of the common room. I didn't notice that it was gone until I was getting ready to leave the next morning. I tore apart my room, searching for it franticly. I could not afford to lose that money! I finally picked up Elijah and left my room, crying, as I searched throughout the shelter. As I walked into the common room, I gasped with relief. My wallet was on the couch, but when I opened it, my heart fell. All the money was gone.

I left the shelter that morning in a state of disbelief, feeling embarrassed because I'd had to borrow bus money. I'd had all my money in that wallet, over four hundred dollars. Christmas was only a few weeks away, and now I wouldn't be able to buy Elijah any presents. I was angry, too. Everybody at the shelter knew my situation, and many of them were people I considered friends. How could someone steal all that money from me, knowing that I was pregnant and had a child? How would I even by Elijah diapers this month? By stealing from me, someone had knowingly stolen from my child! *"What kind of heartless jerk could intentionally steal from a child"* I wondered furiously, as the bus clanked along and Elijah stared up at me with wide, trusting, eyes.

As I watched him smile, coo, and chatter, my bitterness grew. *"Damn-it!"* I thought. *"Not only have I been robbed of my money, but I've also been robbed of my joy! My little boy is happy and healthy, and I can't even enjoy it because of some idiot!"* Suddenly, my anger began to shrivel as I realized how ridiculous my thoughts were. I was the one being an idiot.

What if something had happened to Elijah and he'd died? Wouldn't I give four hundred, four million, four *billion* dollars for just one more precious moment with him? The truth was that if Elijah had died, I'd have been willing to trade *anything* for the ability to bring him back, if only for one or two fleeting moments. But right now, he was right here in front of me; I had countless moments to spend with him! And I was sitting here crying over *money?* I'd been without money lots of times and had always been okay. I'd have money again, but I never knew how many minutes I'd have with my son. As I looked over at him, he giggled and smiled again. I smiled back.

The realization that I'd always be okay as long as my kids were okay was an important one that has carried me through some hard times and helped me set many priorities. But at the same time, it was incredibly scary, because it also worked the other way around. I had a feeling that if for some reason, some day, one of them weren't okay; I'd NEVER be okay again. My children were my first experience with loving someone so much that protecting them became vital to my existence.

I decided that eleven-month-old Elijah and unborn Dawn would have the best lives possible. I was still angry with myself for losing so much money, but I was no longer devastated.

Elijah did receive Christmas presents that year. When my family heard what had happened, they all chipped in to give me back some of the money that had been stolen, and people at the shelter rallied around me, buying baby things for Dawn and Christmas presents for Elijah. But although I was extremely thankful for their generosity, I had no idea who'd stolen my money and wasn't sure whom I could trust.

Adding to my discontent with my living situation, one of the woman staying there went into labor, and I saw her bring her newborn home to live its first days among the noise, unhappiness, and general chaos of shelter life. As people flooded into her room to see the new arrival, I wondered how the new mother felt about so many people touching her baby. Wasn't she worried about germs? Also, as with any group living situation, the bathroom and washing facilities weren't the cleanest. Where would she bathe her baby? As I contemplated this woman's situation, I shuddered at the thought of giving birth while still living at the shelter. I wanted Dawn's first days on earth to be spent in a healthy, clean, private environment.

Gary and I still saw each other often because we wanted to be friends when the baby came. Since residents weren't allowed on the shelter's premises during the day, I would often go to his house when I had nowhere else to go, and on weekends he usually came to visit me at the shelter. On one of these occasions, Gary asked me to marry him. It wasn't a new question; he'd asked many times before, but I'd always put off answering him. This time, however, as I imagined Dawn starting out her life in a shelter, I said yes, although marrying Gary was the last thing I wanted to do. I also said that I wasn't willing to get married until we had our own place and had saved up some money. Due to Gary's past inability to sustain work or save money, I was counting on the probability that he would be unlikely to ever meet those two conditions.

Gary told his parents our news, and just a few months before Dawn was due to be born, Elijah and I moved back to Gary's.

25

It's a Girl

Father's story

After a few months in the shelter Jasmyn told us she was moving back into Gary's parents' home. Once again, we didn't question what was happening. Jasmyn was taking care of herself. She hadn't lived there very long when Dawn was born. Dawn was a beautiful baby girl with a wisp of fine blond peach fuzz for hair. She had delicate little feminine fingers and toes. From the day she was born, she was a beauty queen. We were all thrilled with the new addition to our family, Gary's mother in particular. She couldn't wait to get the new baby home and start taking care of her. I told Lynn that I thought Jasmyn would have a hard time with this woman if she ever wanted to move out. This prediction turned out to be true. Not long after Jasmyn and the baby returned from the hospital, Jasmyn and Elijah were kicked out once again. Jasmyn and Gary had a fight and decided to break up. Gary's parents told Jasmyn if they weren't together, she would have to leave with Elijah. Since she had nowhere to go, Dawn could stay with her dad. Jasmyn had no choice. She packed up her things and left. She had a little money put away and was able to stay in a motel room for a few days.

Daughter's story

Living at Gary's was still hard. He was still doing drugs regularly and refused to save any money. At one point he enrolled in a program to get his GED but almost immediately dropped out because the teacher was "mean." Judy was disappointed that he chose to leave the program, but she also believed that his decision was the teacher's fault.

I was amazed at Gary's consistent refusal to take any responsibility for his own life or decisions, and even more amazed that his mother constantly reinforced this attitude. Gary seemed to believe that life was something that was happening TO him, and the people around him seemed to participate in this belief. Therefore, I reasoned, Gary would always be in the same position: dependant on his parents and unable (unwilling) to change his position. If nothing was his fault, then he had no way of changing it. His belief in his own faultlessness would leave him crippled, without control, and unable to make decisions. I did not want to marry someone like this. If I did, I would be the only adult in the marriage, with no one to lean on or consult. In my mind, our "engagement" (there was no ring and no talk of setting a wedding date), was only temporary—something to worry about someday after the baby was born.

Dawn's birth was short but not easy. I wanted an epidural, as I'd had with Elijah, to ease some of the pain of the contractions, but the only technician available to perform the procedure was busy while I was in labor. When I found out I would not be getting one, I did something I have done only a few times in my life. I sat up in a rage, and screamed at the people around me at the top of my lungs.

"What? You all said I could have one! You LIED to me! I'm leaving!" I tried to scoot off the bed.

"Jasmyn, calm down," said my mom, who was there for the birth. I wasn't having it, though. I was out of here. Nothing anyone could have said could have stopped me, except—

"She's crowning! Lie down, you're squishing her head," snapped one of the nurses.

I immediately fell silent and lay down, my eyes filling with tears, only minutes before Dawn was born. I was terrified I'd hurt my baby. I wanted to ask, but couldn't, because suddenly everybody in the delivery room was yelling at me to push, push harder, harder! Someone must have informed Gary's parents that the moment had arrived, because as I was pushing down with all my might, my knees on my chest and my legs splayed open as wide as they could go, I noticed Gary's mom and (could it be?) his *dad* come bursting joyfully into the room! I stopped pushing and let out my breath, and with it came my voice in a big giant gush.

"GET THEM OUT OF HERE!"

"Jasmyn, they just wanted to see their granddaughter be born," my mom reproached as a nurse ushered them out. I felt slightly guilty, as I hated to be the source of anyone's hurt or a barrier to their joy, but after all, it was my body on display. No one had even asked me if it was okay for them to come in. Was it strange that I didn't want Gary's dad to see me all spread open and practically naked? I wouldn't even have wanted *my* dad to see me like that, much less someone else's. I hoped they would understand, and resumed pushing. Moments later, my baby was born.

My worry about hurting her had been unfounded. Dawn was born unharmed and absolutely perfect. She had my body (I immediately recognized her legs, bottom, and thighs as minute replicas of my own), her father's EXACT face, and long, slender, piano-playing fingers, topped with almond shaped, graceful fingernails that were all her own. She'd emerged from my body with an angry red face, a bald head, and a full set of manicured nails.

As I held my new daughter and observed her miraculous features, I voiced only one thought to the people around me. "I'm NOT pregnant anymore!" This fact was almost as amazing to me as my daughter's birth. I was eighteen years old and had been pregnant for almost two years straight.

I'd wanted to breast feed Dawn, but my experience trying to nurse Elijah had left me feeling unsure about my success. So I was pleasantly surprised and filled with delight when Dawn latched on almost instantly, closing her brilliant blue eyes and snuggling close, as if she was an extension of my own body and we'd always been connected in this manner.

As excited as I was to finally meet my baby girl, giving birth had left me feeling drained and exhausted, so I was surprised when Gary's mom asked him if he was going to go home and get some rest. When he started to say good-bye to me, I gaped at him open mouthed. I had assumed he was going to spend the night with us in the hospital. If he left, who would bring me the baby if she woke up and cried? Who would change her diaper in between feedings so that I could get a little bit of sleep? Gary read my look and asked me if I wanted him to stay. I said yes, and he reluctantly agreed.

When Dawn awoke that night, however, Gary didn't quite provide the support I was hoping for. Instead of bringing me the baby, he angrily muttered that he was too tired. When I asked him to change her diaper, he pretended to be asleep. "Geez," I thought angrily, as I painfully got up and did these things myself, "I carried her for nine months and pushed her out of my body; the least he could do is help out a little." But Gary continued to either sleep or pretend to sleep throughout the whole night with one exception. At one point he did rouse himself for about two minutes in order to complain about his sleeping arrangements. Apparently the hospital-provided cot/chair was uncomfortable. I rolled my eyes and wished he'd gone home.

When we left the hospital and went back to Gary's, it became apparent that his house was not the ideal place to raise my new baby. Gary loved Dawn and loved showing her off to his friends, yet he didn't seem to feel that it was his responsibility to help take care of her. When I asked him for more help, he complained that since he worked, he should be able to relax and be with his friends when he got home. I didn't see working four hours a day as a relevant excuse for neglecting his share of the parenting duties. We got into many fights over this issue, and after our first slightly physical altercation, our fights almost always seemed to follow the same general pattern.

"I'm going to a friend's!" Gary informed me shortly after getting home from work.

"Wait!" I protested, exhausted from the responsibilities of caring for two infants on my own all day. Dawn was about three weeks old and still waking up every night, and Gary's routine of sleeping all night and smoking weed almost all day hadn't changed since her birth. "Going to a friend's" for Gary usually meant being gone all day and then coming home with his friends and sitting out in the driveway smoking weed with them until late at night. "You said you would help with Dawn tonight!"

"Well, damn! I changed her diaper, and she'll go to sleep soon! What else does she need?"

"She's not gonna sleep all day! It's only two o'clock!"

"No, you know what, I'm going! I already told Nate I'd be over there. I need to relax after working all day!" At this point his voice started to rise defensively; as always when people elevated their voices, I consciously lowered my own.

"Working *all day?*" I asked incredulously. "You slept till nine and then you worked *four-hours!* Plus, you got a *break!* I was up with Dawn from five to six this morning and then Elijah got up at seven. Dawn was up again at eight, and I took care of her so that sweet little Gary could get his rest. And do you think I get a break during the day? No! I'm lucky if I even get to go to the bathroom. And don't expect me to be *grateful* that you go to work when that has nothing to do with the kids and me! I pay rent for the kids and me, plus I pay for all the stuff Dawn needs! You want me to be proud that you buy your own fast-food and weed?"

"Shut the heck up, bitch!" he hissed. "My parents will hear you. What the heck? Are you trying to get us kicked out?"

"This conversation is over," I said. Although it happened almost daily in Gary's family, for some reason I was always surprised and newly offended when Gary started calling me names.

"No, forget that, bitch!" He yelled, grabbing me as his voice rose with fury. "You started this conversation, and now you're acting like a prissy little bitch!"

"Just go to your friend's," I said icily, pulling away from him and attempting to walk out the door. "We don't need you here."

"Don't walk away from me!" he screamed, lunging after me noisily and pulling me back into the room. Then his mom came in. This was the first time she had intervened during a fight, and afterward I felt like I was in some twilight zone, or like Alice, but instead of falling into Wonderland, I had somehow made a wrong turn and ended up in Crazyland.

"What's going on?" Judy asked. Gary had been squeezing my upper arms and yelling into my face, but he let go when he heard his mom's voice.

"I'm just trying to finish our freakin' conversation and she's too busy acting like prissy to even freakin' listen to me!" he yelled, spinning to face his mom.

"I won't listen to anyone call me names," I said, in what was, I thought, a reasonable tone.

"Names?" He sounded genuinely confused. "What did I call you?"

"You called me a bitch, like *five* times!"

"I didn't say you *were* a bitch, you idiot! I said you were *being* a bitch!"

"Yeah," I replied sarcastically, "big difference. Plus, you just called me an idiot, which is what I would be if I continued to listen to you."

"Now Jasmyn," Gary's mom interjected wearily, "I heard Gary from the kitchen, and he didn't call you anything; he just said that you were being a bitch. There really is a difference. What we've learned from a lot of the counseling work we've done in our family is that you have to listen very carefully to what the other person is saying and not put words in his mouth."

"Well," I shot back haughtily, straightening to my full height, "I didn't go to counseling, but in *my* family, no one calls each other names. I've never heard my dad call my mom a name, and I don't have to listen to some *guy* call me anything, at any time, for any reason!"

I hated talking to his mom like that, but I felt like my pride was being attacked. Judy seemed to think it was okay for Gary to say these things to me, and she practically accused me of overreacting by being offended.

She later pointed out that both Gary and his father had said worse things to her, and told me that although Gary still often did, she actually was the one who came out on top by just ignoring it. "When he yells and curses at me," she confided, "I just go into the other room. He thinks I'm listening, but I'm really not. But I'm not making it worse either. You need to learn to do that instead of talking back and making the situation worse."

Yeah, right. Learning to let people treat me like garbage on a daily basis was not one of my aspirations. Still, I was living in Judy and her husband's house, and although I was paying rent, I didn't feel comfortable talking back to either of them. They were, after all, Gary's parents, and that alone in my eyes put them in a position commanding respect. I didn't feel comfortable acting disrespectfully toward my own parents, let alone someone else's.

"Okay," Judy said after my small stab at defending my dignity. She sighed. "What was the problem in the first place?"

Gary was still furious. "Well, I promised Nate I would go to his house, and Jasmyn acts like it's a freakin' crime for me to hang out with friends for one day!"

"He hangs out with his friends every day," I argued. "He promised he would help out with Dawn today! I just had a baby three weeks ago, and Elijah's only fourteen months old. Dawn is Gary's baby, too. I need some help."

"I was only going to go for a few hours!" Gary yelled at me. "If you wouldn't have started this stupid fight, I'd be almost back by now! Damn! And Nate thinks I'm meeting him at the bus station. You're making me freakin late!"

"What time are you supposed to meet Nate?" Judy asked Gary.

"Like, ten minutes ago."

Judy said, "I'll drive you to the light-rail station so that you won't miss Nate. And Jasmyn, when Dawn wakes up, I'll take her for a while to give you a little bit of a break, okay?"

I nodded, not feeling like I had much of a choice. If I said no, it would invalidate my whole argument about needing help with the kids and make me seem petty, when I already felt guilty for being disrespectful to an adult and embarrassed about being called names. But I didn't want Judy to take Dawn. I wanted Gary to keep his promise to take on a small amount parental responsibility for Dawn. Why wasn't Judy supporting that? Instead of encouraging her son to become a strong, responsible father, she was acting like it was a ridiculous goal and actually helping him act *irresponsibly.*

After a few hours, I went downstairs and got Dawn. Judy reluctantly gave her to me. She had always wanted another daughter, and now that Dawn had been born, Judy often said she felt she and Dawn had an extra special connection. Sometimes, after Gary had yelled at her, or when she'd had an especially stressful day, she would immediately pick Dawn up and hold her close, as if deriving comfort from the baby. She also often "accidentally" referred to herself as "mommy" when talking to my daughter.

Although I was glad Dawn had so many people who loved her, I wasn't sure that Judy's feelings toward Dawn were especially healthy and was reluctant to leave them alone together for long amounts of time. When Gary was around, and Judy had taken Dawn down to her room, I would often have him go get her for me. Although Dawn was my daughter, I was living in Judy's house and didn't feel comfortable going into Judy's room to get her.

On this day, however, I did go to get the baby. Gary arrived home later, apologized for going to his friend's, and promised to get up with Dawn during the night so that I could get some sleep. I was still breastfeeding, but Dawn was an extremely adaptable baby and was able to eat with equal ease from breast or bottle. I agreed that Gary should get up during the night and accepted his apology, although it was conveniently made after he had already gotten to do what he wanted.

But that night when Dawn woke up, Gary pretended to be asleep.

"Gary!" I finally said, nudging him.

"What?"

"Dawn is crying!"

"Then get her!" he snapped.

"You said you would get up with her tonight."

"I have to freaking work in the morning. Quit being a bitch and get your daughter."

"You're calling me a bitch when you won't even bother to be a dad?" I hissed, getting up to get Dawn. She was hungry, and I wasn't going to ignore her just to prove a point.

"Just shut her up; I'm trying to sleep!" I sat down on the bed and brought my crying daughter to my breast. She latched on and quieted immediately.

"Damn, that's better!" Gary commented, rolling over and closing his eyes. All was quiet—for about thirty seconds.

"What the hell?" Gary rolled over and glared at me.

"What?" I had absolutely no idea what his problem could be.

"You're making her do that on purpose!" "Making her do what? I'm not making her do anything."

"That sucking sound; you're making her do that to keep me awake."

"That's what she *sounds* like when she's eating. You would *know* that if you ever bothered to get up with her at night."

"Not that loud! You're trying to keep me awake!" He accused again, this time more loudly.

"I'm *not!*" I protested. "I don't *want* you to be awake! I don't even *like* you!"

"You don't like me?" he shouted, pulling me up by the arm and jarring Dawn so that she came unlatched and started to cry. "Then get the hell out of my room!"

"Okay!" I'd go downstairs, finish feeding Dawn, and then sleep with her on the couch.

"You get back here!" Gary shouted, grabbing me and pulling me back into the room.

"Gary," I said, trying to calm him. Dawn was still crying, and our argument was scaring her. I hated myself when this happened. Sometimes I was so concerned about pushing what I thought was right and not being taken advantage of, that I let things develop into arguments in front of my babies. "It's okay. I'm just going to bring Dawn downstairs and feed her. You go back to sleep. I really don't mind."

"If you don't mind, why the hell did you have to wake me up? I was SLEEPING! I'll take her!" He grabbed roughly for the baby.

"It's okay," I said, attempting to walk out again. "I didn't realize you were so tired; I'm sorry. I'll just finish feeding her."

"You're not going anywhere with my daughter, bitch!" he screamed, pushing me into the bed. I tried to turn to protect Dawn as I fell, but I was a second too late and her head grazed the headboard. Her cry turned from a normal infant cry to the high-pitched, piercing cry babies use when they're in pain. I started crying too.

I was in a crappy relationship, and my *child* was getting hurt. I wanted to leave; I hated living in this house, subjecting my kids to such unhealthy dynamics, but where could I go? I didn't have money for an apartment, and if I moved the kids into a shelter, I knew that Judy could easily get custody of Dawn. My dad, step-mom, and I were just barely on speaking terms again, so I didn't feel I could ask them for help, and my mom and I weren't close anymore at all. It seemed that if I wanted to keep both my kids, my only option was to continue living with Gary.

As I tried to comfort Dawn, Gary started apologizing while at the same time trying to rewrite what had happened. "I'm sorry, Jasmyn. I was trying to give you guys a hug, and you pulled away and fell onto the bed. Are you okay? Is she okay?"

I was concentrating on Dawn and didn't answer him. I didn't even notice that Gary's parents were in the room until his dad spoke.

"What was all that banging? What happened in here?" He looked at Dawn and me, still crying on the bed.

"Jasmyn wanted me to get up with Dawn, and she was being all loud, so I got up to get her, but when I tried to take her, Jasmyn wouldn't let me. She said she wanted to take her downstairs to feed her. So I tried to give them both a hug before Jasmyn went downstairs, but she pulled away and they fell onto the bed," Gary said.

"Yeah, right," I said, explaining what had really happened.

"Jasmyn," Judy asked, "is it possible that Gary was trying to give you a hug but you just thought he pushed you?"

"No," I said firmly.

"Well, look," Gary's dad said. "You guys can't get up in the middle of the night and make all this noise. You're waking the whole household up. I have to get up at four-thirty in the morning and go to work. I'm going back to bed."

Judy watched him go with a sigh and then turned to me. "Jasmyn, when two people are in a relationship with kids, the mother's responsibility is to take care of the kids and the father's responsibility is to go to work. Gary needs to get his sleep so that he can go to work. You just have to get used to that. And it should be okay if he wants to relax with his friends after work."

"Well, yeah," I said, trying to stop crying. "The father's responsibility is to go to work if he's helping to pay the finances for the family, but I pay for everything for the kids out of Elijah's welfare money. And I can't get anything for Dawn because then Gary would have to pay the state. Since Gary isn't helping financially, he should help with the responsibilities. Why should

I have to do everything just because Gary is earning his own spending money?"

"It's not just spending money, Jasmyn," Judy said. "Gary owes his father and me a lot of money that he needs to pay back."

"Well, fine. But he's still a parent, and it's not unreasonable for me to expect him to act like one once in a while," I insisted.

"Jasmyn, that's just how it is," Judy repeated. "The mom takes care of the children."

"That's not true!" I argued. I couldn't believe we were even having such an illogical conversation. "My dad took care of me by himself after he and my mom got divorced. Whether you're a mom or a dad, you're still a parent!" (Judy must have told my mom about this part of the conversation, because the next day my mom called to tell me that my dad had actually had a nanny.)

"Well, maybe that was an exception. That's not how it usually works." Judy continued, "And, we've been meaning to talk to you anyway. Since you're not working, we expect you to do more around the house. Everyday we'd like a list of things you've done around the house aside from the care of your children." She turned to Gary. "Now why don't you go sleep on the couch so that Jasmyn can finish taking care of Dawn."

These kinds of fights became a common occurrence while we lived with Gary. He would often yell at me or push me in front of the kids and later try to reconstruct what had actually happened. His mom would usually try to rationalize his behavior or try to find a way to give him what he wanted in order to calm him down. When we were alone in the house, there were times I had to lock the kids and myself in a room to stay safe.

Another thing we fought about was whether or not I should be allowed to see friends outside the house. Gary got extremely jealous and suspicious when I did anything that didn't involve him, and during my pregnancies I'd grown apart from all my previous friends. Recently, however, I'd started getting to know a girl named Shelly, a friend of Gary's who lived across the street from him.

At first we didn't like each other. Before I'd met Shelly, Gary often went over to her house to complain about me, and upon returning, he told me Shelly didn't like me and thought I was a bitch. Despite our first impressions, we started getting to know each other during the last month of my pregnancy, when I'd bring Elijah out into the front yard to play, and she'd pick him up and talk to him. She was extremely good with him, and it was hard for me to dislike someone who was so nice to my son.

We slowly became acquaintances and began hanging out together, though I still thought of her as Gary's friend. Gary usually didn't mind her coming over to his house, but if I went over to her house, he would call every few minutes or so, asking what I was doing, what we were talking about, and when I would be home.

One night after Dawn had been born, Shelly and I were planning to go out. Gary had been out the previous night and had promised that I could go out on this night in return. He'd also said he'd get up with Dawn during the night so that I could sleep in. Shelly and I didn't have any specific plans, but I was excited to be going somewhere without Gary or the kids. I put the kids down around 7:30 and got dressed. Gary was out front with a group of his friends. As Shelly and I started to leave, he told me he didn't want me to go after all.

"What?" I asked. "You're gone all the time. You already agreed that I was going tonight!"

"You just want to go flirt with guys!" he accused.

"Oh my gosh! You always do this! It's not my fault you're insecure! I can't go anywhere without you freaking out!" I yelled, hoping if I embarrassed him in front of his friends, he'd want me to just leave.

"Gary," asked Daryl, one of Gary's friends, "why don't you just let her go?"

Daryl and Gary had been friends for a long time. Daryl was a natural-born leader and the only one of us with a car. He seemed to be the unofficial leader of Gary's little group, and all the guys looked up to him.

"Look how she's dressed!" Gary said. I was wearing jeans and a spaghetti-strapped tank top.

"All right," Daryl said. "Jasmyn, change your shirt and then go."

Everybody looked at Gary, who didn't say anything. I walked back into the house and put on a sweatshirt to hide my original outfit, feeling like an idiot for acting like a rebellious teenager. I wanted to punch Daryl in the head. Who did he think he *was* to decide what I should do?

Shelly and I finally left. All we did was get on and off the bus a few times and walk around. Even though we didn't really go anywhere, it felt so good to be out of the house and walking around with a friend like a normal person.

We got back to the bus stop at about ten after eleven and waited for the bus to arrive. The schedule said the bus would arrive at 11:54, which would get us back home around midnight, which was good. Even though Gary often arrived home at two or three in the morning, Gary had told me that on this day his mom had decided to enforce a twelve o'clock curfew.

We arrived home about 12:05, and I was surprised to find both Gary and his mom waiting on the front lawn. Gary immediately started yelling that I was late, and accusing me of being an irresponsible slut who didn't care about the kids.

"I don't have to listen to this!" I said angrily, trying to walk past him.

His mom was right behind him. "Yes, you do, Jasmyn," she said. "You are late, and Gary woke me up because he was worried!"

"It's *five* minutes past twelve!" I protested.

"Late is late," Judy said. "You're a mom, and you can't just leave your kids with Gary and not be back when you're supposed to."

She continued to lecture me as Gary glared at me smugly.

After she finished, I apologized and we went inside. Gary turned to me as we went upstairs.

"Since you kept me up all night worrying, don't expect me to get up with Dawn for you tonight."

Between the fights over Gary's possessiveness, and our constant disagreement on how to divvy up parental responsibility, it seemed like we were fighting all the time. The situation was getting increasingly worse, Gary was getting more explosive, and I felt like even if there had been someone I could ask to help me get out of it, it would be too late. How could I explain the situation without admitting that I'd had my kids in a bad situation and not done anything about it? Didn't that make me a bad mom? My biggest fear was that if I tried to explain the situation to anyone, they would think I was a bad mom and take my kids.

Eventually, though, I'd had enough. When Dawn was a little over two months old, the kids and I went on a weeklong camping trip with my dad and Lynn's family. The relief I felt to be away from Gary made me realize how tense I usually was from all the fighting when we were together. Instead of missing Gary, I enjoyed the peacefulness of a week without him and dreaded going back to his house.

After we returned, the tension got worse. Jed moved back into the house and Gary was constantly suspicious that he and I were flirting.

"Why do you keep looking at him?" Gary asked one day when he and Jed were playing Nintendo.

"I'm not looking at him; I was watching the screen," I snapped.

"Whatever, you freakin bitch," he muttered, walking out of the room. Jed followed.

I sat there in Gary's empty room, which was still decorated with teenage paraphernalia, listening to the repetitive carnival-like drone of Nintendo music, and I started to think about my life. If I stayed with Gary, my kids would think it was okay for him to call me names. They would grow up thinking that's how relationships were supposed to work. This would be our *life*. What was I *doing*? I knew who Gary was, and I couldn't change him. The only thing I could do was decide whether or not the kids and I would be a part of it. By the time Gary came back into the room, I'd made a decision.

"Look, I'm sorry," he said. "I shouldn't have called you a bitch. You're not one."

"I know," I said.

"Are you mad?" he asked, when I didn't say anything else.

"I'm not mad at you," I answered, "but I'm not with you anymore, either."

"What do you mean? You're breaking up with me?"

"Yep. I'm not willing to be called names or have the kids grow up thinking that fighting all the time is normal."

"Babe, you know I'm working on my anger."

"That's great," I said. "But I'm still not with you."

"Fine, but we'll be back together in a few days," he said, leaving the room.

I let out a sigh of relief. I knew he had taken it so well because he hadn't believed me, but I was still happy that it hadn't turned into a big fight. I knew I would never get back together with him, and I hoped that this way, the realization would come gradually for Gary, allowing us to skip a big blow-up.

The assumption that I would give in and get back with Gary eventually was one his parents seemed to share as well. Since they didn't believe our relationship had truly ended, they continued to let me live in the house for a few weeks after we had broken up. During this time, Gary alternated between courting me and threatening or intimidating me.

One day when Dawn woke up from her nap, Gary picked her up and started to bring her downstairs.

"What are you doing?" I asked, surprised that he hadn't given her to me. It was almost time for him to leave for work, and he'd been getting ready.

"I'm bringing her to my mom," he said. "If you're not going to be with me, you're not going to take care of my daughter, either."

I stopped myself from pointing out that she was my daughter, too. I would *not* fight in front of my babies anymore. They didn't deserve it. I decided to wait until Gary left for work and then go down and get Dawn, even if it meant annoying Gary's mom. But that was unnecessary.

"Mom's not home," Gary announced, breezing into the bathroom empty-handed.

"Where's Dawn?" I tried to sound unconcerned.

"I brought her over to Shelly's so that I could go to work. I told her *not* to give her to you."

I waited until Gary left for work, put Elijah's little shoes and socks on, and walked with him over to Shelly's. "Where's my daughter?" I asked when she answered the door. Without a word, she went into the house and got Dawn for me.

"What are you going to do?" she asked.

"I don't know," I said. "Gary's seriously freaking out because I won't get back together with him. Maybe I'll call my grandma, and see if I can stay with her for a while."

"Yeah," Shelly said. "Gary told me you were just trying to teach him a lesson but that you'd eventually get back together with him."

"Nope," I answered, as Eli started to fuss. "I already have two kids; I don't have time to try to teach Gary things, too."

Shelly nodded, and I said goodbye, explaining that I needed to feed Elijah and put him down for a nap.

I fed Elijah and got him settled down; then I strapped Dawn into her electric swing so that I could clean up around the house. The house was always a mess, and it was not unusual to find three or four days' worth of dishes strewn in and around the sink.

As I scrubbed at the dry food caked to the dishes, I thought about how rare it was to have a moment like this when both my children were sleeping at the same time. I deeply resented the fact that I was the only one required to do the cleaning around the house, and that I was thought lazy if all I had time to do was tend to two infants on my own all day. I was, after all, the only one paying rent. Why did Gary's four hours of work a day count so much that it got him out of parental duties, plus housework, while my much more grueling twenty-four hours a day of childcare was regarded as lacking unless I did additional work.

My thoughts were interrupted by the sound of the front door opening, which was strange because nobody in the family was supposed to be home for hours. I'd barely had time to wonder who it was when Gary came barreling into the kitchen and started yelling.

"Shelly called me at work and told me you came and got Dawn! What the hell? And you're planning on taking her to your grandma's?"

"Damn, Gary!" I protested. "I was just thinking out loud. I can't stay here and have the kids watch you freak out all the time!"

Suddenly, my head snapped back and I felt a pain spread throughout my jaw. It took me a second to even realize what had happened, but when I did, I was dumbfounded. He had *punched* me. In the *face!* Besides stupid childhood fights, no one had ever punched me in the face before. And I'd never seen one adult do that to another. I couldn't believe it. Before I had time to react, Gary was on his way out the front door.

"You can leave whenever you want, bitch!" he yelled in my direction before he slammed the door. "But you'll never, *ever,* take my daughter!"

After he was gone, I checked on the kids, who were both still sleeping, and went back to the dishes, my mind racing. I knew I should leave right then, but where could I go? And what if Gary came back and saw me as I was leaving? I knew he would take Dawn from me, and it would turn into another big fight in front of the kids. Or what if he tried to hurt me while I was holding one of them? If I left with Dawn, I knew Gary and his parents would try to get custody. I was nineteen, on welfare, and had two kids with two different dads. A few times after Dawn was born, I drank alcohol with Gary and his friends, although I was underage. Add all that to the fact that I had no stable place to go, and I figured they could probably make me look pretty bad in court.

I felt I had no choice. Unless I wanted to give up being a full-time mother to Dawn, I would have to stay at Gary's.

A few days later, however, Gary's parents, realizing our breakup was permanent, informed me that since he and I no longer had plans to marry, Elijah and I would have to leave. They said that they understood that I didn't have anywhere to go, so they would help Gary take care of Dawn until I found a place.

I packed up as many of Elijah's things as I could in one backpack along with a change of clothes for each of us, kissed Dawn, and left. I had grabbed Eli's playpen as I left, as well as a stroller. The bus stop was only about two blocks away, but I kept dropping things, and it took me about half an hour to get Elijah and all our things there.

Once we'd reached it, I sat on the bench, exhausted and crying. I was sure I'd never get Dawn back. I couldn't believe I was leaving without my child. But I couldn't force my newborn daughter to be homeless, lugging her on and off the buses and into cheap, dirty, hotel rooms. It was already bad enough that I was doing it to Elijah.

A few days later, when I called to check on Dawn from my hotel room, I found out from Judy that Gary had been kicked out of the house as well. I was relieved that the situation would be less explosive with him gone, but I also worried about what Judy's hopes were for Dawn. I pointedly thanked her for keeping Dawn *until I found a place*, and told her I would give her as much money toward Dawn's care as I could.

I hung up the phone with a feeling of apprehension and shame. I was running out of money, still had nowhere stable to go, was barely taking care of my son, and was sure I'd lost my three-month-old daughter.

26

The Psycho Boss

Father's story

Jasmyn knew she needed to find a job and a place to stay. She had hit what she thought was rock bottom. She was on the street with her one-year-old son. Her newborn daughter was living with Gary's mother. Jasmyn bought a newspaper and answered a few ads for live-in nanny positions; within a few days, she found a job working for a single woman named Nancy. Jasmyn could live in her garage with Elijah and take care of Nancy's two children while Nancy worked for the county as a social worker. Jasmyn was also responsible for keeping the house clean and the children quiet. There was no salary. Jasmyn worked in exchange for room and board. She was supposed to have evenings and weekends off, and Jasmyn accepted the job thinking she could visit Dawn in her off time. She moved in and started work.

It wasn't long before Jasmyn realized she was in a bad situation once again. Nancy was a very strange woman. She checked for dust with a white glove. Her children had very nice toys but couldn't play with them because she feared they would break or look sloppy. Worse than her peculiar behavior, Nancy would come home from work and tell Jasmyn she was going out. Jasmyn would have to stay and watch her children. Nancy was gone every weekend. Jasmyn was treated as her live-in slave. There wasn't much of an alternative for Jasmyn. As bad as it was with Nancy, at least she wasn't on the street.

Then Nancy came home with a plan she had cooked up. She had found out about a program Jasmyn could apply for through social services. Since Jasmyn was a single mom with no income, she was eligible to receive assistance with money for daycare so she could work. Here was the really good part, according to Nancy. Jasmyn would receive four hundred dollars a month that she could then turn over to Nancy for rent. Nancy would then be able to pay Jasmyn twenty-five dollars a week. Nancy was thrilled with her genius. Jasmyn went along with the plan, seeing no alternative. Together, Nancy and Jasmyn filed the necessary papers to get Jasmyn into the program. Since Nancy was a social worker, she was able to expedite the procedure.

A few weeks later, Jasmyn was scheduled to have Sunday off to finally spend some time with Dawn. When the day arrived, Nancy informed Jasmyn that she didn't feel well and wanted to spend the day in bed, so Jasmyn would have to cancel her plans and take care of Nancy's kids. Jasmyn refused. She told Nancy that she had to see her daughter and was not available. She had been working for Nancy for over a month with no time off. Enough was enough. Nancy was furious. Slaves were not allowed to rebel. She fired Jasmyn and told her to get out.

Daughter's story

My time working as a nanny at Nancy's house was extremely hard, but I was grateful not to have Elijah on the street. Besides caring for Nancy's four-year-old and six-month-old sons during the day, I was also expected to get up and feed the younger one three or four times at night. I would often wonder whether Dawn was up, too, and who was feeding her if she was.

I missed her desperately, and my longing was made worse by the fact that I had no hope of getting her back anytime soon. I made no salary at Nancy's and had been giving Judy about half of Elijah's welfare money for Dawn, while using the other half to pay for necessities such as shampoo, hygienic supplies, and diapers for Elijah. I was supposed to have time off to see Dawn after work and on the weekends, but Judy often changed her plans without notice, demanding that I work the extra hours.

When I complained, she informed me that if I didn't like it, I could leave. As a result, I didn't get to see Dawn even half as much as I would have liked, and even when I did see her, the visits were startlingly lacking contrasted with the full-time care I was used to giving my daughter.

Eventually, after about a week of changed plans resulting in missed visits, I defied Nancy's orders and went to see Dawn, leaving Nancy's children with her. When I returned, most of my things were on the driveway, and Nancy said that Elijah and I would have to leave. I was extremely surprised, since Nancy had worked out a plan so that she would have gotten paid four hundred dollars a month by the state for me to watch her kids, but I left as she asked.

Once again Elijah and I were on the streets with no place to go. I wasn't sure what to do, but finally decided I needed to ask somebody for some suggestions, even if doing so would be uncomfortable for me. I couldn't just keep missing out on my daughter's life and bouncing my son from place to place. I wanted a better life for them. I swallowed my pride and called my parents.

Father's story

Jasmyn called Lynn and me in tears. She had tried her best but found herself on the street again. She wanted to know if she could come over and ask us for some advice.

For the first time, Jasmyn was asking for help. Lynn and I were thrilled! I dropped what I was doing and went to get her. Looking back, I see this moment as a turning point in Jasmyn's life.

Daughter's story

When I called my parents' to ask for advice, I was surprised by their reaction. Lynn did not act judgmental like I'd expected her to; instead, she invited me to bring Elijah over and suggested that she, my dad, and I sit down and brainstorm some solutions. When I got to their house, Dad and Lynn invited us to spend the night, and the next morning, they asked me what I wanted to do.

I explained that I wanted to find a job so that I could get a place for the kids and me to live. They told me that they had discussed it the night before and had decided that if I really wanted to get my life together, Elijah and I could stay with them for a while. They would drive me to job interviews, help me get my driver's license, and watch Elijah while I did these things.

I was extremely touched and grateful for their offer. I knew my dad had to work, and so when they said they would help me do all these things, it was really Lynn who would do most of the driving and babysitting. She and I hadn't gotten along in years, and I was amazed that she was willing to do all that for me.

I readily accepted their offer and started looking through the want ads for a job that day. My parents had asked me how long I thought it would take to get my life together, and we had agreed that I would stay for three months initially, but that if, at the end of that time, they saw that I was really serious about my goals, they would allow me to stay longer if I needed to.

Once I'd set up my first job interview, Lynn took me shopping to get some professional-looking clothes. To my surprise, we had a great time. She and I started talking to each other more often, and I was astonished to find that we could have entire conversations without fighting! I found myself gradually relaxing and even enjoying my time around her.

Dawn visited my dad's house often. During one of these visits, as I played with her on the floor, I told Lynn that even after I had an apartment and a steady job, I was worried Judy would be extremely reluctant to give her back to me.

Lynn agreed that that could be a problem and suggested I keep Dawn with me.

"You mean, right now?" I asked, feeling like I'd won the lottery.

"Sure," she replied. "You have a safe, stable place for her now, and Judy knew you were going to take her back once you did."

I was overjoyed. I'd been living away from Dawn for almost three months and had been worried that Dawn would feel less bonded to me as time went on.

I tried to call Judy to tell her I'd be able to keep Dawn with me now, but she wasn't home. I'd have to tell her when she came to pick Dawn up. I wasn't looking forward to it. I knew how much Judy liked to care for Dawn, and although I didn't think that was the healthiest place for a six-month-old baby, I *was* grateful for all the care Judy had given her.

When Judy rang the doorbell, I answered the door reluctantly. Even though she and I hadn't gotten along very well much of the time, I wasn't looking forward to telling her something that I knew would cause her pain.

"Is she ready?" Judy asked when I opened the door.

"Uh, actually, I have some good news," I said tentatively. "My parents have decided that she can stay here with Elijah and me until I get an apartment, so I can take care of her now."

"But we just bought her a crib!" Judy exclaimed.

"I'm sorry," I said, feeling extremely guilty. "But she'll always be able to visit you guys, and she can use the crib then."

"So, you're just going to keep her now?" she asked.

"Well, yeah," I answered. "The agreement was that you were only going to keep her until I had a place to bring her, and now I do."

"But I…didn't know it was going to be so soon."

"I'm sorry," I repeated, feeling horrible that they'd just spent a bunch of money on a new crib. But I couldn't give up my child just because someone had bought a crib. And Judy had known since before Dawn was born that my intention had always been to take care of her, so why had she bought the crib in the first place?

As guilty as this exchange made me feel, it confirmed my anxieties that Judy had been hoping to keep Dawn long term and made me extremely relieved to have her back in my care. I was still worried about whether Gary or his parents would decide to pursue custody, and that worry helped me to compound my efforts to build the best life I could for my children as quickly as I could.

After about three job interviews and one day at a dead-end commission-only job that my parents advised me not to pursue, I found a wonderful job in sales, complete with benefits. The Saturday after I'd accepted this job, my parents went out for a while and came back with a surprise for me. They led me outside and showed me a humungous white station wagon. I immediately fell in love with my first car. My dad taught me how to drive it, and the day before I was to start my new job, he took me to get my license.

The next day, I went to work at the job I would keep for the next two years. I easily learned about the product I would be selling and found working in sales easy and exciting. My ability to read people and my flirtatious nature made me a natural in sales, and I would finally be able to save some money. I'd been at work less than a week when I started looking at apartments.

During this time, I was also looking for childcare. Lynn had offered to watch the kids until I found reliable daycare, but I didn't want to take advantage of her generosity. I had already looked at a few daycares but found them incredibly wanting. I was nervous about putting Elijah and Dawn in a facility anyway, as they were too young to communicate to me if there was a problem or they were being treated badly.

Not surprisingly, Gary called me and told me that his parents had let him move back into his house, and he wanted to share custody of Dawn. Still wanting to stay out of court, I came up with a compromise: he could have her while I was at work and for an afternoon every other weekend, and I would have her otherwise. This way, we would both have her about half time and she wouldn't have to go to daycare. He agreed, and we started our shared custody arrangement. Most of the time when I picked Dawn up after work, however, I'd arrive to find Gary out and Judy actually caring for Dawn.

Now that I had childcare for Dawn, a car, a job, and a driver's license, I was able to concentrate on finding an apartment and childcare for Elijah. Lynn asked around and gave me the number of a longtime family friend who was a stay at-home-mom and might be able to use the extra income that caring for Elijah would bring.

I called the woman, whose name was Katy, and after meeting with her and her family agreed that she would take on the care of Elijah on a trial basis. Everything was falling into place; shortly afterward, I found an apartment as well. The moving date was set. My parents had given me three months to get everything together; it had actually only taken two.

Shelly came over and spent the night at my dad's to help me on moving day. She and I had grown pretty close, and she was the only person I really ever hung out with. In the last few months, I'd thought a lot about my life and what it meant to be a parent, especially after my fears of losing Dawn. I'd realized that there was a huge difference between actually being a parent and just some person who happened to have kids. I wanted to create a life for Dawn and Elijah and had decided that having a social life was not on my list of priorities. Neither was dating.

I had read somewhere that children of single parents were much more likely to be subjected to abuse and molestation than children growing up in two-parent families. I had concluded that this phenomenon wasn't as much a result of family structure as it was a result of the lifestyle often led by single parents. If a mother was dating, leaving her children with numerous babysitters, and bringing various people into the house where her children lived, it made sense that those children had more opportunities—and were therefore more likely—to be abused than children who were living continuously with the same two people. So, when moving into my own apartment, I decided my home would be a place where my children truly felt that life was predictable and safe. I wouldn't date, hire babysitters, or go out with friends.

I moved into my apartment and settled into this new chapter of my life with pride. At nineteen, I had both my kids with me, and I had a great job that could eventually turn into a career. I was also no longer on welfare, which was a huge relief. The only thing I still felt uneasy about was the situation with Gary. He had recently been asking for more time with Dawn, probably at Judy's urging, and threatening to take me to court for full custody if I said no. He said his parents would pay for him to hire a lawyer, which was something I couldn't afford, and I was afraid that if we went to court, they would win and I would lose Dawn. For this reason, I tried to keep my relationship with Gary as civil and friendly as possible.

One morning when Dawn was about seven-months-old, Gary called me and asked if he could take the kids and me to breakfast. I agreed, and since he didn't have a car, I got the kids ready and went to pick him up.

He came out of the house just as I pulled up. "Hey, do you think this shirt's cool?" he asked.

"Well," I answered, looking at his long-sleeved flannel shirt, "it might be a little hot for that."

"Whatever," he muttered angrily, going back inside to change. I turned in my seat, rolled down the kids' windows, and started playing with them. A few minutes later, Gary returned, got into the car, and sat stonily as I pulled away from the curb.

"So, where we going?" I asked, trying to sound cheerful.

"I don't care," he muttered.

"Look," I said, after a moment of silence, "if you're in a bad mood or whatever, we can do this another time."

"I'm fine," he snapped. "I just really like that shirt, and you made me feel stupid for wearing it."

"But you're the one that *asked* me about the shirt," I pointed out, astonished. "I just said you might be hot."

"Well, you didn't have to be such a stupid bitch about it!" he shot back, his voice suddenly rising.

I glanced into the rear-view mirror; Elijah was watching us intently from the backseat. He was twenty-one months old, and I didn't want the words "stupid-bitch" to be included in his steadily increasing vocabulary.

"You know what," I said, pulling over, "I don't want the kids to learn this. Please get out." When he said no, I pulled into the street again and drove back to his house.

"What the hell are you doing?" "I told you," I repeated calmly to avoid scaring the kids, "I want you to get out. If you yell at me and call me names, and then I just go to breakfast with you as if we're buddies, the kids will think what you are doing is okay. That's wrong, and I'm not willing to teach them that."

Gary stared at me for a moment, then suddenly lunged over and grabbed my car keys out of the ignition. "What, you don't want him to know that his mom *is* a stupid bitch?" he asked tauntingly, dangling the keys. I refused to grab for them, as he obviously wanted me to. I wasn't going to start a physical altercation in front of the kids.

When I failed to react, Gary grabbed my purse and threw it out his open window onto the lawn. He then flung open his door and, still holding my car keys, went into his house.

I turned in my seat again and started trying to distract the kids, who were getting fidgety. I considered calling the police from my cell phone but worried that doing so might be an overreaction to the situation. As I was considering my options, Gary came back outside, opened the passenger door, and tossed my purse inside. I asked him for my car keys, which he refused to give me.

"Alright," he said finally, "I'll give them to you if you and the kids will come back later and we can go do something."

"No," I said. "I'm not going to let the kids see me just hang out with you as if what is happening right now is a normal part of life. I don't want Elijah growing up thinking it's okay to treat woman this way, and I definitely don't want Dawn to think it is normal to be treated this way. Now please give me the keys! The kids are hungry, and they need a nap!"

He refused again and started yelling that I had already agreed to go out to eat with him and the kids, so now I had to go. He said he'd give me the keys if I would just stop being a bitch and bring the kids inside so that he and I could sit and talk.

Finally, I got out of the car, blinking back tears. The kids were starting to cry, and I didn't want them to hear him yelling. It was hot, they were probably hungry, and I needed to check Dawn's diaper. I made a quick grab for the keys, and Gary pushed me away. I leaned against the car, not sure what to do.

Gary's mom came out and asked what was happening.

"I won't go anywhere with Gary when he's calling me names," I said. "The kids are hot, cranky, and probably scared, and he won't give me my keys so that I can get them home!"

"I'd give her the damn keys if she'd stop being a bitch and just talk to me!" Gary exploded. "I simply asked her to come in and talk to me, or go out to breakfast with me and the kids like she *already agreed to do*, but she's being so damn freakin' unreasonable that she won't even do *that!*"

Although Gary was talking to his mom, he pushed his face into mine as he yelled so that his whole forehead was pushing my head backwards. I again grabbed at the keys, and almost had them, but I was a second too late, and Gary pulled them behind his back just as my fingers closed around them.

Judy had been trying to get in between us; now she reached behind his back and plucked the keys out of his hands. "Gary," she implored, "please calm down."

I was glad to see that Judy had the keys. "Thanks," I said, reaching for them.

To my surprise, she pulled them out of my reach and refused to give them to me. "Judy," I said, exasperated, "I need to put the kids down for a nap. This isn't okay."

"You can put them down here," she said. "Just come in and talk to Gary. He wants to work this out."

"What Gary wants is not my responsibility," I said angrily. "Dawn and Elijah are my responsibility, and right now I need to get them home. *Please* give me my keys."

When she refused again, I got back into my car and started looking for my cell phone. Judy finally relented and gave me my keys, but as soon as I put them into the ignition, Gary jumped back into the passenger seat again. I silently chided myself for not locking the doors and again asked Gary to get out.

He reached over, grabbed my arm, and started to twist it, with no apparent goal in mind. "Let go of me! Get out of my car!" I yelled. After about thirty seconds, he jumped out of the car. I thought about locking the doors, but remembered the kids' windows were open and decided to just get out of there. Then Gary opened the back door and removed Dawn. He took her into the house.

I stopped the car and got out. Ignoring Judy, I knocked on the front door. Gary came to the door, holding Dawn. "Alright, I'll come back after the kids' nap, and we can talk if you give me Dawn right now," I said, although I had no intention of doing so.

Gary looked out toward the street, where his mother was still standing, and suddenly thrust Dawn at me, turned around, and slammed the door. As I walked back toward the car, I saw why. A police car was pulling up in front of the house. Apparently one of the neighbors had called the police.

The officer got out and asked what had happened. As I recounted the story, he turned to Judy in disbelief. *"You* wouldn't give her the car keys either?" He asked, with furrowed brows.

"Well, I just wanted her to come in and talk to Gary!"

"Ma'am," said the officer, "your son is abusive, and you're *enabling* him. You need to get some counseling or something."

He then asked her to go get Gary, but when she returned, she reported that it looked like he had taken off out the back door.

"Well," asked the officer, looking at me, "do you want me to write this up so that you can press charges?"

"No," I said, "I just want to get the kids home and out of the car."

"Well, "he said, "how about if you pull the car into the shade and sit in the car with the kids while I get some information. I'm going to write this up whether you press charges or not. That way, if this happens again, you'll have a record of it happening before."

The officer's decision to write up the report turned out to be a fortunate one for me when, five months later, a similar incident occurred. By this time, Katy was watching both Elijah and Dawn during the day because Gary had decided to look for daytime employment. Since Gary was no longer getting time with her during the day, we had agreed that he could have Dawn overnight every Wednesday.

The deal was that he would keep her from Wednesday night to Thursday morning, when I would pick her up from his house and drop her off at Katy's before starting my 45 minute commute to work. Gary was supposed to have fed Dawn and dressed her before I arrived. Unfortunately, this was rarely the case. Gary still liked to sleep in, and on most Thursday mornings I would find Gary in bed and Dawn still in her crib, lying awake with a wet diaper and last night's old bottle of formula beside her.

I had repeatedly asked Gary and his mother not to give Dawn a bottle while she lay in her crib because it was bad for her teeth and contributed to earaches. I also felt it was a choking hazard. When I complained to Gary about finding bottles in the crib on Thursday mornings, he said that his mom gave Dawn the bottles at night when he was asleep and he couldn't stop her.

Also, when Katy had agreed to watch the kids, it was understood that they were to arrive at her house fed, dressed, and ready for the day. Gary's failure to get Dawn ready on Thursday mornings meant that instead of just picking her up and leaving, I first had to get Elijah out of the car, dress Dawn, get both kids back into the car, and then stop somewhere and feed her before dropping the kids off and heading to work. Being late for work every Thursday became a pattern.

After a few weeks, I told Gary that I wouldn't allow Dawn to spend the night at his house during the week anymore if he continued to ignore her morning needs. He promised to get her ready on time. The Wednesday after this conversation took place, I dropped Dawn off at his house and reminded Gary of the conversation.

"Look," he said, "I said I'd have her ready in the morning, and I will. You don't have to be so controlling."

"I'm not being controlling," I said, "but it's just really essential that I get to work on time tomorrow. I have an appointment with a really important client."

"Okay, fine. I'll have her ready!"

Despite Gary's promises, I was still doubtful he would follow through, so I called his house about half an hour before I was to pick Dawn up to make sure he was awake and remind him to have her ready. There was no answer.

As I continued to get Elijah ready, I called the house every few minutes, but still did not get through. I finally packed Elijah into the car and drove over to Gary's house, hoping that the reason Gary hadn't answered the phone was that he had been busy getting Dawn ready.

No such luck. After banging on the door and ringing the doorbell for about five minutes with no response, I grabbed my cell phone to call again. As the phone started to ring, Gary's brother Jed flung open the front door and started to yell and curse at me, asking why the hell I had been making so much noise.

"I'm sorry," I replied, "but Gary's supposed to have Dawn ready right *now*. I'm going to be late for work. Where's Dawn?"

"She's been awake in her crib for like, two hours," Jed answered angrily. "It's freaking annoying! I keep trying to wake Gary up to go take care of her, but he just screams at me to *get the hell out*! I'm not getting her. Why the hell should I have to take care of his kid while that lazy punk sleeps? He knows she's up!"

"I'll get her dressed," I said, walking past Jed into the house. "I have to get to work." I had parked my car in the driveway, and since I was already late and could see the car from Dawn's window, I decided not to get Elijah out while I ran upstairs to dress Dawn.

Gary stumbled out of his room as I was changing Dawn. "Oh," he said. "Sorry, I didn't realize she was awake."

"Jed said she's been awake for two hours!" I shot back. "And even if she hadn't been, you were supposed to get her up and feed her. You *can't* just leave her in her crib all morning. She has a poopy diaper, a rash, and she's been crying. You're supposed to take *care* of her!"

"Look, Jasmyn," he said, as I grabbed some clothes for Dawn and picked her up out of the crib, "I'm sorry I slept in. Next time I'll have her ready on time."

"There's not going to be a next time," I replied, and started to walk out of the room. I didn't have time for this. I'd dress Dawn in the car. "She's not staying overnight on Wednesdays anymore."

"You can't do that to me! She's *my* daughter," he said loudly, following me toward the stairs.

"We'll talk about it later," I said. I could tell he was about to start yelling and didn't have the time or the desire to fight with him.

"Well, she's staying here today! You're not taking her anywhere!" he yelled. "Since you're such a selfish bitch who obviously doesn't care about anybody but yourself, I'm taking her away from you!"

He was sputtering and stomping around. Still holding Dawn, I tried run down the stairs, but Gary put his arm around my throat, roughly pulling me backwards and yelling, "You better give her to me or I'll kick your ass!" Dawn was screaming at the top of her lungs by now, frightened and confused.

I twisted out of Gary's grip and again tried to leave, but he continued to grab me, push me, pull my hair. Throughout the whole incident, he yelled, threatened, and screamed, saying that I was a selfish, bad mother, that he was going to take Dawn away from me and keep her, and that he would kill me if I ever tried to stop him or keep her from him.

At the height of this tirade, Gary grabbed Dawn's upper arms and started trying to pull her away from me. His face was set angrily, and as Dawn started to cry, I realized that he either didn't notice or didn't care that he was hurting her. I handed her to him so that he would stop pulling on her arms and ran downstairs and out the door to call the police.

Gary followed me out the door with Dawn and continued to yell as I dialed 911. As the dispatcher picked up, Gary tried to wrestle my cell phone out of my hand. Dawn was crying, emitting enormous, terrified sobs. "You're scaring her!" I hissed at Gary, pulling away with the phone.

"No, I'm not! Are you scared?" he asked, looking at our one-and-a-half year old daughter.

"Yes," she squeaked in a small voice, choking back a sob.

"No, you're not!" he snapped at her. Dawn resumed screaming, I started crying, and the dispatcher asked what the address was and said she was sending a car.

"The police are on their way," I said to Gary.

"That was the *police?*" he asked, shoving Dawn at me. I gratefully took her and got into the car to comfort her. I locked the doors as Gary continued to yell. "I don't know why the hell you had to call them! I was trying to give her to you. I just wanted to give her a hug first! Well, you can deal with them yourself! I'm out of here!"

By the time a police officer arrived, Gary was gone and no action was taken, although the officer did tell me how I could get a restraining order.

After he left, I called Katy and told her why we were so late. She told us to come over, and when we arrived, asked why I hadn't gone to court to get legal custody of Dawn. As I explained my worries about losing, I realized I wasn't in as precarious a position as I had been when Gary and I had first broken up. I was now leading a stable life, I had a reputation at work as being professional and responsible, I made sure my kids had all their shots and checkups, and being twenty, I was no longer under the stigma of "teen parent."

Also, because of the report the police officer had insisted on writing a few months before, I knew that there was now at least one record of Gary's violent behavior. (When my attorney went to get the police report, I was surprised to find out that there were other records of Gary's violence that hadn't involved me. There were records of Gary punching and choking his mom, fighting with his dad, and hitting his brother in the back of the head numerous times with a garden tool.)

Instead of going to work that day, I went down to the courthouse and filed for an emergency restraining order as well as sole legal and physical custody of Dawn. I was immediately granted the restraining order, which meant that Gary couldn't be near the kids or me.

Although it took a few months, I was eventually granted the custody order as well. During the course of the trial, I was extremely afraid that I would lose and be ordered to leave Dawn at Gary's where she would not get proper care.

Gary could be extremely charming when it suited him, and I was worried that since he was liable to be on his best behavior in front of court officials, they wouldn't understand the importance of his not receiving the custody he was asking for. Gary and his attorney had proposed an arrangement where he and I would get equal custody of Dawn, each keeping her at our house for a week, every other week. I was terrified of this arrangement, as I felt it would rob Dawn of the stability and security children need in order to thrive.

My worries about Gary's behavior turned out to be unfounded. During the trial, he accused me of using drugs, refused to take the drug tests we were both ordered to submit to in response to his accusations, and got angry and stalked out of the courtroom anytime something didn't go his way.

He was granted supervised visitations and ordered to pay child support.

27

The Turn Around

Father's story

Immediately after Jasmyn asked for advice, Lynn and I decided it was time for us to help. We decided Jasmyn would stay at our house while we came up with a plan. Together, we asked Jasmyn what she wanted to do. Jasmyn said she wanted to get a job, get her own place, and get her daughter back. She told us the story of her experience with Nancy. Together we came up with a plan of attack. Lynn and I would give Jasmyn four months to get her life together. She needed to find a good job and move toward independence. As long as she was making progress, we would be happy. Jasmyn agreed happily and moved in with Elijah.

Things were different than before. Jasmyn was in our home by her choice. She had asked for our assistance. She was grateful and showed it at every opportunity. After a few days, Jasmyn told Lynn how concerned she was about Dawn. She feared every day Dawn spent at her "in-law's" home would make it harder and harder to regain custody. Jasmyn was worried Judy would claim Jasmyn deserted Dawn and therefore custody should be awarded to her. Lynn agreed and told Jasmyn to call Judy and tell her she was coming over to pick her up. I don't know how Judy took the news, but that evening when I returned from work, there was another member of the family living in our home.

Jasmyn was getting her life back together. We decided she needed to learn how to drive in order to get around for work. I started teaching Jasmyn how to handle a car, and I enjoyed my time with her. Actually, I had always enjoyed her company, but now the chip that had been permanently affixed to her shoulder was gone. She learned to drive quickly with one minor problem. On a few occasions, Jasmyn confused the gas pedal and the brake pedal. We pulled into our driveway in Lynn's new Acura and as we got close to Joshua's

206

vintage Mustang, Jasmyn punched the gas. Boom! We nailed the back of Joshua's car. I was livid. I told Jasmyn that was it. She was too stupid to drive a car. Later I apologized for the remark, and we resumed her lessons. She passed her driving test on the first try.

Jasmyn started looking for a job as soon as she got her driver's license. She went on her first interview and was very proud to tell us about her first job offer. She had interviewed with the very same company Robert worked for selling vacuum cleaners. As with Robert, the job was commission only and door-to-door. Seeing Jasmyn's enthusiasm, I was very careful telling her what I thought. I explained that this was Jasmyn's one chance to get a good start in life. We were helping to take care of Elijah and Dawn while standing by her. She shouldn't be looking for a job but a career, something with a steady paycheck and benefits. If she was going to support Dawn and Elijah, she needed a reliable paycheck.

Much to our amazement, Jasmyn agreed. This was truly the new and improved Jasmyn. She decided to continue the search. Lynn took her out to the thrift shops in town, and together they purchased a complete new interviewing wardrobe. Jasmyn modeled the new clothes for me and was excited about getting out in the world. Even more exciting for me was the relationship that was steadily building and improving between Lynn and Jasmyn. After years of fighting and tension, they were now becoming the best of friends. They shopped together, took care of the babies together, and laughed together. For me, it was a dream come true.

Jasmyn kept checking the papers for jobs. She landed an interview for a sales position at a cellular phone company. She was very nervous about the interview because she had no real job experience. Lynn coached her as to how to interview. She told Jasmyn to look the interviewer in the eye and tell him if he gave her a chance, he wouldn't be disappointed. The next day Jasmyn came home with the job. She was so excited. She was bubbling over when she told Lynn that she had said exactly what they practiced and got the job on the spot. She would be making more money than she ever had, enough money for her own apartment and support for both her children. She was to start in a week.

The next day Lynn and I went to the battered women's charity car auction. We found an older big white station wagon in great condition. We purchased it and brought it home for Jasmyn. She couldn't believe she had her own car. She absolutely loved that wagon and drove it for years. Jasmyn had been living with us for two months and had regained her daughter, earned her driver's license, found a job, and gotten a car. After a few weeks at work, she found that she was excelling as a sales associate. It was time to find an apartment for her.

Jasmyn called Eden and asked for her help. Together they looked at a small one-bedroom apartment that was managed by the company Eden worked for. It was located only a few miles from Eden's home and ours. Jasmyn was moving into her own place. The garage sale crew swung into high gear. Lynn and her sister Anne seized the opportunity to help out as much as humanly possible by purchasing all the necessities of life at local garage sales. Jasmyn was thrilled with the help and soon was settled in her new life.

With Jasmyn settling into her new life, I felt a heavy burden had been lifted from mine. My professional life, however, was about to take a series of detours. I received a call from a gentleman asking me if I would be interested in consulting on a new audio/video product. He said they were very interested in my opinions as one of the leading custom electronics retailers in the area. I was flattered and accepted the offer. There was also a small compensation for each meeting as well as stock options in the new company.

At the first meeting the entire staff of this new company was introduced—a grand total of seven people. The product they described was new and revolutionary. It would have the ability to pause TV and skip over commercials. As I listened, I decided I had to go to work on this new technology full time. Because I have a very strong personality, I dominated the meeting with marketing and engineering ideas. I went home that afternoon hoping I could figure out a way to become more involved with this new venture.

The next day my phone rang again. The founder of the company wanted to have lunch. At the meeting, he told me that all who met me yesterday were impressed by my ideas and industry knowledge. Would I be willing to join the team full time? I couldn't believe my good fortune. The decision was an easy one. I sold out of my company and started my new career as a marketing professional.

The company and my role in it grew very quickly. My marketing efforts helped gain massive press coverage and awards for best of show at the consumer electronics show in Las Vegas. The stock market was also growing in the tech sector with the same feverish pace. We were soon a company of 150 employees, and those of us from the original ten started dreaming of an initial public offering (IPO) on the stock market and the millions of dollars we would make. The most respected venture capital firm in the country approached us about taking us public.

The investment dollars poured in and the management team started to grow out of control. The VC firm decided to remove the CEO and replace him with a known name in the entertainment industry. This created a rift in the senior management ranks, and the company was in turmoil for six months. The old and new CEO fought continuously, resulting in very few decisions being made. The IPO was delayed by months. Then the bottom fell out and the tech market crashed. The company was up to 300 employees and running out of money.

I decided to make a move. I made a few calls and was offered a job the following week as VP of an Internet media company. I was assured they were well funded and had a proven product. I took the position and soon found both claims were greatly exaggerated. I worked hard for the next six months trying to secure financing for my new employer. The search took me to all over the country as well as to Europe for weeks at a time. The extensive travel coupled with the pressure was taking a toll on my life both professionally and privately. The collapsing tech market was also taking a toll on the local economy and real estate market. Lynn and I decided it was time to leave California. I sent out feelers to the areas we were interested in. Within weeks, Lynn and I were flying to our new prospective home to check out the local community. I was offered a position, and we decided to make the move.

The local economy was also affecting Jasmyn. We informed her of our plans to move. She was also planning on making a move. She had friends who were relocating to Colorado. The cost of living was quite a bit less than California, and Jasmyn was considering going with them. The new home Lynn and I purchased had a guesthouse in the yard. It would be perfect for Jasmyn and the two kids. We suggested to Jasmyn that it might be easier on her to come with us. After all, she would have family a stone's throw away. She agreed and we were all off to our new home in a new state.

Jasmyn decided she wanted to go to school and become a social worker. She located the community college and enrolled. She arranged daycare at a co-op. She also applied for and received grants and student loans. She had become an extremely resourceful young woman. At this writing Jasmyn has just completed her second year at school. She has maintained a 3.8 GPA and is in the process of transferring to the local university. Elijah and Dawn continue to excel as well.

Daughter's story

After the stress of the custody battle had passed, life settled into a smooth routine for the kids and me. They continued to go to Katy's, whose family was by now a sort of second family to them. I continued to excel at work and, in the course of two years, received three raises and a promotion.

As the Silicon Valley economy started to slow down, business slowed as well and I was able to leave work earlier and earlier. This was great for me. I was on a monthly salary plan as opposed to an hourly one, so fewer hours had little effect on my paycheck. Less business did affect the company, however, and people were starting to get laid off.

Although I was slightly worried about how this would affect me professionally, I was greatly enjoying the extra hours with my kids. I got into the habit of bringing them to the park after I picked them up, where we would all play together until it got dark. Afterward we would go home and eat; then I would give them a bath before getting to my favorite part of their bedtime routine: story time. I loved how they cuddled up, one child on each side of me, and lay their little heads on my chest as I read to them. I loved to see them laugh and point in excitement at the pictures in the books. I loved being a mom.

I didn't have much of a social life; work and the kids took up almost all of my time. I didn't mind, though. I was growing extremely close to my family and felt that I had a full life. The kids and I often stopped by my dad and Lynn's house, where Elijah and Dawn would play with my little brother and sister while I chatted with Lynn or went to a movie with her or my dad.

One day, they told me that my dad had gotten a great job offer and they were going to relocate. They wanted the kids and me to go as well, but I was reluctant at first to make any changes. I had worked hard to build a stable, safe life for the kids, and I was worried that if I moved I would have to start over. But, as more people in my company started to get laid off, I decided this might be a good time for a change. I also wanted my kids to grow up with Dad and Lynn's kids, as they had known each other all their lives and were extremely close. When my dad and Lynn found a house that was actually *two* houses on the same lot, I decided to go with them.

When we arrived in the new state, I immediately started looking for a job. I soon found out the job market in our area was extremely sparse. Even fast food places only had part time positions available and didn't pay enough to cover childcare for two children.

I went down to the employment office and, while looking through various employment pamphlets, came across a financial aid application for college. The idea to go back to school hadn't occurred to me until now, but I called the college to get some information. I found out that the new term would start in four days. I filled out the necessary paperwork that day, and by the next day was taking my placement tests. To my surprise, since I had not been in school in years, I did extremely well on the tests. By the following week I had found a co-op daycare where I felt comfortable leaving the kids and was already attending classes.

I had enrolled in a community service program with the hope of becoming a social worker. As a single young mother, I feel extremely lucky to have such a strong support system of family members whom I can depend on for solid emotional support and advice. I feel proud that my kids are happy and thriving, and I recognize that this most likely wouldn't be the case had I not had the family support that I do. Since a lot of young parents don't have that, their kids are missing out on the wonderful, stable lives they deserve. I'm not sure whether I want to work with young kids or teen parents, but either way my goal will be to give support to others the way that my family gives support to me.

Epilogue

Father's story

The writing of this book has served more than one purpose. My daughter and I took on this project to try to help other families with similar situations. We both believed, and still do, that showing the generational differences in point of view could lead to a much deeper understanding of conflicts. What I did not anticipate was the extent to which I misunderstood the signs being given to me throughout my daughter's upbringing. With the benefit of hindsight and the sections authored by my daughter in this book I can now see forks in the road where I took a wrong turn.

Jasmyn is very intelligent. Many of her mischievous behaviors were rooted in boredom. My reaction to her self-destructive behavior was usually a punishment consisting of grounding her for long periods of time. When this punishment proved to be ineffective I followed it up with more of the same. We have all heard the saying pertaining to the definition of insanity. "Insanity is doing the same thing over and over and expecting different results." This is a classic example of my actions.

What could I have done differently? I believe my most damaging error was not channeling my daughter's energy and intellect into an activity or activities that would constantly and consistently challenge her. She was left on her own to fill the void that was the basis of her boredom. Her reaction was to become involved in alcohol abuse followed by drug abuse. Once consumed by these influences her downhill slide turned into a freefall.

The credit for her turn around belongs to Jasmyn. She has worked through the challenges her poor life choices created. My wife and I are amazed on a daily basis how dedicated Jasmyn is to making a quality life for herself and her children. Her everyday actions not only fill me with pride but also give me a sense of satisfaction. She was listening to the life lessons my wife and I were trying to convey. I also believe the unconditional love that was always waiting at home for Jasmyn was the beacon that helped guide her out of the abyss.

978-0-595-36991-1
0-595-36991-X

Made in the USA
Monee, IL
26 February 2022

91907962R00132